Digital Literacy, Inclusivity and Sustainable Development in Africa

Every purchase of a Facet book helps to fund CILIP's advocacy, awareness and accreditation programmes for information professionals.

Digital Literacy, Inclusivity and Sustainable Development in Africa

Edited by
Helena Asamoah-Hassan

facet
publishing

Published by Facet Publishing
7 Ridgmount Street, London WC1E 7AE
www.facetpublishing.co.uk

Facet Publishing is wholly owned by CILIP: the Library and Information Association.

British Library Cataloguing in Publication Data
A catalogue record for this book is available from the British Library.

ISBN 978-1-78330-511-7 (paperback)
ISBN 978-1-78330-512-4 (hardback)
ISBN 978-1-78330-513-1 (PDF)
ISBN 978-1-78330-524-7 (EPUB)

First published 2022

Text printed on FSC accredited material.

Typeset from the editor's files by Flagholme Publishing Services in 10/13 pt Palatino Linotype and Open Sans.
Printed and made in Great Britain by CPI Group (UK) Ltd, Croydon, CR0 4YY.

Contents

Figures and Tables

Figures

Tables

Notes on Contributors

Editor

Helena R. Asamoah-Hassan is the Executive Director of the African Library and Information Associations and Institutions (AfLIA). Prior to this, she was the University Librarian of the Kwame University of Science and Technology, Kumasi, Ghana. She was President of Ghana Library Association 2003–06; member of the Governing Board of the International Federation of Library Associations and Institutions 2007–11; member, and later chairperson, of eIFLnet Advisory Board 2007–11; member, and later chairperson, of UNESCO's International Advisory Committee on the Memory of the World Program 2013–2015; chairperson, Management Committee, Consortium of Academic and Research Libraries in Ghana (CARLIGH) 2004–13. She was also the Ghana Country Coordinator for INASP Programme for the Enhancement of Research Information (PERI) and also for eIFL.net 2003–13; the 1st Emerald Regional Advisor for Africa 2011–13. She received the 2011 BioMed Open Access Advocate of the Year and the IFLA Service Medal for her significant contribution to IFLA and international librarianship.

Currently Helena serves as the chairperson of the Ghana Library Authority Board, having done so since March 2018; chairperson of the Ghana National Committee of UNESCO's Memory of the World Program; Secretary-General of UNESCO's African Regional Committee of the Memory of the World Program; member of the Appeals Board of the Kumasi Technical University, Ghana; member of the Management Committee, School of Communication and Information Studies, University of Ghana, Legon, Accra; editorial consultant to the *Ghana Library Journal*; member of the editorial board of *Library Trends*. She has written three books, a chapter in each of three books, 19 refereed conference proceedings and journal articles. She also has 112 conference papers and 20 major commissioned reports. She is a consultant to some international organizations on library and information issues and has served and still serves on several other committees at national, regional and international levels.

Contributors

Oluwaseun David Adepoju is a Global Challenges faculty member at the African Leadership University, Kigali Rwanda. Before joining the University, he was the founder and the manager of TECHmIT Africa, a technology and innovation ecosystem advocacy organization in Nigeria. He has a Bachelor's degree in Library and Information Science and a Master's degree in the same field from the University of Ibadan, Nigeria, a Master's in Public Policy (Technology Policy) at the Korean Development Institute School of Public Policy and Management South Korea, and is currently a PhD researcher in Creative Technologies at the COLAB, Auckland University of Technology, New Zealand.

Najeh Aissaoui is an expert in digital economy, professor at the Higher School of Communications of Tunis, University of Carthage, holder of a doctorate in economics (University of Sfax) and associate researcher at the LARIME laboratory (Higher School of Economics and Business). His research interests focus on the digital economy, inequalities in development economics, entrepreneurship and sustainable development.

Godfred Anakpo has a doctorate in Economics at the University of the Witwatersrand and is currently a postdoctoral research fellow in the Economics Department at Nelson Mandela University. He has done extensive studies on technological innovation and economic growth, and on the application of artificial intelligence and automation for economic development in the developing economy, culminating in journal papers. He has published extensively. His current research area and projects include behavioural and experimental economics, digital inclusion for small, medium and micro enterprises and the informal sector, and the sustainability of informal financial institutions. He is a mentor and supervisor/co-supervisor of several Bachelor's, Master's and PhD students.

Rachel Andisi is a librarian at the Kenya National Library Service at Lusumu branch in western Kenya, where she is in charge of all library operations at the branch level. She holds a Master's degree in Library and Information Science and has completed other short courses in line with her professional and career development.

Okwuoma Chidumebi Chijioke holds Bachelor's and Master's degrees in Library and Information Science from the University of Nigeria, Nsukka, where she is also currently a part-time doctoral student. She is an Assistant Chief Librarian in the National Library of Nigeria, Enugu State branch. She is an alumnus of AfLIA's International Network of Emerging Library Innovators, Sub-Saharan Africa, Cohort 2.

Na'angap Daship works with the National Library of Nigeria as an Assistant Chief Librarian. He holds a Bachelor's of Library and Information Science from Ahmadu Bello University, Zaria and a Master's of Library and Information Science from the University of Nigeria Nsukka. He is also an Alumnus of the AfLIA Leadership Academy, Cohort 2 and presently the Plateau State chairman of the Nigerian Library Association. He has published in journals and also presented academic papers at conferences.

Lanre Abubakar Folorunso has Bachelor's and doctoral degrees in Library and Information Science and is a chartered librarian. He began his career at the University of Ilorin, Nigeria, from where he gained practical knowledge as a library and information science educator. He has authored/co-authored publications in library and information science journals. Presently, he is Librarian in Charge of the National Institute for Sports, Lagos, Nigeria.

Eric Nelson Haumba is a Senior Librarian at the Law Development Centre as well as a Library and Information Science trainer in Uganda. He is a professional librarian administrator, with experience in building and developing the library into a fundamental constituent of university education and student academic success. He is also an experienced copy-editor and author. He holds a Master's of Science degree in Information Science from University of Pretoria. He is also a PhD candidate at the University of Cape Town, South Africa. He is the public lead, Creative Commons Uganda Chapter, AfLIA East Africa Representative and a freelance blogger.

Priti Jain is a professor of Information and Knowledge Management in the Department of Library and Information Studies, University of Botswana. She holds BA (Hons) and LL.B. degrees from Meerut University, India, a Master's in Library and Information Studies from the University of Botswana, and a DLit et Phil (Doctor of Literature and Philosophy) from Unisa, South Africa. Priti has published extensively in refereed journals and has presented several papers at international conferences. She serves on five editorial boards in international journals. Priti is engaged in various community initiatives, and teaches and researches in knowledge management and information science courses. Her areas of research interest are: knowledge management, open access, institutional repositories and digital scholarship.

Lynn Jibril is a librarian and an educator, currently employed by the University of Botswana Library. She has teaching experience spanning over 25 years in secondary schools. She holds a Master's degree in Library and Information Studies as well as a Diploma in Secondary Education. She is passionate about the teaching of information and digital literacy skills to both undergraduate and graduate students of the University. Her interests are research data management and open science issues. She is also the current president of the Botswana Library Association.

Sarah Kaddu holds a Bachelor's of Library and Information Science degree, Master of Arts in Information Studies and a PhD in Information Science. She is currently chair of IFLA Sub-Saharan Africa; chair of the Library and Information Science Section, AfLIA; immediate past president, Uganda Library and Information Association (ULIA); former secretary-general, ULIA; current chair, AfLIA LIS Education and Training Section; and an AfLIA Governing Council member. Sarah is also a reviewer of the IFLA/OCLC Jay Jordan Early Career Fellowship programme.

Syden Mishi holds a doctorate in Economics and is currently an associate professor of Economics and acting head of department at Nelson Mandela University, where he leads a research group in Behavioural and Experimental Economics. His research interest is in development economics, applying novel techniques to study issues like poverty, inequality, unemployment and irrational decision making.   He is the author to over 25 peer-reviewed journal articles and has contributed to book chapters. Syden is a guest editor for a special issue of Emerald Publishing's *African Journal of Economic and Management Studies*, has been a member of the Eastern Cape Province Economic Commission since 2020 and has been a member of the BRICS Ministers Expert Forum on Youth Employment since 2018.

Emmanuel Omeiza Momoh has a Bachelor's degree in Librarianship with additional certifications in leadership/team management, communication and project management. He is a chartered librarian by the Librarian Registration Council of Nigeria and has published articles on critical areas in librarianship. He is currently a member of the World Literacy Foundation and the Young African Library Leaders Fellowship, as well as of the Global Schools Advocacy Programme, where he and others assist in raising awareness on the United Nations' Sustainable Development Goals and the importance of the library in society.

Miriam Mureithi has a Bachelor's degree in Information Science from Moi University and a Master's degree in Knowledge Management from Kisii University. She has 19 years' experience in information technology, records management and librarianship. She is a Principal Librarian at Kenya National Library Services, Thika and has steered the library services, leading to recognition and awards at local and international levels. Miriam is passionate about youth empowerment programmes in the library. As a beneficiary of the African Library and Information Association and Institutions Leadership Academy cohort 1, she started a highly successful digital skills youth empowerment programme in 2018.

Faridah Muzaki holds Bachelor of Library and Information Science and Master of Science in Information Science degrees, both from Makerere University, and is currently an assistant lecturer at the East African School of Library and Information Science.

Ngozi Ogechukwu Nwogwugwu holds a Master's degree in Library and Information Science, and a doctorate in Business Administration, both from Nnamdi Azikiwe University, Awka, Anambra State, Nigeria. Ngozi is the librarian in charge of Confucius Institute Library at Nnamdi Azikiwe University.

Jeff B. Nyoka is a librarian from Durban, South Africa. He has a degree in Library Science from Durban University of Technology. He has worked at the eThekwini Municipality Libraries and University of KwaZulu Natal libraries and resource centres and has been the e-Learning manager for the City of Johannesburg Municipality Public Library Services, since 2016. Jeff also holds a Management Development Program Certificate and is currently running a Master's degree course in ICT Policy and Regulation, focusing on Digital Literacy, at the University of Witwatersrand. Jeff is an award-winning librarian who has implemented digital literacy courses, coding programs and other online courses in libraries.

Joshua Onaade Ojo, PhD, is a senior librarian with the University of Lagos Library, Nigeria. He holds degrees in Library and Information Science and in Sociology. He has worked in public, private and non-governmental organizations and is currently working in the technical services department of the library. Joshua is interested in resources management, information brokerage and information for development. He has attended local and international conferences and has published extensively at local and international levels. He is the chairman of the Nigerian Library Association, Lagos State.

Glory Odochi Okeagu is on the staff of the National Library of Nigeria, Abuja. She has Bachelor's of Library Science and Master's of Library and Information Science degrees from Abia State University and the University of Ibadan. She enjoys mentoring young librarians and using technology for the innovative dissemination of information.

Solape Oshile is a graduate of Computer Science from the University of Ilorin and is currently running a programme for a Master's degree in Information Management in Ahmadu Bello University, Zaria. He is a member of Computer Professionals Registration Council of Nigeria, deputy director and head of ICT at the National Library of Nigeria and has vast experience in database administration, systems analysis and design.

Hayford Siaw is the Executive Director of the Ghana Library Authority. He holds a Bachelor of Business Administration from Sikkim Manipal University; an Executive Master of Business Administration, Project Management specialization from the University of Ghana Business School; and a Certificate in Non-Profit and Public Administration Management from the School of International and Public Affairs, Piket Centre, Columbia University. Hayford is a trusted social entrepreneur and a development consultant with a wealth of experience spanning 15 years. He founded and served as the Chief Executive Officer of the Street Library Ghana and Volunteer Partnerships for West Africa.

Introduction

Access to information is an acknowledged human equalizer and enabler of development. Technology is aiding the increased spread and wide reach of information as never before. This leads to faster development outcomes and social changes that have a great ability to spawn transformed and inclusive communities. Robust economic growth, opportunities for the betterment of life and job creation can also be achieved through digital transformation as people access critical information that can breed innovative solutions to development challenges. Technology is also aiding the spread of information as never before to communities which may be considered marginalized development-wise.

For Africa to fully tap into the digital economy that will drive development in all facets of human life, the need to address deficits in digital infrastructure and skills is obvious. Internet access is the backbone of the digital economy. There are other challenges of cost and space for connecting mobile devices with the internet. Africa has wholly embraced mobile telephony; it is estimated that there will be 475 million mobile internet users in sub-Saharan Africa by 2025 even as internet penetration in the continent was measured at 39.3% in the first quarter of 2020.

Digital infrastructure without commensurate digital skills is a great mismatch. While formal education offers some help to those of school age to learn basic digital skills, there are millions of Africans in workplaces, in governance, involved in commercial activities at various levels, out of school, in rural communities and in cities who need to learn these skills and how to apply them so that they can operate optimally in digital spaces, whether accessing the internet via fixed or mobile devices.

Furthermore, development in the 21st century is intentional and methodological. Research as an integral part of development requires that citizens have access to skills for searching out, using and building on available knowledge. Digital literacy skills are needed to adroitly mine (search, evaluate, use, adapt and share) the internet for information as part of the research process. This is critical at the tertiary education level, where a strong national system/infrastructure of innovation can be instituted by empowering academics with above-average digital literacy skills for knowledge production/sharing that will support quality education through providing students with enhanced learning experiences and informing the field of new and best discoveries/practices.

The COVID-19 crisis brought to fore the digital gap in the African continent as schools, markets, workplaces and other physical meeting places shut down. Teaching, learning, research, communication and all forms of engagement went online and the need for digital literacy at all levels became glaring. Chapter 1 discusses the digital gap in Africa, how the COVID-19 pandemic has widened the gap and the attendant inequalities caused by this. Chapter 2 narrows down the digital gap to Tunisia, North Africa and looks at how the lack of digital skills can affect workers' wages. The book also delves into how libraries are engaging with different sections of African communities to inculcate digital skills.

Kenya's economic blueprint, the vision 2030, identified information and communication technology (ICT) as crucial for attainment of the goals and aspirations of the Kenya Vision 2030. One of the core pillars of this vision is to turn Kenya into a knowledge economy. Chapter 3 discusses how Kenya National Library Services, Thika has been running digital skills programmes for different groups in the city. The content of the programmes is clearly outlined, as well as the collaborations that gave birth to the programmes.

The City of Johannesburg embraced e-learning and the library played critical roles in ensuring that citizens had access to digital infrastructure and acquired the requisite digital skills. The story of how this happened – the steps, the challenges, successes and disappointments – is succinctly shared in Chapter 4. The chapter provides an example of how libraries lead in digital transformation, pre and post the COVID-19 crisis.

There are two chapters about how libraries in West Africa are inculcating digital skills. The National Library of Nigeria recognizes that lack of digital skills can breed inequalities. Chapter 5 details how the Library, through the innovative services introduced by librarians within the system who had attended AfLIA's (African Library and Information Associations and Institutions) International Network for Emerging Library Innovators, Sub-Saharan Africa and the AfLIA Leadership Academy, were able to teach digital skills to job seekers and some marginalized sections of the community. The Ghana Library Authority has been growing in leaps and bounds, and Chapter 6 outlines how the Library has been driving digital literacy in different parts of Ghana, with impressive outcomes.

Digital skills are viewed from various perspectives by different people, professions and groups. Chapter 7 provides a rare view of how librarians and educators in Botswana view the digital divide in the country and the impact of COVID-19 on teaching, learning and the use of library facilities and resources. Chapter 8 projects another perspective as digital skills as an entity are viewed through the prism of Library and Information Science undergraduates in Makarere, Uganda.

In ensuring that no one is left behind, Chapter 9 presents how a library in Kenya (Lusumu Branch, Kenya National Library Services) helps those with hearing impairments to acquire digital skills.

Chapter 10 argues that communities are the driving force for the acquisition of digital literacy. Chapter 11 provides an exposition of how creativity is fuelled by digital skills, the importance of knowledge sharing and how libraries play a role in enhancing this, while Chapter 12 links the high rate of unemployment in developing countries to lack of digital skills. Chapter 13 proposes a backwards modelling design for digital literacy in Africa. The chapter points out that there needs to be a measurement of the technology readiness and digital infrastructure development in Africa before the drive for digital literacy can have sustainable outcomes.

Digital Gap in Global and African Countries: Inequalities of Opportunities and COVID-19 Crisis Impact

Syden Mishi and Godfred Anakpo

Abstract

This chapter provides a critical review of the digital gap and how the COVID-19 crisis has impacted on the digital gap globally, with particular focus on developing countries. It begins by providing a comprehensive overview of the emerging trends and nature of the digital divide in the 21st century. It then details the COVID-19 crisis and the paradigm shift to a 'new normal', with a highlight on the technology in use and digital gap in the 'new normal'. It examines the ex-ante and ex-post inequalities of opportunity in relation to the digital economy amid the COVID-19 shock; barriers to digital application amid COVID-19 and related crises; and the prospects for and roadmap to digital application for sustainable development. It identifies critical issues on how the COVID-19 crisis has impacted on the digital gap both globally and in developing countries. While the chapter highlights the digital gap from a global perspective, there is a particular focus on African countries. The outbreak of COVID-19 has exposed the underlying socio-economic problem of inequality of opportunities, which have further widened and deepened the digital gap across the social and economic spectrum. Despite various interventions by government and non-governmental agencies to mitigate the impacts, barriers to digital application still exist, especially in Africa and in the developing world in general. This requires bold and coordinated action by governments as well as private industrial partnerships to achieve digital inclusion and sustainable development.

Keywords: Digital gap, global perspective, digital divide, African countries, inequality of opportunities, COVID-19 impacts, ICT, internet.

Introduction

While over 71% of the African population lack internet connectivity (International Telecommunication Union, 2019), the Internet of Things (IoT) is dominating and permeating everyone's life, and the issue of digital divide has become extremely important for actions toward inclusive growth and sustainable development. This is more critical now than ever as the wind of COVID-19 continues to blow, moving physical connectivity to virtual, online connection, thus engendering another dimension to inequality among people.

Inequality varies across countries, the most unequal countries being South Africa, Angola and Brazil and the most equal ones being Norway, Slovenia and Iceland, based on the Gini Coefficient (Scott, 2019; Worldbank, 2021). The world over, the call has been for inclusive growth, which will help to reduce socio-economic ills such as inequality, poverty and unemployment. Although efforts are being made to reduce inequalities, it has become evident that such efforts are often contested (for instance, land expropriation without compensation in some African countries), or they fall short of addressing the problem holistically. It is imperative to note that access to opportunities may be the necessary dimension to consider. Access to opportunities does determine livelihood and well-being outcomes, and the opportunities may differ even before effort is considered (ex-ante) or when effort is taken into account (ex-post). The latter is considered fair, but the former is unfair and is the basis of the inequalities seen in most developing countries at present (for example, as an outcome of the exclusionary pioneer and colonizers' policies).

Technological development is inevitable, its ubiquitous edge enabling greater productivity for individuals and firms, yet access has likely followed the pathways of existing inequalities. In effect, access to technology (the internet, for example) can be taken as an opportunity, with access being unequal in some instances before any effort is considered. The digital gap can therefore be attributable to inequality of opportunities, and evidence shows that the inequalities are both ex-ante and ex-post (unequal effort producing unequal outcomes). As such, the emergence of the digital economy has widened existing inequalities across different sectors and social spectrums. Many services and activities within the economy have migrated to the digital space, with more and more being added daily; and many new activities, goods and services have been created to meet the needs of the growing digital economy. Notable examples are how reading materials have become mainly available solely in digital spaces, with limited hard copies, and libraries have transformed their stock to match the changing times. The shift to the digital economy should match the adaptability, learning abilities and access of society at large, so as to avoid catastrophic exclusion, which would lead to further widening of inequalities. Resultantly, either any shock and reactions to such shocks within the economy can exacerbate the inequalities, or policy makers and development practitioners can consciously respond, taking it as an opportunity to fast track redress of the inequalities. There is a possibility that interventions may widen the gap if they are not carefully thought through. Further, not fully understanding the digital gap and its causes may enable it to persist.

This provokes critical consideration of questions such as the extent of the digital gap, especially in African countries; the ways in which COVID-19 creates and further widens digital inequality; and the existing interventions and roadmaps to eliminating the digital gap and promoting digital literacy for inclusive growth and sustainable development. The purpose of this chapter is to provide answers to the above critical questions.

This chapter provides a critical review of the digital gap and how the COVID-19 crisis has impacted on the digital gap globally, with particular focus on African countries, and addresses the roadmap for inclusive digital applications. It begins by providing a broader view of emerging trends and the nature of digital divide in the 21st century, giving a general overview and grasp of the state of the art. It then details the COVID-19 crisis and the paradigm shift to a 'new normal', highlighting the technology in use and the digital gap in the 'new normal'. The chapter further examines the ex-ante and ex-post inequalities of opportunity in relation to the digital economy, barriers to digital application amid COVID-19 and related impacts. Lastly, interventions by government and non-governmental agencies and a roadmap for digital application for inclusive growth and sustainable development are highlighted.

Emerging trends and the nature of digital divide in the 21st century

The definition of digital divide, also known as digital gap, evolves over time, from century to century (Rouse, 2014). One frequently used definition in the 21st century characterizes it as differences and inequality in access, skills, use and benefit of modern information and communications technology (ICT) (internet connection) due to race, economic status, gender, physical ability, nationality and geography (Van Dijk, 2020). Prior to the 20th century, digital divide was mainly used to refer to the gap between those with access to the telephone and those without access. However, due to technological advancements, especially in the late 1990s to the 21st century, the term has been used to describe the gap between those who have access to and use internet and those without access to or use of the internet (Rouse, 2014). The digital divide has been identified as one of the pressing problems of the 21st century in the face of a digital-driven economy both globally and, especially, in African countries (Rai and Sharma, 2019).

From the global perspective

The use of modern ICT has witnessed exponential growth, especially since the beginning of the 21st century, and this trend is predicted to increase. The adoption and the use of ICT since the start of the century has had significant impacts on many aspects of life, including business activities and socio-economic growth around the globe (Acilar, 2011). As a result of recent advancements in the technological space, a significant knowledge and skills gap in ICT and its complementary assets exists between the rich and poor countries, and this has led to some countries being excluded from fully participating in the global village enabled by ICT (Iskandarani, 2008).

Table 1.1 documents percentages of internet usage (via computer, internet-enabled mobile phone and other devices) globally and by continents and regions. It is interesting to note that while internet usage is on an increasing trend in each category, the proportion of the population using the internet is much higher for the developed world than the developing world and for continents such as Europe and Americas than for Africa. For instance, over 80% of people in the developed world have been using the internet since 2017, while in the developing world less than half the population has internet access. Continents such as Europe and the Americas were in the lead. Africa, however, recorded the least number of people with internet usage (21.8% in

Table 1.1 *Internet users: worldwide, continent and region*

Internet users	2005 percentage of population	2010 percentage of population	2017 percentage of population	2019 percentage of population
Worldwide	16.0	30.0	48.0	53.6
Africa	2.0	10.0	21.8	28.2
Americas	36.0	49.0	65.9	77.2
Arab states	8.0	26.0	43.7	51.6
Asian and Pacific	9.0	23.0	43.9	48.4
Commonwealth of Independent States	10.0	34.0	67.7	72.2
Europe	46.0	67.0	79.6	82.5
Developed world	51.0	67.0	81.0	86.6
Developing world	8.0	21.0	41.3	47.0

Source: International Telecommunication Union (2019).

2017 and 28.2% in 2019), a record that is below the world averages of 48.0% and 53.6% for 2017 and 2019, respectively. Furthermore, the rate of increase in internet usage is much higher for the Americas and Europe than for Africa. The developed world had about 81% and 86% of its population with internet access and use in 2017 and 2019, respectively. All these statistics epitomize a wide range of digital disparity between the richer continents (Europe and America) and poorer continents such as Africa, and between the developed and the developing worlds. This disparity can be explained by the theories of technology and diffusion of innovations (DOI) theory (Rogers, 2005).

While the theories of technology explain how technological innovation is produced, and the factors that shape it and its impacts on the society and culture, DOI theory seeks to explain how, why and at what speed or rate new technology innovation spreads through society and cultures. In his theory, Rogers documented five fundamental factors that drive the dissemination and adoption of innovative technology: 'the innovation itself, adopters, communication channels, time, and a social system, all of which rely heavily on human capital'. To be self-sustaining, the innovation must be broadly embraced and used by many people. Diffusion takes several forms and is very dependent on the kind of adopters and innovative decision-making process (Rogers, 2005). In this context, there is a high level of variability in terms of the rate of adoption of ICT globally, and among continents, regions and countries, that accounts for the digital gap, and this is largely attributed to economic, social, geographic, educational and demographic factors (Cruz-Jesus, Oliveira and Bacao, 2018). Authors have also found evidence that countries in which English is the native language are more willing and inclined to digital adoption, since that language is often used as a medium of scientific communication and technological innovation propels economic development and industrial outputs (Anakpo and Oyenubi, 2020; Anakpo and Kollamparambil, 2020).

This partly explains why Africa recorded the highest gender gap in terms of internet usage among all the continents in 2013 and 2019 (Figure 1.1 on the next page). This shows that the inability to use technologies is incrementally creating an entirely new group of disadvantaged persons.

From the African countries' perspective

In contrast to the enormous success of the developed countries in the ICT space, the digital divide in African countries is both widening and deepening. It is widening because access and use of ICT is limited to a small group of people (as seen in Table 1.1), despite efforts at bridging the gap, and it is deepening in the sense that the ultimate consequence of the majority not

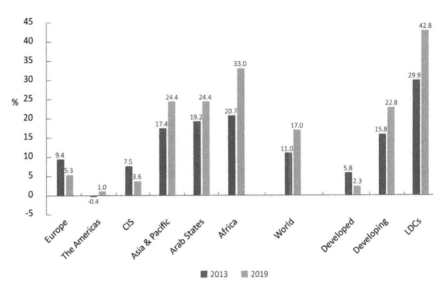

The Internet user gender gap (%), 2013 and 2019*

Figure 1.1 *Internet usage by gender*

Source: International Telecommunication Union (2019).

accessing and using ICT is far reaching, with enduring effects. Figure 1.2 shows internet usage by five African sub-regions: North, West, Central, East and Southern Africa. The figure indicates an increasing trend of internet usage for North Africa since 2011. However, the trend is constant for Central, East and Southern Africa and on a downward trajectory for the West Africa sub-region from 2017 to 2019, prior to the declaration of COVID-19 as a pandemic in 2020. By implication, these four African sub-regions are more likely to be hardest hit by the outbreak of COVID-19, at least in the short term. In general, Figure 1.2 opposite shows that North Africa continually records the highest growth in user numbers from 2011 to 2019, followed by Southern African, whereas Central Africa recorded the lowest growth over that period. This indicates that even among the sub-regions in Africa, which is often ranked as the poorest continent, there is a high level of intra-regional digital disparity and this may get worse.

There is high digital disparity not only between rich countries and African countries but even within African countries (Table 1.2). One thought-provoking question is: Why is Africa of special interest on this subject? According to the United Nations Human Development Report (UNDP, 2005), sub-Saharan African is the least developed region in the world, characterized

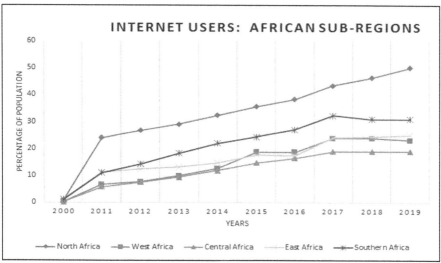

Figure 1.2 *Internet usage statistics for Africa*

Source: Compiled using data from Worldbank (2021).

by low income, school enrolment and life expectancy. As a continent with low income level (per capita), Africa generally lacks adequate infrastructural capability and the commitment to create the innovative technology (for instance ICT) that has become a necessary precursor and driver for high productivity and socio-economic growth. Further, the high initial investment cost associated with the creation and diffusion of innovative technology is seen as a big burden to the already poor continent, making the adoption rate of technology drastically low in comparison to the developed world.

Table 1.2 *Percentages of population of African countries using the internet*

Country	2000	2011	2013	2015	2017	2018	2019
North Africa							
Algeria	0.49	14.9	22.5	38.2	47.69	59.57	59.57
Egypt. Arab Rep.	0.64	25.6	29.4	37.82	44.95	46.92	57.28
Libya	0.18	14.0	16.5	19.02	21.76	21.76	21.75
Mauritania	0.19	4.5	6.2	15.20	20.80	20.80	20.80
Morocco	0.69	46.1	56.0	57.08	61.76	64.80	74.38
Tunisia	2.75	39.1	43.8	46.50	64.19	64.19	66.70
West Africa							
Benin	0.22	4.15	4.9	11.25	20.0	20.0	20.0
Burkina Faso	0.08	3.00	9.1	14.0	16.0	16.0	16.0

Table 1.2 *Continued*

Country	2000	2011	2013	2015	2017	2018	2019
Cabo Verde	1.82	32.00	37.5	42.68	57.16	58.17	58.17
Cote d'Ivoire	0.23	2.90	12.0	38.44	43.83	46.82	36.45
Gambia, The	0.92	10.87	14.0	16.50	19.83	19.83	19.84
Ghana	0.15	9.0	15.0	25.0	39.0	39.0	39.0
Guinea	0.09	2.0	4.5	8.20	18.0	18.0	18.0
Guinea-Bissau	0.23	2.67	3.1	3.54	3.93	3.93	3.93
Liberia	0.018	2.5	3.2	33.0	7.98	7.98	7.98
Mali	0.14	2.2	3.5	10.33	13.0	13.0	13.0
Niger	0.04	0.9	1.15	2.48	10.22	5.25	5.25
Nigeria	0.06	13.8	19.1	36.0	42.0	42.0	42.0
Senegal	0.40	9.8	13.1	27.0	46.0	46.0	46.0
Sierra Leone	0.12	0.9	4.0	6.34	9.0	9.0	9.0
Togo	0.8	3.5	4.5	7.12	12.36	12.36	12.36
Central Africa							
Burundi	0.07	1.11	1.26	4.86	2.66	2.66	2.66
Cameroon	0.25	5.0	10.0	20.68	23.20	23.20	23.20
Central African Republic	0.05	2.2	3.4	3.8	4.33	4.34	4.33
Chad	0.035	1.9	2.5	3.5	6.5	6.5	6.5
Congo, Dem. Rep.	0.01	1.2	2.2	3.8	8.62	8.62	8.61
Equatorial Guinea	0.13	11.5	16.4	21.32	26.24	26.24	26.24
Gabon	1.22	18.0	30.53	45.78	62.0	62.0	62.0
East Africa							
Comoros	0.271	5.5	6.5	7.45	8.48	8.47	8.47
Djibouti	0.19	7.0	9.5	11.92	55.68	55.68	55.68
Eritrea	0.13	0.7	0.9	1.08	1.31	1.30	1.31
Ethiopia	0.02	1.1	4.6	13.85	18.62	18.61	18.62
Kenya	0.32	8.8	13.0	16.58	17.83	17.82	22.56
Madagascar	0.19	1.9	3.0	4.17	9.8	9.8	9.8
Mauritius	7.28	34.95	40.12	50.13	55.40	58.59	63.99
Rwanda	0.06	7.0	9.0	18.0	21.76	21.76	21.76
Seychelles	7.39	43.16	50.4	54.25	58.76	58.76	58.76
Somalia	0.02	1.25	1.5	1.76	2.00	2.0	2.0
South Sudan	..	..	3.83	5.5	7.97	7.97	7.97
Sudan	0.02	17.46	22.7	26.61	30.87	30.87	30.87
Tanzania	0.12	3.2	4.4	20.0	25.0	25.0	25.0
Uganda	0.16	13.01	15.5	17.83	23.70	23.70	23.71

Table 1.2 *Continued*

Country	2000	2011	2013	2015	2017	2018	2019
Southern Africa							
Angola	0.11	3.1	8.9	12.4	14.33	14.33	14.34
Botswana	2.90	9.0	30.0	37.31	47.0	47.0	47.0
Lesotho	0.21	7.0	15.0	25.0	29.0	29.0	29.0
Malawi	0.13	3.33	5.05	5.3	13.78	13.78	13.78
Mozambique	0.11	4.3	7.29	16.93	10.0	10.0	10.0
Namibia	1.64	12.0	13.9	25.68	51.0	51.0	51.0
South Africa	5.34	33.97	46.5	51.92	56.17	56.16	56.16
Eswatini	0.93	18.13	24.70	25.64	47.0	47.0	47.0
Zambia	0.19	11.5	15.4	21.0	27.85	14.3	14.3
Zimbabwe	0.40	8.4	15.5	22.74	27.05	27.05	27.05

Source: Worldbank (2021).

Additionally, due to low school enrolment rates, the digital literacy rate is extremely low in Africa as compared to developed countries, and this affects ICT or internet usage proportionally (UNDP, 2005). The low life expectancy also adversely affects technology transfer. Other factors such as age, gender, educational level and rurality are significant determinants, especially in Africa (Acilar, 2011).

Furthermore, internet shutdowns (in some African countries) have profound direct and indirect impacts which could be short term (such as disengagement and exclusion of individuals, businesses, or countries from participating in the digital-driven world as long as the shutdown persists), long-term (through effects on the economy, business activities and missed opportunities that may never be regained) or a combination of both, and this can further widen and deepen the digital divide. Internet-driven businesses are hardest hit by internet shutdowns which adversely affect productivity and monetary returns, especially in time-sensitive transactions. Sometimes, in the face of persistent shutdown, individuals lose jobs and become incapable of affording access to ICT. For instance, in 2017 the internet shutdown in the Anglophone regions of Cameroon for 240 days led to a number of ICT/internet-related job losses, which are precursors of digital disparity (Thijmen, 2017). Additionally, internet shutdowns are estimated to have a deleterious economic impact, due to disruption of business operations. For instance, according to West (2016), the global cost of internet shutdowns in 2015–16 was estimated at $2.4 billion. Also, internet shutdown per day costs an estimated $3.1 million in Ethiopia, $2 million in the Democratic Republic of Congo, $1.7million in Uganda and $1.67 million in Cameroon

(Anglophone) (CIPESA, 2019). Shutdowns have a direct impact on countries' gross domestic product (GDP).

Beyond macro-economic impacts, shutdowns also result in loss of earnings in the digital economy and of government revenues which could otherwise be used for investment in digital infrastructure. They also affect the informal sectors of the economies of different countries, worker productivity, supply chains, manufacturers and service providers, investor confidence and foreign direct investment (Mare, 2019). Even an internet shutdown for a short period of time affects many facets of the national economy and this tends to persist far beyond the period for which access is disrupted. Internet shutdowns can also lead to political impacts (civil unrest, causing vulnerable groups to become more vulnerable and further removed from digital space), technical impacts (such as collateral damages and blocking of websites due to internet disruption) and social impacts (such as inability of individuals to complete online job applications, applications for basic identity documents, submission of school and college assignments and transfer of remittances), as witnessed in countries such as Ethiopia, the Democratic Republic of Congo, Uganda, Cameroon, Tanzania and other countries. All of these could further widen and deepen the digital divide between individuals, business entities and countries and geographical areas. With the digital economy growing ubiquitously, the power to connect people across socio-economic divides instantaneously has been viewed as an enemy in weak democracies where propaganda and state-controlled media dominate. As a result, such shutdowns will continue to be witnessed, and some institutions (such as the judiciary) have to be strong and independent to prevent persistent use of this approach.

COVID-19 crisis and a paradigm shift to a 'new normal'

Following the outbreak of the COVID-19 pandemic, global and country-level response measures, sharply contrasting with 'normal' life, were put in place to mitigate the spread of the deadly virus. Firstly, social distancing protocol was implemented to minimize the risk of spreading the virus through contact with infected persons. This was accompanied by rules to prohibit hand shaking and touching surfaces exposed to the public. Subsequently, with the astronomical increases in confirmed cases and rising death tolls, complete lockdowns were enforced that inevitably compelled businesses and institutions into complete shutdown, with the exception of those classified as essential and providers of critical services or goods. Thus, physical activities in the 'old normal' came either partially or completely to a halt. While these interventions contained the outbreak, they posed a severe threat to the survival of businesses, institutions and individual lives. Consequently, a paradigm shift to a 'new normal' has emerged, where internet connection and online activities have dominated, are gradually replacing the old physical way of doing things and are more than ever becoming an essential part of life (Anakpo and Mishi, 2020). People relied on the internet for access of updates on what is happening in the world, and it became an important information and learning tool.

ICT products became a necessity, yet for some they are generally beyond reach and people are not acquainted with their use, even if access is granted as a public good (proliferation of free Wi-Fi zones in some cities; the top 10 cities with free Wi-Fi zones in public spaces are in developed continents (Marcus, 2014), with capped access growing at a snail's pace in African cities (Mzekandaba, 2018)). Those who relied on previously public spaces for free Wi-Fi access – such as libraries and internet cafés – were cut off, because such areas and 'services' were not categorized as essential. The essentiality and continuity of services has become pronounced and understood by many but, unfortunately, public sites of internet access have never earned that badge. Industries and organizations were forced to embark on a new business model called 'working from home' (WFH); most schools and universities moved to online classes and assessment of students, webinars and other online engagement, while individuals used the internet to reach out to their loved ones.

Digital gap amid the COVID-19 'new normal'

Despite the recent increase in internet usage to embrace the 'new normal' spiked by the outbreak of COVID-19, the pandemic has exacerbated the digital divide by limiting opportunities and benefits for the poor (who cannot access the online platform), while the rich get richer through the opportunities and benefits of internet access. COVID-19 has fast tracked a fourth industrial revolution.

Global digital gap amid COVID-19

Prior to the declaration of COVID-19 as a pandemic, in 2019 the world's population without access to modern ICT and internet connection was recorded at 46.4%. This, by implication, indicates that about 46.4% were at higher risk of being marginalized and excluded from participating in the technology-driven economy through online activities, at least in the short-term. It is important to note that while the COVID-19 pandemic has widened and deepened the digital gap globally, the impact is much less significant in the developed world than in the developing world, especially in Africa. For instance, as at the end of 2019 and beginning of 2020, only 13.4% of the developed world did not have access to or use internet. More specifically, only 17.5% of the population in Europe were without internet access, while 22.7% of the population in the Americas were not using internet at the beginning of 2020. However, the digital disparity in the developed world is predominantly an urban–rural digital disparity (Lai and Widmar, 2020), and the COVID-19 pandemic continues to widen and deepen urban–rural digital disparity in the developed world. For instance, in the developed world, like the USA, for many rural residents, internet access and speed is a major challenge (Lai and Widmar, 2020). It has been documented that only 51.6% of those in the rural areas of the USA had 250/25 megabits per second (Mbps) internet access in 2018, as compared to 94% of urban residents (Federal Communications Commission, 2020).

African countries' digital gap amid COVID-19

In a time when social distancing, minimal social gathering and lockdown restrictions are enforced by governments, digital technology has become the only option for continuation of work, education, economic activities and communication. However, the vast majority of Africans without access to and use of modern ICT were more likely to experience the adverse economic impacts, at least during the initial stage of the lockdown restrictions. As at the end of 2019 and beginning of 2020, about 71.8% of the African population did not have access to or were not using the internet and therefore could not participate in the technology-driven world through online platforms. Africa is a continent classified as poorest (UNDP, 2005), with poor infrastructure and a low level of digital literacy. The COVID-19 pandemic with its related restrictions poses a great work challenge to Africa's people, due to the inability to afford the right technology, including internet, to participate in the 'new normal' driven by digital technology. In 2019 only 10 out of 45 African countries tracked by the Alliance for Affordable Internet were able to afford internet connectivity (defined as 1GB of mobile prepaid data costing 2% or less of the average monthly income) (Lai and Widmar, 2020).

Table 1.3 opposite shows internet penetration rates at the beginning of 2021. It shows that about 46.2% of the African population uses the internet. While this figure is an improvement on the 28.2% recorded for Africa in 2019, the increase is mainly among males and urban populations, further widening and deepening gender and urban–rural disparity, as a majority of the population are still excluded from the ever-growing digital world and its enormous socio-economic benefits. Over 85% of the population in African countries, such as Congo, Madagascar, Togo, Chad, Guinea-Bissau among others, are still

Table 1.3 *Africa internet usage, 2021 population statistics and Facebook subscribers*

Africa	Population (2021 est.)	Internet users 31-Dec-2000	Internet users 31-Dec-2020	Penetration (% population)	Internet growth % 2000–2020	Facebook subscribers 31-Dec-2020
Algeria	44,616,624	50,000	25,428,159	57.0%	50,756%	25,140,000
Angola	33,933,610	30,000	8,980,670	26.5%	29,835%	2,831,000
Benin	12,451,040	15,000	3,801,758	30.5%	25,245%	1,538,500
Botswana	2,397,241	15,000	1,139,000	47.5%	7,493%	1,139,000
Burkina Faso	21,497,096	10,000	4,594,265	21.4%	45,842%	1,998,200
Burundi	12,255,433	3,000	1,606,122	13.1%	53,437%	667,700
Cabo Verde	561,898	8,000	352,120	62.7%	4,302%	287,000
Cameroon	27,224,265	20,000	7,878,422	28.9%	39,292%	4,267,000
Central African Rep.	4,919,981	1,500	557,085	11.3%	37,039%	135,700
Chad	16,914,985	1,000	2,237,932	13.2%	223,693%	443,200
Comoros	888,451	1,500	193,700	21.8%	12,813%	193,700
Congo	5,657,013	500	833,200	14.7%	166,540%	833,200
Congo, Dem. Rep.	92,377,993	500	16,355,917	17.7%	3,271,083%	3,800,000
Cote d'Ivoire	27,053,629	40,000	12,253,653	45.3%	30,534%	5,860,000
Djibouti	1,002,187	1,400	548,832	54.8%	39,102%	258,100
Egypt	104,258,327	450,000	54,741,493	52.5%	12,064%	48,830,000
Equatorial Guinea	1,449,896	500	362,891	25.0%	72,478%	120,900
Eritrea	3,601,467	5,000	248,199	6.9%	4,864%	6,200
Eswatini	1,172,362	10,000	665,245	56.7%	6,552%	339,900
Ethiopia	117,876,227	10,000	21,147,255	17.9%	211,372%	6,745,000
Gabon	2,278,825	15,000	1,367,641	60.0%	9,017%	830,000
Gambia	2,486,945	4,000	442,050	19.0%	11,713%	419,100
Ghana	31,732,129	30,000	14,767,818	46.5%	49,126%	7,944,000
Guinea	13,497,244	8,000	2,551,672	18.9%	31,795%	1,938,000
Guinea-Bissau	2,015,494	1,500	250,000	12.4%	16,566%	140,000
Kenya	54,985,698	200,000	46,870,422	85.2%	23,335%	10,444,000
Lesotho	2,159,079	4,000	682,990	31.6%	16,974%	490,900
Liberia	5,180,203	500	760,994	14.7%	152,098%	658,200
Libya	6,958,532	10,000	5,857,000	84.2%	58,470%	5,857,000

Table 1.3 *Continued*

Africa	Population (2021 est.)	Internet users 31-Dec-2000	Internet users 31-Dec-2020	Penetration (% population)	Internet growth % 2000–2020	Facebook subscribers 31-Dec-2020
Madagascar	28,427,328	30,000	2,864,000	10.1%	9,446%	2,864,000
Malawi	19,647,684	15,000	2,717,243	13.8%	18,015%	637,600
Mali	20,855,735	18,800	12,480,176	59.8%	66,284%	2,033,300
Mauritania	4,775,119	5,000	969,519	20.3%	19,290%	927,300
Mauritius	1,273,433	87,000	919,000	72.2%	956%	919,000
Mayotte (FR)	279,515	n/a	107,940	38.6%	n/a	95,500
Morocco	37,344,795	100,000	25,589,581	68.5%	25,489%	21,730,000
Mozambique	32,163,047	30,000	6,523,613	20.3%	21,645%	2,756,000
Namibia	2,587,344	30,000	1,347,418	52.1%	4,391%	792,000
Niger	25,130,817	5,000	3,363,848	13.4%	67,177%	577,800
Nigeria	211,400,708	200,000	203,168,355	96.1%	101,484%	31,860,000
Réunion (FR)	901,686	130,000	608,000	67.4%	367%	608,000
Rwanda	13,276,513	5,000	5,981,638	45.1%	119,532%	806,200
Saint Helena (UK)	6,086	n/a	2,300	37.8%	n/a	2,300
Sao Tome & Principe	223,368	6,500	63,864	28.6%	882%	60,800
Senegal	17,196,301	40,000	9,749,527	56.7%	24,273%	3,802,000
Seychelles	98,908	6,000	71,300	72.1%	1,088%	71,300
Sierra Leone	8,141,343	5,000	1,043,725	12.8%	20,774%	833,400
Somalia	16,359,504	200	2,089,900	12.8%	852,550%	2,089,900
South Africa	60,041,994	2,400,000	34,545,165	57.5%	1,339%	24,600,000
South Sudan	11,381,378	n/a	900,716	7.9%	n/a	436,600
Sudan	44,909,353	30,000	13,124,100	29.2%	43,647%	1,300,000
Tanzania	61,498,437	115,000	23,142,960	37.6%	20,024%	5,223,000
Togo	8,478,250	100,000	1,011,837	11.9%	912%	860,500
Tunisia	11,935,766	100,000	8,170,000	68.4%	8,070%	8,170,000
Uganda	47,123,531	40,000	18,502,166	39.3%	46,155%	3,328,000
Western Sahara	611,875	n/a	28,000	4.6%	n/a	27,000
Zambia	18,920,651	20,000	9,870,427	52.2%	49,252%	2,543,000
Zimbabwe	15,092,171	50,000	8,400,000	55.7%	16,700%	1,303,000

Table 1.3 *Continued*

Africa	Population (2021 est.)	Internet users 31-Dec-2000	Internet users 31-Dec-2020	Penetration (% population)	Internet growth % 2000–2020	Facebook subscribers 31-Dec-2020
Total Africa	1,373,486,514	4,514,400	634,863,323	46.2%	13,963%	255,412,900
Rest of World	6,502,279,070	356,471,092	4,463,600,449	68.6%	87.5%	2,474,111,201
World total	7,875,765,584	360,985,492	5,098,463,772	64.7%	100.0%	2,729,524,101

Source: Internet World Statistics (2021).

without access to the internet (at the time of this writing) and the majority of these are from rural areas (Internet World Statistics, 2021). Table 1.3 shows the sharp digital disparity among African countries during the COVID-19 period. Additionally, the gap is expected to be wider between genders (as lockdown forces many women into housework and unemployment), urban and rural areas, various economic groups and so forth.

Ex-ante and ex-post inequalities of opportunities and implications of the digital gap

Prior to the outbreak of the COVID-19 pandemic, inequality was an issue of great concern in the developing world, especially in Africa. While there was a significant increase in internet usage during the outbreak, the pandemic has greatly heightened socio-economic and digital inequality, especially in Africa, at least in the short and medium terms.

Jobs

The vast majority of workers in Africa are in the informal sector, most of whom depend on daily wages and casual work for a living. The lockdown regulations and movement restrictions during the pandemic have caused significant job losses among this group, rendering them unemployed with no protection. For instance, in South Africa the rate of employment decreased from 57% to 38% within two months of the COVID-19 outbreak (Ranchhod and Daniels, 2020), while Kenya's unemployment rate doubled to 10.4% in the second quarter of 2020, compared to 5.2% in the first quarter (Huaxia, 2020).

Digital and asset inequality

The pandemic is leading to inequality of assets such as digital devices, which enables some to access and use the internet, whereas others who cannot afford them are rendered helpless. For instance, richer people, especially, in the developed world, can buy digital devices to participate in the ever-changing digital world. Consequently, they reap the benefits of participating in technology-enabled platforms and engagements and are able to expand their asset base, thus increasing relative advantages, while the poor have limited options and are faced with affordability challenges. More specifically, digital devices and internet connections are more, than ever, outside the reach of rural people (Tshabalala, Anakpo and Mishi, 2021). During the COVID-19 pandemic, digital inequalities may be further reinforced by a lack of access to digital support (Nguyen et al., 2020).

Restrictions in movement meant that access to the internet through friends, school, work, community library, internet café, among others was no longer possible. A smart gadget within the household was needed to enable continued access. In some households, one gadget ended up serving more than six people, for school and university-level education, for work and for everyday keeping in touch with family and friends afar. Besides the limited availability of devices, internet costs are beyond the reach of many, making access unsustainable or, worse still in the short run, displacing other essential household goods and services. Internet data is most expensive in developing countries (Facebook, 2016), for example, African countries with the most costly internet data are Swaziland and Zimbabwe, where 1GB of data cost $21.39 and $16.95, respectively in 2019 (Gilbert, 2019).

While efforts to obtain devices (government, non-governmental organizations and institutions of higher learning on their own or partnering with the private sector; as well as employers intervened vigorously) and costs are subsidized or budgetary sacrifices are made, the infrastructure in some areas is non-existent or not good enough to support the increased demand. Network spectrum became a stumbling block. Such challenges are common in already poor and marginalized communities (ex-ante inequality), and the efforts to obtain devices and meet the costs (effort) reduced ex-post inequalities. Interventions should not come at the tail end of the problem, to address the ex-post inequalities; they must start with redress of the ex-ante inequalities. ICT infrastructure is driven by profit, rather than being viewed as a public service provided by government (Rangaswamy, 2008). This view needs to radically change if inclusive growth is to be realized as the majority of economies become digitized.

Gender gap

Women are often disadvantaged in society, and this is expected to be more pronounced in the era of COVID-19. USAID (2020) documented that even though numbers of internet users have generally increased in the year 2020 above the statistics recorded in the previous years, the majority of this growth is among males and from urban areas. Thus, the problem of gender digital disparity persists in the COVID-19 era. This could be partly attributed to the fact that a large number of women generally work in the retail and hospitality industries, where working remotely is almost impossible during lockdown regulations, and are more likely to suffer job loss than are their male counterparts. Also, with many schools closing down, girls are at higher risk of not returning to school and this may affect their employment prospects in the long term.

Economic inequality

In a time of social distancing and lockdown regulations, making digital technology the only option for survival, rich people and countries can afford to embrace the new trend and reap the benefits associated with it, thereby making them richer. However, low income earners, poor people, less developed countries, those who live in rural areas and who either depend on a daily wage or do physical work or other offline activities, and who cannot afford digital devices to embrace the online model of the 'new normal', cannot reap the economic benefit. This exacerbates the existing economic disparities.

Interventions by governmental and non-governmental agencies and how they are mitigating the digital gap in Africa

The outbreak of COVID-19 spiked responses from governmental and non-governmental agencies to put in place interventions targeted at containing the spread of the virus and minimize related impacts such as the digital gap. This has encompassed investment and provision of remote working infrastructure, reinforcing and modernizing the role of libraries, capacity building for staff, providing relief to the vulnerable, financial bailouts for businesses and measures to contain the virus.

Investment and provision of remote working infrastructure

A major intervention during the outbreak of the pandemic was heavy investment in remote infrastructure. Both government agencies and organizations in the private sector, in an attempt to keep up with changes due to the pandemic, have invested in digital devices and internet infrastructure so as to adopt the WFH models of the 'new normal'. This also includes providing free community internet and other online resources. For instance, the South African government increased the free internet zone so as to create wider coverage, provided digital devices to staff in various public institutions and expanded infrastructure in schools, hospitals and other locations to enable the application of digital technology (Western Cape Government, 2020). Additionally, governments worked closely with key players in the telecommunications industry to provide short-term/emergency spectrum licences to mobile network operators to access any portions of unallocated spectrum, facilitate and expedite access to the backhaul spectrum and to extend deadlines for any ongoing transitions or renewals for licensees to provide high-speed broadband. Additionally, companies spent around US$15 billion extra each week on remote infrastructure to adapt to the new changes (KPMG, 2020).

Interventions of libraries towards digital inclusion in time of COVID-19

Libraries play a very critical role during the COVID-19 pandemic towards digital inclusion in the following areas.

Digital literacy and competence development

The COVID-19 pandemic reinforces even more the crucial role of academic libraries in helping students, staff and other users to search and develop information and acquire digital literacy skills so that they can be well equipped to independently select, access and use accurate, reliable, trustworthy and credible sources of information, not only for their studies but also for their own well-being (Martzoukou, 2020). For instance, the City of Johannesburg Library has been driving the city's e-Learning initiative by equipping users with digital information retrieval and management skills, using the digital platform which is so critical to participating in the digital world.

Provision of more wireless internet services

Libraries also play a critical role in providing wireless internet services to users (Jaeger et al., 2012). Since the outbreak of the COVID-19 pandemic and subsequent distancing protocols and government-enforced lockdown regulations, online activities have taken the place of the former physical ways of doing things, and these have helped those without access to the internet to participate in the 'new normal'. The provision of wireless internet services in libraries makes it more possible for the marginalized to participate and gain the benefit of being online. For instance, since the outbreak of the pandemic,

South African public libraries such as Central Library Cape Town, Strandfontein Library and Johannesburg City libraries have been providing free services to assist students and the general public in the 'new normal'.

Facilitation of collaboration with publishers

In response to the measures that were imposed on universities during the COVID-19 outbreak, university libraries liaised with publishers and suppliers, who offered on a temporary basis increased or free access to resources to support students and academics with online teaching, beyond their normal offerings to most university libraries, including those in Africa (a few indicative examples include ScienceDirect eBooks, EDP Sciences Journals, JSTOR public health journals, Microbiology Society, Pharmacy Knowledge, among others) (Robert Gordon University Library, 2020; Martzoukou, 2020).

Provision of institutional support to academic researchers

Before the outbreak of COVID-19, academic libraries were involved in the core mandate of providing resource materials and facilities to researchers for the sharing of knowledge for the benefit of the wider public good. Additionally, during the outbreak, libraries provided more internet services to help researchers navigate through any barriers to search and retrieval of information and, more importantly, renewing institutional subscriptions, regulating and updating their database periodically with information on all happenings during the outbreak.

Community service

Libraries, especially community libraries, provide services to various communities, especially those in rural areas, to update information on COVID-19 and to access internet connections. This narrows the digital disparity between urban and rural areas. The distance to the library, number of people per digital gadget and literacy levels may still hinder access, and the digital gap persists.

Communication and dissemination role

During the pandemic, academic libraries were actively involved in providing additional services, especially on curation of resources related to the COVID-19 outbreak to assist academics and other researchers in advancing their understanding, as well as to help them increase awareness of the importance of information evaluation for the public as a protective mechanism against the COVID-19 'infodemic' (Rafiq et al., 2021). The University of Cape Town Library, WITS Library and Nelson Mandela University Libraries among others were frequently sending out updates on pertinent issues related to COVID-19.

Capacity building for staff

Government and non-governmental organizations (NGOs) have also undertaken several initiatives on capacity building for staff to embrace the changes. This enhances inclusivity and participation in the digital world (Rallyware, 2020; Smith, 2020). Opportunities are being made more equal, to the extent that effort does not really define the inequalities, implying that any existing gaps are more historical and structural, engraved over longer periods of deprivation and distorted market prices. Therefore, the efforts by government and NGOs are welcome to increase access by a historically neglected group of people.

Containment measures of the virus and providing relief and financial bailouts

Since the outbreak of the pandemic, governments have taken measures to minimize the impacts of the disease. Beside the regulatory measures, governments also provide some reliefs such as income to the vulnerable and financial bailout to businesses. The effort by government to acquire vaccines for vaccination of people against the deadly virus is a major step to prevent future infection and disadvantages to the vulnerable.

Barriers to digital application amid the COVID-19 crisis

Despite various interventions by government and non-governmental agencies (indicated above), barriers still exist that greatly limit digital participation in Africa as compared to the rest of the world. This is evident in over half of the African population without access to internet as at the beginning of the year 2021. Thus, there is a wide gap in access to and usage of digital infrastructure and services between individuals, households, businesses, nations, continents and geographical areas. In this section, four major barriers to inclusive digital application are identified.

Lack of digital infrastructure and services

One main challenge to digital application in the developing world, especially in Africa, is a lack of digital infrastructure, specially relating to network connection to digital devices and to software and applications. For instance, it was documented that more than 50% of the world population do not have a network connection (Facebook, 2016). Additionally, in places where network connection has been extended, there is a big challenge in high-speed connection unlike in the developed world (Shenglin et al., 2017). These infrastructure challenges, coupled with the challenges of access to sustainable energy, further widen digital gaps not only between Africa and the rest of the world but even more so between urban and rural Africa.

Lack of affordable network services, devices and applications

In places where network connection is available, the majority cannot afford to pay for it. A study conducted by Facebook (2016) revealed that over two billion people could not afford a mobile device let alone pay for an internet connection. This further reinforces an earlier assertion (UNDP, 2005) that Africa is the poorest continent, heavily weighed down by poverty in all its forms.

Lack of digital skills to create or add value

Africa faces challenges of digital skills that will enable citizens to fully tap into digital technology and create added value within the ICT or internet domain. According to Shenglin et al. (2017), physical access to internet is a necessary condition, but insufficient skills to fully benefit from the digital-driven economy are a major challenge. For instance, in Africa, less than half of those with physical access to the internet have up-to-date skills to keep up with the ever-changing digital world. It is worth noting that without proper digital education and skills training, it is difficult to harness digital technology to the fullest.

Lack of coordinated efforts to foster social and economic equality

In most developing economies, especially in Africa, there is a substantial lack of coordinated effort by government, industry, research institutions and civil society organizations to foster social and economic inclusion and equality. For instance, when internet service providers (ISP) make possible wider access to the internet by many people, but without an oversight role for relevant government agencies of the activities of these service providers, the result can be greater control by the ISPs, rather than digital empowerment and inclusion. Similarly, absence of checks and balances of companies enjoying economies of scale can lead to a market monopoly that is often characterized by inefficiency due to lack of competition (Shenglin et al., 2017).

Prospects and roadmap to digital application for sustainable development

In the face of the digital challenges confronting developing countries, especially those in Africa, short- to long-term actions can be taken to significantly drive inclusive digital application and to narrow the digital divide.

Investment in digital and energy infrastructure

The first task toward inclusive digital application is the provision of universal digital infrastructure. This can happen through public-private partnership where government takes the lead and plays a critical role in providing funding commitment, policy and incentives to run in collaboration with the private sector for sustainability. It is also government's responsibility to draw investors through its policy action, a congenial investment climate and incentives to partner with other international corporations for mutual benefit. Key industrial players include those in the telecommunication industry, working harmoniously with government to achieve universal access to the internet and other ICT by people in both urban and rural areas. It also requires investment in sustainable energy infrastructure to power the operation of digital installations, apparatus and related devices.

Harnessing Television White Space for universal internet access in rural Africa

As documented earlier in this chapter, the trends in the digital divide are wide and deep in most African countries, where over 60% of the population reside in rural areas that are characterized as having low literacy, high poverty levels and limited telecommunication infrastructure support (Opawoye et al., 2015). Therefore, harnessing Television White Space (TVWS) could be a suitable solution for providing affordable universal access in rural Africa. TVWS refers to vacant, unused or interleaved frequencies located between broadcast TV channels in the Very High Frequency and Ultra High Frequency (VHF/UHF) range (which can be found between 54 MHz and 806 MHz (Andersson, 2014). TVWS is an invaluable technology system that has highly favourable propagation characteristics, such as a better signal that has the ability to pass through obstacles (such as buildings, weather, foliage), and allows for wireless broadband deployment with a greater range of operation or catchment area, unlike ordinary Wi-Fi, which has obstacle challenges, with a narrow range and poorer signal.

It has since been researched and proven (such as in pilot rollouts) that this unused spectrum can be harnessed to provide universal broadband internet access while operating harmoniously with surrounding TV channels. For instance, pilot projects were carried out to bring broadband internet access to rural areas in some African countries such as South Africa (connection of about ten selected schools, extension to some rural areas in Limpopo province, machine-to-machine communication), Kenya, Malawi, Nigeria and Tanzania which have proven to be successful in providing wider internet connectivity (Oliver and Majumder, 2019; Microsoft for Afrika Initiative, 2013). Furthermore, large-scale rollout of TVWS application can bring internet access to over 60% of the African population residing in rural areas, contribute significantly to economic growth (including the rural economy) (Wall, 2014), improve the capacity and quality of networks in public agencies, promote education (schools and universities), bring new services and applications to consumers, enhance mesh networking and promote security applications and reduction in energy consumption (due to reduction in the number of cell/sites needed to cover a geographical area). This can contribute significantly to bridging the digital divide between urban and rural areas, between countries and geographical locations, while at the same time ensuring proper planning for primary users and deployment mechanisms for secondary users.

Connecting the unconnected

The next action is to connect the unconnected people. For instance, since 2011, China has made it a major priority to connect all villages to the internet and this has been done through collaboration between central government, local government and the telecommunications industry, resulting in all the villages being connected to the internet connection. Africa can also achieve the same in several ways, including through government subsidies whereby internet connection and related services are made cheap and affordable.

Industry innovations

Industry innovations help break barriers and remove bottlenecks for digital inclusion. It is notable that during the early years of personal computers (PCs), access to the internet was mainly through computers and was limited to the few who could afford it. Later, mobile phones such as smartphones and other mobile devices were invented. Consequently, low-income people who could not afford PCs were able to acquire smartphones with which to access and use the internet. This innovation was a major breakthrough that has enabled adults, minorities and even those in rural areas to be connected through mobile devices.

Digital literacy

Digital literacy is an essential precursor for digital application. While physical access to the internet is a necessary condition towards digital application, it must be augmented with digital literacy to reap the full benefits. This involves both formal and informal education and training on digital skills and application, creating added value in the digital space.

Education should be dynamic and stay ahead

Technology is ever changing and growing exponentially, therefore education must be dynamic so as to stay in tune with the change. As technology progresses, some skills become obsolete and therefore continuous skills and knowledge update is required to keep up in the ever-changing technology-driven world. For instance, over three decades ago, the typewriter was widely used, but the computer has now taken over, rendering those with typewriter skills jobless. Goldin and Katz (2010) documented the dynamics in the labour market as a 'race between education and technology'. It is essential therefore that education be dynamic so as to meet specific sets of skills needed in each phase of the digital world.

Technology decision and budgeting

Universal technological application is important for the sustainable development of every developing economy in the age of the digital economy. However, for this to be achieved universally, conscious efforts through decision making and budgeting are a prerequisite. Governments must budget adequately for technology use and detail a practical course of action for its implementation. This includes investment in technology research (Anakpo and Oyenubi, 2020), providing the necessary equipment and facilities and promoting education at all levels.

Coordinated efforts

There must also be harmonious collaboration between government, researchers and industry players, and exchange of feedback among the parties. For instance, the government needs suitable policies involving market competition actions for universal access and affordability, and at the same time providing incentives to industry players. Furthermore, researchers need to tailor their research so that outcomes will be of use to industry and drive technology innovation. This coordinated effort is needed at global, national and local levels, involving the developing of policies, standards and regulations to ensure a high degree of competition, making services accessible to all.

Conclusion

In the ever-changing technological world, the digital gap between rich and poor countries and within poor countries is still widening and deepening. The outbreak of COVID-19 has made this more serious, as the vulnerable become even more vulnerable and deprived from engaging fully in the 'new normal' driven by digital technology. Africa remains the most affected, as over half of its population, due to inequality of opportunities, are still without ICT, internet connection, access to and participation in the digital-driven economy. While interventions are made governmental and non-governmental agencies, such as investment in remote working infrastructure, reinforcing the role of libraries, capacity building for staff, relief, financial bailouts and containment measures, some barriers (such as lack of digital infrastructure and services, lack of affordable network services, devices and applications, lack of digital skills to create or add value and lack of coordinated efforts to foster social and economic equality) still exist. To stay in tune with the digital-driven economy and universal digital application, bold actions – such as investment in digital infrastructure, TVWS application, connecting the unconnected, industry innovations, dynamic digital literacy education, technology decisions and budgeting and coordinated efforts – need to be taken for digital inclusion and sustainable development, especially in Africa.

Acknowledgements

This work is based on the research supported wholly by the National Research Foundation of South Africa (Grant Number 121890).

References

Acilar, A. (2011) Exploring the Aspects of Digital Divide in a Developing Country, *Issues in Informing Science and Information Technology*, 8 (April), 231–44, doi: 10.28945/1415.

Anakpo, G. and Kollamparambil, U. (2020) Effect of Artificial Intelligence on Unemployment: The Case of Southern Africa. Manuscript submitted for publication.

Anakpo, G. and Mishi, S. (2020) Business Response to COVID-19 Outbreak: Effectiveness Analysis in South Africa. Manuscript submitted for publication.

Anakpo, G. and Oyenubi, A. (2020) Technological Innovation and Economic Growth in Southern Africa: Application of Panel Dynamic OLS Regression. Manuscript submitted for publication.

Andersson, K. (2014) Using TV White Spaces for Rural Broadband, Carlson Wireless Technologies white paper, www.carlsonwireless.com/wp-content/uploads/2014/10/White_Spaces_White_Paper.pdf.

CIPESA (Collaboration on International ICT Policy for East and Southern Africa) (2019) *Despots and Disruptions: Five Dimensions of Internet Shutdowns in Africa*, https://cipesa.org/2019/03/despots-and-disruptions-five-dimensions-of-internet-shutdowns-in-africa.

Cruz-Jesus, F., Oliveira, T. and Bacao, F. (2018) The Global Digital Divide: Evidence and Drivers, Journal of Global Information Management, 26 (2), 1–26, doi: 10.4018/JGIM.2018040101.

Facebook (2016) *State of Connectivity 2015: A Report on Global Internet Access – About Facebook*, https://about.fb.com/news/2016/02/state-of-connectivity-2015-a-report-on-global-internet-access.

Federal Communications Commission (2020) Broadband Deployment Report No. FCC 20-50, www.fcc.gov/reports-research/reports/broadband-progress-reports/2020-broadband-deployment-report.

Gilbert, P. (2019) *Digital Inclusion: The Most Expensive Data Prices in Africa - Connecting Africa*, www.connectingafrica.com/author.asp?section_id=761&doc_id=756372.

Goldin, C. and Katz, L. F. (2010) *The Race Between Education and Technology*, Harvard University Press.

Huaxia (2020) Kenya's Unemployment Rate Doubles to 10.4 pct in Q2 due to COVID-19, www.xinhuanet.com/english/2020–09/03/c_139339492.htm.

International Telecommunication Union (2019) *Facts and Figures: Measuring Digital Development*, https://news.itu.int/measuring-digital-development-facts-figures-2019.

Internet World Statistics (2021) *Africa Internet Users, 2020 Population and Facebook Statistics*, www.internetworldstats.com/stats1.htm.

Iskandarani, M. Z. (2008) Effect of Information and Communication Technologies (ICT) on Non-industrial Countries – Digital Divide Model, *Journal of Computer Science*, **4** (4), 315–19, doi: 10.3844/jcssp.2008.315.319.

Jaeger, P. T., Bertot, J. C., Thompson, K. M. and Katz, S. M. (2012) The Intersection of Public Policy and Public Access: Digital Divides, Digital Literacy, Digital Inclusion, and Public Libraries, *Public Library Quarterly*, **31** (1), 1–20.

KPMG (2020) COVID-19 Forces One of the Biggest Surges in Tech Investment in History, Finds World's Largest Tech Leadership Survey, KPMG Global, https://home.kpmg/xx/en/home/media/press-releases/2020/09/covid-19-forces-one-of-the-biggest-surges-in-technology-investment-in-history-finds-worlds-largest-technology-leadership-survey.html.

Lai, J. and Widmar, N. O. (2020) Revisiting the Digital Divide in the COVID-19 Era, *Applied Economic Perspectives and Policy*, **43** (1), 458–64, doi: 10.1002/aepp.13104.

Marcus, L. (2014) San Francisco Gets Free Wi-Fi: Check Out these 9 Other Connected Cities, www.cntraveler.com/stories/2014–10–03/10-cities-with-free-wifi.

Mare, A. (2019) The Effects of Internet Shutdowns on Societies: Lessons for SADC Member States. Paper presented and submitted to the Southern Africa Regional Dialogue on Internet Access, Johannesburg, 5 November 2019, www.ngopulse.org/sites/default/files/attachments/THEMATIC%20PAPER_The%20effects%20of%20Internet%20shutdowns%20on%20societies_SADC%20Lesson%20by%20Dr%20Admire%20Mare.pdf.

Martzoukou, K. (2020) Academic Libraries in COVID-19: A Renewed Mission for Digital Literacy, *Library Management*, doi: 10.1108/LM-09-2020-0131.

Microsoft for Afrika Initiative (2013) White Space Project, www.microsoft.com/africa/4afrika/white_sp ces_project. aspx.

Mzekandaba, S. (2018) Minister Calls for More Public WiFi Zones, www.itweb.co.za/content/GxwQDM1AXVpMlPVo.

Nguyen, M. H., Gruber, J., Fuchs, J., Marler, W., Hunsaker, A. and Hargittai, E. (2020) Changes in Digital Communication During the COVID-19 Global Pandemic: Implications for Digital Inequality and Future Research, *Social Media and Society*, **6** (3), doi: 10.1177/2056305120948255.

Oliver, M. and Majumder, S. (2019) Motivation for TV White Space: An Explorative Study on Africa for Achieving the Rural Broadband Gap. In *2nd Europe – Middle East – North African Regional Conference of the International Telecommunications Society (ITS): Leveraging Technologies for Growth*, Aswan, Egypt, 18–21 February.

Opawoye, I., Faruk, N., Bello, O. W. and Ayeni, A. A. (2015) Recent Trends on TV White Space Deployments in Africa, *Nigerian Journal of Technology*, **34** (3), 556–63.

Rafiq, M., Batool, S. H., Ali, A. F. and Ullah, M. (2021) University Libraries Response to COVID-19 Pandemic: A Developing Country Perspective, *Journal of Academic Librarianship*, **47** (1), 102280, doi: 10.1016/j.acalib.2020.102280.

Rai, A. and Sharma, A. K. (2019) Digital Divide and Libraries: A Systematic Literature Review, *Library Herald*, **57** (3), 402, doi: 10.5958/0976-2469.2019.00026.5.

Rallyware, R. (2020) *Digital Transformation of Employee Training and Engagement – Rallyware*, www.rallyware.com/blog/knowledge-retention-strategy.

Ranchhod, V. and Daniels, R. C. (2020) *Labour Market Dynamics in South Africa in the Time of COVID-19*, Coronavirus Rapid Mobile Survey.

Rangaswamy, N. (2008) Telecenters and Internet Cafes: The Case of ICTs in Small Businesses, *Asian Journal of Communication*, **18** (4), 365–378, doi: 10.1080/01292980802344208.

Robert Gordon University Library (2020) Resources Related to the COVID-19 Outbreak, https://library.rgu.ac.uk/c.php?g=679488&p=4889976.

Rogers, E. M. (2005) *Diffusion of Innovations* (5th edn), Free Press.

Rouse, M. (2014) *What Is Digital Divide? Definition from WhatIs.com*, Techtarget.com, https://whatis.techtarget.com/definition/digital-divide.

Scott, K. (2019) *South Africa Is the World's Most Unequal Nation. 25 Years of Freedom Have Failed to Bridge the Divide*, https://edition.cnn.com/2019/05/07/africa/south-africa-elections-inequality-intl/index.html.

Shenglin, B., Simonelli, F., Ruidong, Z., Bosc, R. and Wenwei, L. (2017) Digital Infrastructure: Overcoming the Digital Divide in Emerging Economies, *G20 Insights*, **3**, 1–36.

Smith, B. (2020) Microsoft Launches Initiative to Help 25 Million People Worldwide Acquire the Digital Skills Needed in a COVID-19 Economy, *The Official Microsoft Blog*, https://blogs.microsoft.com/blog/2020/06/30/microsoft-launches-initiative-to-help-25-million-people-worldwide-acquire-the-digital-skills-needed-in-a-covid-19-economy.

Thijmen, C. (2017) Cameroon Shut Down the Internet for 240 Days, https://techtribes.org/cameroon-shuts-down-the-internet-for-240-days.

Tshabalala, N., Anakpo, G. and Mishi, P. S. (2021) Ex Ante vs Ex Post Asset-inequalities, Internet of Things, and COVID-19 Implications in South Africa, *Africagrowth Agenda*, **18** (1), 18–21.

UNDP (United Nations Development Program) (2005) *UNDP Annual Report 2005*, United Nations Development Programme, www.undp.org/content/undp/en/home/librarypage/corporate/undp_in_action_2007.html.

USAID (2020) *USAID Digital Strategy*, www.usaid.gov/sites/default/files/documents/15396/COVID-19_and_Gender_Digital_Divide.pdf.

Van Dijk, J. (2020) *The Digital Divide*, John Wiley & Sons.

Wall, M. (2014) Africa's Mobile Boom Powers Innovation Economy, www.bbc.com/news/busines28061813?oci d=africa outbrain_ techbiz.

West, D. M. (2016) *Internet Shutdowns Cost Countries $2.4 Billion Last Year*, Center for Technological Innovation at Brookings, www.brookings.edu/wp-content/uploads/2016/10/intenet-shutdowns-v-3.pdf.

Western Cape Government (2020) *Switching on Public Wi-Fi Hotspots across the Western Cape*, www.westerncape.gov.za/general-publication/switching-public-wi-fi-hotspots-across-western-cape.

Worldbank (2021) *GINI Index (World Bank Estimate),*
     https://datacatalog.worldbank.org/search?search_api_views_fulltext_op=AND&
     query=GINI+&sort_by=search_api_relevance&sort_by=search_api_relevance.

e-Skills and Wages in Tunisia

Najeh Aissaoui

Abstract

This chapter analyses the impact of employees' e-skills on wages. The estimation of a logit model on Tunisian data allowed us to identify two main results. First, digital skills are very important and required in the Tunisian labour market. Second, informational and strategic digital skills play a determining role in wages evolution.

Keywords: ICT, e-skills, wages, technological bias, inequality.

Introduction

Tunisia is currently going through a complicated period on all fronts. The main difficulties encountered by the country are linked to the health crisis and the economic models put in place at the end of the Arab Spring, demographics, poor governance and human capital. This, despite the good quantitative performance achieved in recent decades, contrasts with the country's difficulty in ensuring strong and sustainable growth. This divergence is partly explained by the low quality of human capital and the mismatch between the supply and demand for skills in the labour market.

Skills development is a necessity to put Tunisia on the path to recovery. However, the jobs and skills required of today are not those of yesterday. The development of the digital economy has rapidly changed the labour market. The capacity of Tunisian companies to grow and face competition has become increasingly dependent on the efficient and innovative use of information and communication technologies (ICTs). Therefore, digital skills are now essential to boost the competitiveness, employability and productivity of the workforce. These developments underline the importance of identifying this type of skill.

This chapter provides a contribution in this area. Using data collected in 2020 on the Tunisian labour market, it analyses the impact of employees' digital skills on wages. Such an analysis makes it possible both to highlight the importance of e-skills, the kind of digital skills required in the Tunisian labour market, and to provide certain recommendations to company managers and political decision makers in order to strengthen this integral part of the human capital.

The estimation of a logit model on Tunisian data allowed us to identify two main results. The first is that digital skills are very important and required in the Tunisian labour market. The second indicates that informational and strategic digital skills play a determining role in the evolution of wages.

The rest of this chapter is structured as follows. The first section presents a review of the literature; the second section is devoted to the state of the digital economy and e-skills in Tunisia; and in the third section we carry out an empirical analysis providing an explanation of the evolution of wages in the Tunisian labour market. The last section is the Conclusion.

Literature review
ICT and wages evolution

The ICT–wage inequality relationship finds its origins in the literature on the phenomenon of biased technological change. The coincidence, in the USA, of the arrival of a wave of technological innovation with the rise in wage inequality between workers has sparked the debate on the existence of a technological bias in favour of skilled workers (Quinet, 2000). Acemoglu (2001) proves the existence of a technological bias in the USA because the increase, since 1960, in the supply of skills has been accompanied by an increase in the skill premium. The biased technological change thesis has been the subject of a multitude of empirical and theoretical works. The main idea of this literature is that new technologies are complementary to skilled labour. Bartel and Sicherman (1997) detect the existence of a significant positive relationship between wages and technological change and attribute this result to the adaptability of skilled workers to new technologies, which is relatively strong. Card and DiNardo (2002) state that workers with a higher level of education are more able to familiarize themselves with ICT and to use computers at work. Thus, the productivity of skilled labour increases and that of the unskilled decreases. This divergence in productivity generates a divergence in wages and inequalities between the two categories of workers (Ben Youssef, 2004).

The diffusion of ICT induces significant organizational changes within companies, which must absolutely redefine their business model. Indeed, digitalization requires companies to completely rethink their processes in order to build, integrate and reconfigure external and internal skills and resources (Benghozi and Cohendet, 1997). Specifically, the implementation of digital technologies paves the way for more autonomy, teamwork, project work, cooperation, job rotation and participation in decision making (Crifo, 2003). Bué et al. (2002) state that the impact of ICT on skills and wages would rather be to look into organizational change.

Digital skills

Digital skills are one of the main factors in conceptualizing the digital divide. The difference in their ownership between employees risks accentuating existing inequalities (van Dijk, 2005; De Haan, 2003). The rapid development of ICTs around the world has shifted researchers' attention from inequalities in material access, known as the first-level divide, to differences in the way ICTs and digital skills are used (second-level digital divide). Initially, the concept of digital skills was limited to the technical dimension, which concerns the basic knowledge necessary for the use of computer hardware (text processing, copying a document to a floppy disk, etc.). Then, researchers realized that this concept goes beyond the determinist vision.

Gilster (1998) defines digital skills as the ability to understand and use information from digital technologies. Steyaert (2002) defined three types of skills: instrumental (operational manipulation of ICT), structural (referring to the structure in which information resides) and strategic (related to the proactive search for information, to decision making based on the available information and to the analysis of the environment for a relevant use of the information). For his part, van Dijk (2005) changed Steyaert's definition by proposing operational skills (the capabilities of using computer hardware and software, and networks), formal informational skills (the ability to manage and understand the characteristics, formal computer and network skills), substantial information skills (referring to the search, selection, processing and evaluation of information) and strategic skills (the ability to use ICT to achieve goals and improve one's position in society). In more recent work, van Deursen and van Dijk (2010) distinguished between four types of skills: operational, formal, informational and strategic. For their part, van Deursen, Helsper and Eynon (2016) identify four categories: operational, informational, social and creative skills.

Digital skills and the labour market in Tunisia

Since the 1980s, Tunisia had started implementing a strategy to strengthen the digital sector that promotes public and private investment in this area, and to gradually liberalize the telecommunications sector. As a result, the ICT sector has experienced strong growth since 2011. Indeed, in 2017, 44.7% of Tunisians have a high knowledge of computer use, and 27.6% use the internet for training and online education, as against 60% in Luxembourg. At the level of e-commerce, there are remarkable differences with advanced countries in terms of the use of the internet to make online purchases (12.5% of Tunisians, as compared to more than 79% of Norwegians in 2018) (CUA/OCDE, 2022). However, the sector is yet to realize its full potential, and its contribution to employment and economic growth has remained relatively low. This is due to the many difficulties including a lack of digital skills, a poor alignment between the demand for skills and the supply of training institutions, and problems in the business environment.

Skills mismatches and the resulting high unemployment rate among young graduates in the labour market are a growing concern in Tunisia. Cumbersome administrative processes limiting the agility of public universities and their ability to quickly adapt their training to the needs of the labour market, the lack of a medium- to long-term vision of the skills that the higher education sector will have to train and the absence of institutional mechanisms and arrangements allowing teacher-researchers to be up to date with recent developments in their fields of expertise are the main causes.

The insufficient availability of digital skills in the Tunisian economy is explained by the small number of courses and capacity-building courses in ICT provided by universities and other institutions (private and public) to meet the needs of the labour market, and by the immigration of Tunisian skills abroad. According to IACE (2019), in 2018, 22.3% of Tunisian private sector companies recruited or sought to recruit people with skills in ICT and engineering. The number of jobs currently vacant stands at 47,026, with 77.5% of the skills required being technical and digital/IT. Regarding the use of digital technology within companies, in 2018, 54% of permanent employees used a computer in their work. Most of them make medium or even very high usage. In addition, 47% have an internet connection at their workplace. In 80.6% of cases, these employees make an average or very high use of Internet. In terms of quality, ICT training generally meets the expectations of companies. However, weaknesses were detected at the level of soft skills. In addition, some skills (especially in cybersecurity and robotics) still mark a rarity.

Empirical study

Our empirical work consists of highlighting the importance of e-skills and identifying the kinds of digital skills required in the Tunisian labour market. To do this, we analysed the impact of different categories of employees' digital skills on wages.

Data and variables

In order to achieve our research objective, we developed a questionnaire that includes 20 questions based on a large review of the literature. The conduct of the questionnaire took place during the year 2020. We opted for three modes of administration: direct distribution of the questionnaire, self-administration and electronic transfer of the questionnaire. Fifteen hundred questionnaires were distributed, from which 919 responses were usable (a response rate of 61%).

The variables used in this study are: variables linked to the characteristics of the employee (age, sex, education, experience, training), of the firm in which they work (size, sector of activity), their access to and use of ICT (phone, mobile phone, computer, laptop, internet social media and other, intranet, intensity of use and experience with ICT at work) and certain organizational forms (teamwork, job rotation, participation in decision making, flexibility, cooperation, work by project, versatility) in which the employee is involved and the salary. The latter is unobservable, but we know that it belongs to one of three categories: the salary is said to be low if it is less than TD600, medium if it is TD600–1200 and high if it is greater than TD1200. One Tunisian dinar is equivalent to USD2.74.

The measure of digital skills was based on the definition put forward by van Deursen, Helsper and Eynon (2016). To assess each of the skill categories, we asked certain questions (see the questionnaire), codified the responses and subsequently calculated a score for each employee. The number of items used is given in Table 2.1.

Table 2.2 on the next page gives the characteristics of the sample and some descriptive statistics.

Table 2.1 *e-Skills measurement*

e-Skills	Number of items
Operational skills	9
Formal skills	10
Informational skills	7
Strategic skills	6

Table 2.2 *Descriptive statistics*

	Obs	Mean	Standard deviation	Min	Max
Salary characteristics					
Sex	919	0,5044	0,5003	0	1
Age	919	0,8902	0,7510	0	2
Education	919	1,7860	0,9267	0	3
Experience	919	0,7517	0,7086	0	2
Training	919	0,6330	0,4822	0	1
Company characteristics					
Sector	919	0,9013	0,7743	0	2
Size	919	1,3769	0,7537	0	2
Use and intensity of use of ICT					
Phone	919	2,1842	1,4543	0	4
Computer	919	2,6367	1,5182	0	4
Internet (social media)	919	1,1696	1,5841	0	4
Internet (other)	919	1,6530	1,4508	0	4
Intranet	919	1,9189	1,7474	0	4
Laptop	919	2,1619	1,6545	0	4
Mobile	919	2,0189	1,7463	0	4
Intensity of use	919	1,8736	1,0070	0	3
ICT experience	919	1,4557	0,7910	0	2
e-Skills					
Operational	919	6,5898	2,4967	0	9
Formal	919	5,4822	2,7569	0	10
Informational	919	4,4379	2,2149	0	7
Strategic	919	2,6818	1,8933	0	6
Organizational practices					
Teamwork	919	1,8991	1,0978	0	3
Rotation	919	0,5854	0,6687	0	2
Participation	919	0,6670	0,4786	0	2
Autonomy	919	1,4335	0,7326	0	2
Cooperation	919	2,7125	1,3024	0	5
Project work	919	0,4956	0,5531	0	5
Versatility	919	1,4634	0,8351	0	3
Wage	902	1,1013	0,6954	0	2

The sample includes 919 employees: 36% belong to the service sector, 38% to the industrial sector and 26% to the administrative sector. About half of the population is female. More than 24% of employees have postgraduate qualifications, about 42% are graduates, 23.5% have a university undergraduate degree and 11.5% have secondary school education. In terms of age, 23% are over 40 years; more than 42% are between 30 and 40 years, and about 34% are less than 30 years. About 16% of the sample of employees have a professional experience exceeding 20 years, 44% have a professional experience of 5 to 20 years and 40% less than 5 years. Concerning firms in which the employees work, 17% are micro-businesses, 28% are small companies and 55% are medium or large businesses.

Results and discussion

For our model, the likelihood ratio and Brant tests are not significant; hence the proportional odds assumption is violated. In this regard, we have chosen to estimate a generalized ordered logistic model. This model developed by Fu (1998) and cited by Williams (2006) is a variant of the ordered multinomial model.

The estimation results of the generalized multinomial logit model are presented in Table 2.3 on the next page. The second column of the table gives the parameters estimated by comparing the probability of being paid a low salary against the odds of receiving at least an average salary (medium and high salary), while the third column gives the probability of being paid at least an average salary (low and middle) versus the propensity to be paid a high salary.

The results obtained show that gender, age, educational level and professional experience play a decisive role in favour of high remuneration. Being male increases significantly the likelihood of an employee earning a middle or high wage rather than a low wage and the probability of earning a high wage rather than the average wage. The older the employee is, the higher their salary.

Education level also plays a huge role in classifying the salary in a different wage category. Indeed, the higher the employee's educational level, the greater their probability of receiving an average (high) salary rather than a low (low or medium) salary. This confirms previous studies which argue that the availability and use of ICT favours the more educated workers by accelerating their productivity and thus increasing their wages (Acemoglu, 1998, 2001, 2007; Bartel and Sicherman, 1997). Therefore, the wage gap between skilled and unskilled workers increases. Regarding the characteristics of the firm, it is the size that plays a significant role in wage determination.

Table 2.3 *Results from generalized multinomial logit model*

Dependent variable: wage	Low vs medium and high (wage)	Low and medium vs high (wage)
Independent variables	Coefficients	Coefficients
Characteristics of the employee		
Sex	0.8749*** (0.1762)	0.8749*** (0.1762)
Age	0.6371*** (0.172)	0.6371*** (0.172)
Education	0.6999*** (0.1693)	0.2578* (0.1403)
Experience	0.6195*** (0.189)	0.6195*** (0.189)
Training	-0.4088* (0.2428)	0.3348 (0.221)
Characteristics of the firm		
Sector	-0.0455 (0.1234)	-0.0455 (0.1234)
Size	0.7475*** (0.1231)	0.7475*** (0.1231)
Use and intensity of use of ICTs		
Phone	-0.2606*** (0.0856)	0.0159 (0.0827)
Computer	-0.0026 (0.0684)	-0.0026 (0.0684)
Internet (social media)	0.1127** (0.0634)	0.1127** (0.0634)
Internet (other)	0.0313 (0.0685)	0.0313 (0.0685)
Intranet	0.1051 (0.0639)	0.1051 (0.0639)
Laptop	0.3556*** (0.0878)	0.0448*** (0.0779)
Mobile	0.1896*** (0.0615)	0.1896*** (0.0615)
Intensity of use	0.1248 (0.1026)	0.1248 (0.1026)
ICT experience	0.0809 (0.1201)	0.0809 (0.1201)
e-Skills		
Operational	0.0738 (0.0529)	0.0738 (0.0529)
Formal	0.0453 (0.0557)	0.0453 (0.0557)
Informational	0.0151 (0.085)	0.4295*** (0.0772)
Strategic	0.3065*** (0.1045)	0.0507 (0.0749)
Versatility	0.4474*** (0.1136)	0.4474*** (0.1136)
_cons	-3.6111 (0.4849)	-9.358707*** (0.6752)
Observations	919	
Pseudo R^2	36.65	
Log likelihood	-573.6847	
LR(34)	663.78	

The results also show that the use of some ICT in the workplace plays in favour of higher remuneration: the use of the phone (landline and mobile) and/or social media and/or laptop at work raises the probability of earning an average (high) wage rather than a low (low or medium) wage. The use of intranet, internet (other than social media), experience with ICT at work and the intensity of using ICT have no significant impact on the salary determination.

Table 2.3 shows that there are two types of skills which are essential in the explanation and evolution of the employee's salary: informational skills (skills for locating information in digital technologies) and strategic skills (skills for using ICT to achieve goals and improve one's position in society). Other types of skills (operational and formal) have no significant effects on the employee's salary. The significant positive impact of the two kinds of digital skills on salary can be interpreted as a form of a technological bias: the capacity to search, select and evaluate information and the ability to use it to achieve goals and improve one's position in society favours some employees compared to others in regard to wages in the Tunisian labour market, and not the intensity of ICT use or its simple manipulation.

Concerning organizational practices, teamwork, autonomy, project work and polyvalence are decisive in wage evolution. The more the employee is involved in one of these organizational forms, the higher the likelihood of their earning an average (high) wage rather than a low (low or medium) wage. Job rotation, cooperation and participation in decision making have no significant effects on the employee's wage.

Conclusion

The main objective of this chapter has been to highlight the importance of e-skills and to identify the kinds of digital skills required in the Tunisian labour market. To do this, using data collected in 2020 on the Tunisian labour market, we analysed the impact on wages of the characteristics of the employee (age, sex, level of education, English language), of the firm in which they work (size, sector of activity), their access to and use of ICT (mobile phone, computer, software, internet, intranet, other, intensity of use and experience with ICT at work) and certain organizational forms (teamwork, job rotation, participation in decision-making, flexibility, cooperation, work by project, versatility) in which the employee is involved. The estimation of a generalized multinomial logit model allows us to identify two main results.

Firstly, the use of ICT, especially mobile technologies, in the workplace increases the employee's chance to access a higher salary. The more the employee uses ICT at the workplace, the more likely they are to have a high salary. Furthermore, employee involvement in some organizational forms (teamwork, job rotation, participation in decision-making, flexibility, cooperation, work by project, versatility) strengthens their chances of earning a high salary.

Secondly, cognitive skills play a huge role in wage evolution: the higher the employee's educational level, the greater their chance of earning a high salary. Even more fundamentally, informational and strategic skills are the digital skills most in demand for our population. That said, what matters today is the capacity to search, select and evaluate information and the ability to use it to achieve goals and improve one's position in society.

References

Acemoglu, D. (1998) Why Do New Technologies Complement Skills? Directed Technical Change and Wage Inequality, *The Quarterly Journal of Economics*, **113** (4), 1055–89.

Acemoglu, D. (2001) Directed Technical Change, *NBER Working Paper 8287*.

Acemoglu, D. (2007) Equilibrium Bias of Technology, *Econometrica*, **75** (5), 1371–409.

Bartel, A. P. and Sicherman, N. (1997) Technological Change and Wages: An Inter-Industry analysis, *NBER Working Paper 5941*.

Ben Youssef, A. (2004) Les quatre dimensions de la fracture numérique, *Réseaux*, (127–8), 181–209.

Benghozi, P. J. and Cohendet, P. (1997) L'organisation de la production et de la décision face aux TIC. In Rallet, A. (ed.), *Technologies de l'information, organisation et performances économiques*: Commissariat général au Plan, 161–230.

Bué, J., Guignon, N., Hamon-Cholet, S. and Vinck, L. (2002) Vingt ans de conditions de travail, *Données Sociales - La société française*, INSEE.

Card, D. and DiNardo, J. E. (2002) Skill-biased Technological Change and Rising Wage Inequality: Some Problems and Puzzles, *Journal of Labor Economics*, **20** (4), 733–83.

Crifo, P. (2003) La modélisation du changement organisationnel: déterminants et conséquences sur le marché du travail, *Actualité Economique*, **79** (3), 349–65.

CUA/OCDE (2022) Africa's Development Dynamics 2022: Regional Value Chains for a Sustainable Recovery, CUA, Addis Ababa/Éditions OCDE, Paris, www.oecd.org/dev/africa-s-development-dynamics-3290877b-en.htm.

De Haan, J. D. (2003) IT and Social Inequality in the Netherlands, *IT & Society*, **1** (4), 27–45.

Fu, V. K. (1998) Estimating Generalized Ordered Logit Models, *Stata Technical Bulletin*, **44**, 27–30.

Gilster, P. (1998) *Digital Literacy*, Wiley.

IACE (2019) Rapport national sur l'emploi 2019, https://iace.tn/rapport-national-sur-lemploi-2019.

Quinet, A. (2000) Nouvelles technologies, nouvelle économie et nouvelles organisations. *Économie et Statistique*, (339–40), 3–14.

Steyaert, J. (2002) Inequality and the Digital Divide: Myths and Realities. In Hick, S. and McNutt, J. (eds), *Advocacy, Activism and the Internet*, Lyceum Press.

van Deursen, A., Helsper, E. and Eynon, R. (2016) Development and Validation of the Internet Skills Scale (ISS), *Information, Communication & Society*, **19**, 804–23.

van Deursen, A. and van Dijk, J. (2010) Measuring Internet Skills, *Journal of Human-Computer Interaction*, **26**, (10), 891–916.

van Dijk, J. (2005) The Deepening Divide: Inequality in the Information Society, *Sage Publications*.

Williams, R. (2006) Generalized Ordered Logit/Partial Proportional Odds Models for Ordinal Dependent Variables, *Stata Journal*, **6**, 58–82.

3

Digital Literacy in Africa: A Case Study of Kenya National Library Services, Thika

Miriam Mureithi

Abstract

The digital literacy gap among the youth is a challenge in the Thika region, Kenya. This is as a result of young people dropping out of school and a lack of information and communication technology (ICT) skills, which are important for individual growth and accessing government services. Currently, technology plays an important role in every aspect of our lives. Research shows that libraries, and especially public libraries, are critical in the achievement of national, regional and international development goals in any country. The Thika library identified the different government agencies such as the Ministry of Education, Ministry of Youth and ICT and other, non-governmental organizations, such as the Digital Opportunity Trust, among others as key partners to achieve the goal. The library now offers the basic packages of computer training and provides access to the internet and ICT devices at no cost. The training programme is designed to take place three days a week for a period of three months, for three sessions a year. Since its inception, a total of 720 (317 male and 403 female) had graduated from the programme as at March 2020. As a result of the project, new programmes have been implemented, more partners started supporting the initiative, library awareness has increased and young people have gained job opportunities. Though the programme targeted young people without ICT skills and school dropouts, older people and professionals continue to enrol. Training all other librarians working in public libraries on how to start such programmes in their respective regions, the recognition of Kenya National Library Services, Thika by the National Examining body and the transformation of the library into a community empowerment centre of choice are the next envisioned steps.

Keywords: Digital literacy, computer packages, Thika Public Library, Kenya National Library Service.

Introduction

Thika is a metropolitan industrial town and a major commercial hub in Kiambu County, Kenya. It is situated in Central Kenya, 42 kilometres north-east of the capital city Nairobi. Thika town is divided into two sub-counties: Thika East and Thika West. Thika is regarded as the Birmingham of Kenya, due to the many industries, from small to multinational. Key among them are Bidco Africa and Del Monte Pineapples, one of the world's producers, marketers and distributors of fresh and fresh-cut fruit and vegetables.

The region has a good number of learning institutions, starting from the basic to institutions of higher learning, both public and privately owned. All the government offices are within a radius of about one kilometre from the Library. Some of the businesses and government institutions surrounding the Library include, Mount Kenya University, Kenya Motor Vehicle Manufacturers (KVM), Thika Level 5 Hospital, Thika Technical Training Institute, Thika High School, General Kago Primary School, churches such as All Nations Gospel Church, African Christian Church and Schools, St Peter's Catholic Church etc., Ministry of Education offices, Government Administration Offices and many other small and medium-scale enterprises.

Kenya National Library Service, Thika

Kenya National Library Services (KNLS) is a statutory body of the Government of Kenya, established in 1965 by Act of Parliament, Cap. 225 of the Laws of Kenya. It is a non-profit-making organization which serves dual roles as a National Library and public library in Kenya. KNLS is open to all individuals regardless of age, tribe, race, religion, national origin and physical status, social and political views.

Thika District Library is one of the branches of KNLS. Thika District Library was built in 1980 by the Danish Government and opened its doors to the public in 1982. It is in Kiambu County, Thika West sub-county, Thika Municipality. It is located one kilometre from Thika Town, along General Kago Road, and next to Mount Kenya University. KNLS Thika library is committed to providing information services and technical advice in all matters relating to libraries within Thika and its environs and the larger part of Kiambu County.

Public libraries

The public library mission has become critical in attempting to help bridge the digital divide in current times (Mackenzie, 2021, 138). As more books, other information resources and government services are being provided online, public libraries increasingly provide access to the internet and computers for users who otherwise would not be able to connect to these services. They also provide community spaces to encourage the general population to improve their digital skills through library clubs and library makerspaces. Almost all public libraries now have computers and are trying to establish computer labs if one does not already exist.

Internationally, public libraries offer information and communication technology (ICT) services, giving access to information and knowledge the highest priority. While different countries and areas of the world have their own requirements, general services offered include free connection to the internet, training in using the internet and relevant content in appropriate languages.

In addition to access, many public libraries offer training and support to computer users. Once access has been achieved, there remains a large gap in people's digital abilities and skills. For many communities, the public library is the only place offering free computer classes, information technology learning and an affordable, interactive way to build digital skills. Current research shows that libraries, and especially public libraries, are critical in the achievement of national, regional and international development goals in any country. A research published online (Lynch et al., 2020) clearly emphasizes the role of libraries in the development agenda. The research further points out that the services of African libraries do often match the goals of development organizations expressed in agendas such as the United Nations Sustainable Development Goals and African Union Agenda 2063.

Digital literacy

Technology plays an important role in every aspect of our lives. It changes how we access education, how we work and how we engage in everyday business. Digital skills are very important to how populations prepare for the economy of the future and the present day as the COVID-19 crisis continues to push engagements of all types to online platforms.

Digital literacy can be defined as 'the ability to use information and communication technologies to find, evaluate, create, and communicate information, requiring both cognitive and technical skills' (Loewus, 2016). In other words, one can say that digital literacy correlates with digital inclusion, where people are able to use and access information and communication technologies, able to do administrative procedures online via e-government services, make payments and access financial services using technology, etc. Digital literacy is therefore no longer an option but has become a fundamental requirement for people when going about their daily lives.

Digital literacy is an ongoing challenge, as digital technology is found in every sector of the economy. A great change is being experienced in the nature of work, and the World Bank (2019) World Development Report on *The Changing Nature of Work* explores how this 'fourth industrial revolution' is shaping the future. Work is constantly reshaped by evolving technologies which have brought opportunities, paved the way to creating new jobs, increased productivity and provided for effective delivery of public services. Governments have adopted technology in all their services and citizens must adapt to the change. People will therefore require digital skills to be able to access jobs and work, in most cases, online. Students are also required to learn, carry out research and submit assignments virtually. Individuals have to adapt themselves to digital life in order to adapt to the digital world.

The digital literacy rate goes hand in hand with access to digital means. According to the Internet World Stats, the internet penetration in Africa in 2020 is estimated to be 47.1%, and at the end of 2019, 45% of the population in sub-Saharan Africa subscribed to mobile services, according to the Global System for Mobile Communications (GSMA, 2020). Despite the lag in internet and mobile penetration in Africa, the curve of growth is increasing and Africans are showing great zeal and commitment to embrace rapid technological change and its versatility and to bridge the global digital divide.

Digital literacy level in Kenya

Literacy is the base on which learning is built, and it provides a way to climb out of poverty, get a revenue stream and be a productive citizen. Learning never stops, and even at old age it's never too late to learn. Van den Berg and Johnston (2020) pointed out that about 65% of children entering primary school today will end up working in a job that does not exist yet. Sub-Saharan Africa will see more than 230 million 'digital jobs'. These jobs will be in all sectors of the economy. Therefore, young Africans need digital skills to enter and remain competitive throughout the economy.

In Kenya, for example, according to World Bank Group, internet users account for only 23% of the total population as of 2019 not only because more than 75% of the population live in remote areas, lacking a stable power supply, but also because many people do not realize the real value of acquiring digital skills. With today's technological society, basic computer literacy is emphasized in every institution (Ezziane, 2007). The advancement of Kenya and the entire continent vis-à-vis economic development lies in the ICT capabilities of its people. The Kenya National Adult Literacy Survey (KNALS, 2007) revealed that only 61.5% of the adult population has attained minimum literacy level, leaving 38.5% (7.8 million) of adults illiterate. It also revealed that only 29.6% of the Kenya adult population has attained desired literacy competency. About 29.9% of the youth aged 15 to 19 years and 49% of adults aged 45 to 49 years are illiterate. A UNESCO 2016 report notes that most computer-literate people in developing countries like Kenya cannot do basic tasks like simple arithmetic on a spreadsheet or writing a basic computer program. Such people may not actively participate in today's digitized global economy, where proper computer literacy is non-negotiable.

Today, when every user holds a computer, computer literacy is defined as an understanding of computer characteristics, capabilities and applications, as well as an ability to implement this knowledge in the skilful, productive use of computers in a personalized manner (Martin and Dunsworth, 2007).

The digital revolution experienced in today's world is pushing governments in developing countries to significantly go digital in their operations. In Kenya the introduction of the e-government platform demands that citizens can mainly access key government services online. Over time, the government has increased the number of services that are available to the public online. Some of these services include payment of taxes through iTax, renewal of drivers' licences, business registration, passport application and application for death and birth certificates, among many more. Apart from government online services, there are services important to individuals, for example, money transfer such as Mpesa, famously known in Kenya for buying and selling online. To access these services, citizens require some basic computer and internet skills.

KNLS Thika, in collaboration with the Department of Adult and Continuing Education Thika, committed to empowering young people by providing free computer training packages and also to equip participants with the desired values, attitudes, knowledge, skills and competencies, particularly in technology, innovation and entrepreneurship.

The prime objective of the computer training packages programme is to prepare participants to competitively thrive within a highly integrated, technologically oriented and information-based economy. The country's economic blueprint, Kenya Vision 2030, has identified ICT as a key enabler to the attainment of the goals and aspirations Vision. The thrust of the vision is to convert Kenya into a true knowledge and information economy by enabling access to quality, affordable and reliable ICT services in the country. In line with this, KNLS Thika embarked on this journey in miniature steps of empowering the youth, as is recorded in the two articles, 'Libraries as Youth

Empowerment Centres' (Mureithi, 2021) and 'Transformed Community Services' (Mureithi, 2020), available on the AfLIA website (www.aflia.net).

The programme has now expanded, bringing about the incorporation of additional related programmes such as online book clubs, data analysis and digital marketing training. Further, the initiative has attracted more partners, including but not limited to eMobilis Mobile Technology Training Institute, Friends of Kipipiri Organization, National Government Constituency Development Fund, Dalworth Organization, Sign Language Society of Kenya, as well as individual members in the community. With these new partners, awareness and the impact of KNLS Thika Library has significantly increased, more people have been attracted to participate in the programme and the job opportunities for programme graduates and access to other government and other online services have been enhanced.

ICT training at Thika Library

The current society demands that every individual should have basic ICT skills, since we are surrounded by ICT devices such as mobile phones, computers, televisions, automated teller machines and laptops, among others. The training is about offering basic ICT skills, chiefly on computer packages. Since the target is young people, some of whom are school dropouts, the content is simplified to their level. The notes that are used have been developed by a trained teacher based on their experience and a combination of different books. The notes have been designed for the basic level.

Training content

The content of the training has been compiled from different computer books. It has been simplified and prepared in Microsoft PowerPoint presentations. During the lessons, the trainer uses a projector so that every participant is able to see clearly.

Introduction to computers and Microsoft Windows

1   Definition of a computer
2   Applications of computer
3   Types of computers
4   Computer hardware
5   Computer software
6   Switching on/off computer
7   Windows desktop

8   Using the mouse
9   Loading programmes
10 Parts of a Window
11 Customizing Windows environment
12 Setting the date and time
13 Creating files and folders
14 Deleting files and folders
15 Saving a file
16 Copying and cutting files and folders
17 Renaming files and folders
18 Checking file and folders properties
19 Identifying file icons and extensions
20 Windows utilities

Microsoft Word

Microsoft Word is a word processing application that allows you to create, edit, format, store and print text.

Areas covered:

1   Overview of Microsoft Word
2   Loading Microsoft Word
3   Saving a document
4   Opening a document
5   Closing a document
6   Formatting text
    • Bolding
    • Underlining
    • Italicizing
    • Changing the font size
    • Changing the font style
    • Changing the font colour
7   Paragraph formatting
    • Bulleting
    • Indenting
    • Line spacing
    • Columns
8   Page formatting
    • Numbering
    • Margins
    • Text alignment

- Headers and footers
- Footnotes and endnotes

9 Page borders tables
  - Creating a table
  - Inserting rows/columns
  - Deleting rows/columns
  - Merging cells
  - Splitting cells

10 Copying and moving text
11 Inserting pictures
12 Word art
13 Auto shapes
14 Printing
15 Mail merge

Microsoft Excel

This is a spreadsheet application that you can use to analyse and represent data.

Areas covered:

1 Loading MS Excel and the Excel screen
2 Creating and saving worksheets
3 Text and number formatting
4 Making simple calculations
5 Inserting and deleting rows and columns
6 Adjusting column width
7 Renaming sheets
8 Auto sum
9 Copying formulas
10 Using the auto fill
11 Relative and absolute referencing
12 Creating and printing charts
13 Setting a print area
14 Auto filter
15 Linking data between Microsoft Word and Excel
16 Functions
17 Automatic recalculation

Microsoft PowerPoint

This is a graphic presentation software used to design presentations that can be used to convey information more effectively.

Areas covered:

1 Starting Microsoft PowerPoint
   - Auto content wizard
   - Templates
   - Blank presentation
   - Opening an existing presentation
2 Creating a presentation using the auto content wizard.
3 Creating a blank presentation
4 Adding a new slide to the presentation
5 Using different PowerPoint views
   - Slide view
   - Outline view
   - Slide sorter view
   - Notes page view
   - Slide show
6 Applying a different design to a presentation
7 Inserting a chart into a presentation
8 Inserting an organization chart
9 Adding a chart box to an organization chart
10 Inserting a table into the presentation
11 Inserting clipart pictures
12 Using the slide master
13 Changing the layout of a slide
14 Entering speaker's notes
15 Deleting slides
16 Animating slide text and objects
17 Setting slide transitions
18 Setting slide timings
19 Running the show

Microsoft Access

Microsoft Access is a database tool that is used to store, maintain and use a collection of information that is organized to serve a specific purpose.

Areas covered:

1   Starting Access
2   Tables
    • Sorting records in a table
    • Sorting more than one column
    • Finding records in a table
    • Matching records
    • Filtering records for viewing
    • Creating a table
    • Creating a table in design view
3   Field names
    • Setting a primary key
    • Entering records in a table
    • Adding records to a table
    • Deleting records from a table
4   Queries
    • Creating a query using design view
5   Total queries
    • Creating a total query
6   Creating a new blank database
7   Forms
    • Controls
      – Labels
      – Text box
    • Creating a form using auto form
    • Add new records to a table by using a form
    • Editing the form design
    • Create a form using the wizard
8   Reports
    • Creating a report using report wizard
    • Previewing and printing a report
      – To preview two pages
      – To preview more than two pages
    • Printing the report
    • Report design view
      – Report header
      – Page header
      – Detail
      – Page footer
9   Report footer

Microsoft Publisher

This is a desktop publishing programme that can be used to create a variety of publications like business cards, greeting cards, calendars, newsletters and much more.

Areas covered:

1 Cards
   • Business card
   • Birthday card
   • Invitation card
   • Postcard
   • Greeting cards
2 Brochures
3 Advertisements
4 Calendars
5 Flyers
6 Labels
7 Letterhead
8 Newsletter signs

Internet and e-mail

Internet

The internet is a network of computers that can communicate with each other. That is, computers can send and receive information.

Areas covered:

1 Web browsers
2 Parts of a web browser
3 Website addresses
4 Internet Explorer buttons
5 Search engines
6 Narrowing searches by using operators
7 Downloading information
8 Downloading web pages without images
9 Bookmarks/favourites
10 Setting a homepage
11 Sending a web page by e-mail

e-Mail

e-Mail is short for electronic mail. This is the transmission of messages over communication networks.

Areas covered:

1 Advantages of using e-mail
2 How to create an e-mail account
3 How to access an e-mail account
4 Reading an e-mail message
5 How to reply to an e-mail message
6 How to forward an e-mail message
7 How to compose an e-mail message
8 How to attach a document to an e-mail message
9 Deleting an e-mail message
10 Creating an e-mail address book

Training duration and mode of delivery

The training takes place over a period of between two and three months, three days a week. The content is delivered in a group setting. Due to the diversified age groups and varied levels of education, delivery is blended with individual support. This personalized support takes place during extra time after the lessons. The trainer and the participant agree on the appropriate time, which should be different from arranged group meetings. The individualized help is to assist the elderly and less advantaged in terms of levels of under-standing/comprehension caused by different reasons which could range from level of education to special needs cases. The elderly and those who dropped out of school do not grasp the ideas at the same speed as those who completed their high school education recently or those who are currently taking a course at a college or university. Extra attention is given to these two categories of participants. They are given extra support in order to be at par with the others.

After every package, the participants are given individual assignments to work on and submit to the trainer within a specified time. During the course, they are also given sit-in examinations after every package. The exam is marked and graded accordingly. The grades attained are recorded on their certificates on completion of the course.

Discipline is not a matter of question. Every participant is expected to demonstrate a high level of discipline and self-control, irrespective of age or status. It is emphasized at the start of the course that a high level of discipline must be maintained. Absenteeism, lateness and failure to complete assignments are highly discouraged. Any participant who misses more than 25% of the total sessions is denied an opportunity to graduate and requested to sign up for the next intake. The reason why absenteeism is discouraged is in order to ensure that every individual takes the training sessions seriously and acquires all the skills imparted.

Statistics on those trained and their demographics

The training started in 2018 as a project which was an integral part of the AfLIA Leadership Academy. The initial intake was a total of 36 participants. The number of participants has been going up gradually and the last intake in 2020 before COVID-19 hit the country, was 202, although only 172 graduated. The trend has been for 85% completion rate of those registered at the start of the course. For various reasons, some people register but do not start the course, others start and drop out along the way. Some of the reasons for the 15% drop-out rate include personal engagements, not being able to adjust to the training times, pursuance of other engagements and, in rare cases, natural attrition. In total, from the training's inception to March 2021, a total of 788 participants have graduated.

The ages of those who have gone through the training range from 17 to 75 years. The young ones are mainly those who join the course after completing their high school education, while the elderly are those involved in adult education and learning. Lifelong learning is encouraged and continuous, as there is no age limit on registering those interested. The programme targeted young people but it has attracted a large number of older people, including professionals and other government workers.

Tables 3.1 to 3.3 following are a summary of all the people trained since the inception of the course, per year.

Table 3.1 *Year 2018*

Intake	Male	Female	Total
January	12	24	36
May	19	22	41
September	19	35	54
Total	**50**	**81**	**131**

Table 3.2 *Year 2019*

Intake	Male	Female	Total
January	65	81	146
May	57	78	135
September	69	67	136
Total	**191**	**226**	**417**

Table 3.3 *Years 2020 and 2021*

Intake	Male	Female	Total
January 2020	76	96	172
January 2021	36	32	68
Total	**112**	**128**	**240**

There are normally three intakes each year, in January, May and September. Marketing and registration of the course take place in the months of November, December, April and August. The training cannot take place during those months, as library usage is at its peak during those times. Due to limited space and furniture, the training is programmed to take place when the library usage is off peak.

Impact of the training

The training has been very effective and has impacted on the lives of many who have gone through it. One of the direct impacts is that the Library does not have to do a lot of marketing, as was the case with the initial class, but now relies on a high percentage of referrals from beneficiaries. The Library has not conducted a survey on the impact, and the impacts here are basically from those reported by people who have come back to the library to give appreciation for what they been able to achieve on completion of the training. Some of the impacts are as follows:

1   Promotion at workplaces. One of the participants, a lady who graduated in March 2020, an employee at the county government, got a promotion after presenting her certificate.
2   Employment. Several young people have come back to the Library to say that they got jobs in cyber cafés, as a cashier in a local supermarket, and another one in a shop.
3   Registering and starting cyber business. One participant started a cyber café business and offers printing, internet and access to government services.
4   Credit transfer. One student joined tertiary college after undertaking the training to undertake a diploma in Information Technology and was given credit transfers after presenting their certificate.
5   Accessing online services. An elderly couple undertook the course and after completion, they were able to apply for passports and visas online and were able to travel abroad.

6 Professional skills for service delivery. A 55-year-old lawyer enrolled on the course in order to acquire the skills and be able to be *au fait* with the technological changes in service delivery in the courts.
7 Enhanced skills in accessing government services.

Partnerships and their roles

KNLS Thika believes in networking and collaboration with other stakeholders because empowering the community is a shared responsibility and is not limited to the four walls of a classroom but also involves other spheres of life. The Library partners with other stakeholders in an effort to fulfil its mandate of becoming a hub of information and knowledge for empowerment.

The Library has been working in partnership with several organizations that have been very supportive in running the youth empowerment programme (Mureithi, 2021). The partners have been supporting the programme in various ways. Some of the partners include: Digital Opportunity Trust, eMobolis, Friends of Kipipiri Organization, Moi University Information Communication and Technology Department, Dalworth Consultants, Malaika Shujaa, Thika Creative Arts, National Authority for the Campaign against Alcohol and Drug Abuse, Ministry of Education and National Government Constituency Development Fund.

Ministry of Education, Department of Adult and Continuing Education, Thika West

The Adult and Continuing Education Department is a government institution under the Ministry of Education in the Directorate of Adult and Continuing Education. Their mandate is to provide literacy and adult education to adults and out-of-school youth, in order to create a well-informed human resource capable of impacting positively on the country's sustainable development. The Department has qualified teachers. When the Library started the youth empowerment programme, the partnership came in handy, since a teacher was available to come and offer training for free.

eMobilis Mobile Technology Training Institute

KNLS Thika has been partnering with eMobilis Mobile Technology Training Institute, located in Westland Nairobi, since 2018. They have been offering a one-day free training to our learners on digital marketing, websites and YouTube creation to enable learners to take advantage of online employment opportunities. Also, through their partner Google, they enable learners from the Library to pursue an online free Google Digital Skills for Africa course in the fundamentals of digital marketing. Given predictions that the digital economy will continue to grow exponentially throughout Africa, digital marketing skills have become important in the job market, and those who acquire these skills can work as consultants or get well-paying jobs in companies or advertising agencies.

According to Kenya National Bureau of Statistics survey report (KNBS, 2015), the rate of youth unemployment stands at 26% and has been increasing every year due to rapidly changing labour markets, technological advancements and globalization. In an effort to help solve unemployment, the Library, assisted by the Department of Adult and Continuing Education, through eMobilis Mobile Technology Training Institute, have been imparting knowledge to learners to help them solve social problems and enable them to create mobile entrepreneurial jobs to employ themselves and others.

Friends of Kipipiri Organization

KNLS Thika started partnering with Friends of Kipipiri Organization in May 2019 to provide free entrepreneurship training to our learners. The entrepreneurship training provided to the participants is designed to introduce them to the idea that they can create and place themselves in today's digital economic reality.

While examining current trends and issues in today's workplace, the learners are challenged to explore their career interests as a starting point for entrepreneurial activities. This course emphasizes the tools for writing a successful business plan.

Upon completion of the course, learners are expected to be able to:

1 Come up with a successful business plan.
2 Identify the personal skills necessary to succeed in an entrepreneurial environment.
3 Examine current business trends and assess their impact and importance to small businesses.
4 Apply business concepts and principles to develop entrepreneurial business goals and strategies.
5 Construct a preliminary set of financial projections to assess the viability of a small business.
6 Complete a feasibility study on a business idea to determine its probability of success.

Digital Opportunity Trust

Digital Opportunity Trust (DOT), an international social enterprise, helps people to create education, economic and entrepreneurship opportunities through application of ICT, and it is in this regard that DOT partnered with KNLS Thika. DOT offered entrepreneurship training to the young people in Thika. Different activities took place in KNLS Thika in collaboration with DOT until the beginning of 2019. Several graduation ceremonies ranging from simple to complex took place in the Library; a very successful business expo also took place at KNLS Thika which attracted prominent people in the region. Several people benefitted from the programme and were able to start their own businesses.

Ministry of ICT and Youth

The Library had been working closely with the Ministry of Youth. The Ministry was later merged with the Ministry of ICT. The Ministry of Youth was referring young people to the Library to acquire the digital skills that the Library was offering in partnership with different organizations. The Government started initiatives for young people geared to making them financially stable and economically independent. One of the initiatives the Government started was 'Ajira'. Ajira is a Swahili word for employment. The Ajira initiative was to empower young people with digital skills in order to start working online. Since the Library had already started the youth empowerment programme, the Ministry of Youth partnered with the Library and identified the library as an Ajira centre.

National Government Constituency Development Fund (NG-CDF)

Every constituency in the country has a Constituency Development Fund (CDF) funded by the Government in order to implement projects geared to bringing services to the individual citizen. In order to support youth initiatives in the Government, each constituency was mandated to establish a Constituency Innovation Hub (CIH) that would be accessible to young people for free. The CIH was to be equipped with laptops and internet access to support the Ajira initiatives. The Ajira Digital Program is a government initiative driven by the Ministry of ICT, Innovations and Youth Affairs to empower over one million young people to access digital job opportunities (ajiradigital, n.d.).

Thika NG-CDF identified KNLS Thika as a partner and library to be a CIH, since the youth programme was already running. The Library therefore benefitted with 13 laptops to be used for the youth empowerment programme and a fibre optic connection for Wi-Fi.

Dalworth Consultants Limited

KNLS Thika partnered with Dalworth Consultants Limited in order to offer data analysis skills to participants. After undertaking basic ICT training in the Library, some participants requested the Library to offer a data analysis course at basic level. The Library through the partnership of peer-to-peer University started offering data analysis through learning circles. This was basically on peer-to-peer learning, and almost all the participants lacked knowledge about data analysis. This necessitated a skilled person to lead in the learning. In the process, Dalworth Consultants Limited came in 2019 and partnered with the Library in the provision of data analysis training. Basic computer skills offered by the Library were the foundational block for the data analysis training.

Other partners

KNLS Thika has been working with other partners including Malaika Shujaa, Thika Creative Arts, National Authority for Campaign against Alcohol and Drug Abuse and individuals. All these play a role in the mentoring part of the training. Every time a new session starts, each Monday is dedicated to mentoring the programme participants. The day is normally referred to as 'Inspirational Monday'. Different groups or individuals are invited to offer life skills and mentoring to the participants. Some of the areas covered are self-esteem, drug and substance abuse, cancer awareness and many more. Thika Creative Arts is a locally based organization that helps young people to identify their talents. They have been very instrumental in identifying and nurturing the talents of the programme participants.

Future plans

The Library is working towards the recognition of the programme by the Kenya National Examination body. The Library aims to be the centre of choice for all in matters of community empowerment programmes. KNLS Thika also looks forward to sharing ideas and providing leadership on how libraries in other regions of Kenya can implement similar programmes.

The Library has not been receiving any funding to support the empowerment programmes, but has been relying on partners to support the programme and other activities related to it. Most of the time, the largest budget has been in conducting graduations. The burden was relieved from the Library when the students were given the opportunity to manage the cost of graduation.

Conclusion

Though the programme initially targeted young people without ICT skills and school dropouts, older people and professionals continue to enrol. Since its inception in 2018, a total of 720 (317 male and 403 female) have graduated from the programme, which translates to an 85% completion rate. The effects of COVID-19 halted most of the Library activities, and the digital literacy programme was no exception. The trainings would have continued on the online platform, virtually, but lack of ICT devices, internet connectivity and the skills required hindered progress.

Access to computers and the internet is now nearly as important to Library users as access to books and other print materials. It is notable that for a public library to deliver efficiently and effectively, there is a need to work in collaboration and with like-minded partners.

References

ajiradigital (n.d.) Online Work Is Work, https://ajiradigital.go.ke.

Ezziane, Z. (2007) Information Technology Literacy: Implications on Teaching and Learning, https://www.academia.edu/55079208/Information_technology_literacy_Implications_on_teaching_and_learning

Kenya Vision 2030 (2007) https://vision2030.go.ke/.

KNALS (Kenya National Adult Literacy Report) (2007) www.eldis.org/document/A31868.

KNBS (Kenya National Bureau of Statistics) (2015) www.knbs.or.ke/?p=1712.

Loewus, L. (2016) What Is Digital Literacy?, www.edweek.org/teaching-learning/what-is-digital-literacy/2016/11.

Lynch, R., Young, J. C., Jowaisas, C., Boakye-Achampong, S. and Sam, J. (2020) African Libraries in Development: Perceptions and Possibilities, *International Information & Library Review*, **53** (4), 277–90, www.tandfonline.com/doi/full/10.1080/10572317.2020.1840002.

Mackenzie, K. (2021) Public Libraries Help Patrons of Color to Bridge the Digital Divide, but Barriers Remain, *Evidence Based Library & Information Practice*, **16** (4), 138–40, doi: 10.18438/eblip30035.

Martin, F. and Dunsworth, Q. (2007) A Methodical Formative Evaluation of Computer Literacy Course: What and How to Teach, *Journal of Information Technology Education*, **6**, https://jite.org/documents/Vol6/JITEv6p123-134Martin217.pdf.

Mureithi, M. W. (2020) Thika Library, KNLS + AfLIA Leadership = Transformed Community Services, https://web.aflia.net/thika-library-knls-aflia-leadership-academy-transformed-community-services.

Mureithi, M. W. (2021) Libraries as Youth Empowerment Centres,
    https://web.aflia.net/libraries-as-youth-empowerment-centres-miriam-w-
    mureithi.

The Mobile Economy (2020) www.gsma.com/mobileeconomy/sub-saharan-africa.

UNESCO (2016) *Education for People and Planet: Creating Sustainable Futures for All*,
    https://en.unesco.org/gem-report/report/2016/education-people-and-planet-
    creating-sustainable-futures-all.

Van den Berg, I. and Johnston, Z. (2020) *Skills for the Digital Economy: Digital Skills in
    Kenya*, https://cenfri.org/publications/skill-for-the-digital-economy_kenya-case-
    study.

World Bank Group (2019) *The Changing Nature of Work*,
    www.worldbank.org/en/publication/wdr2019.

4

Digital Transformation in City of Johannesburg Library Services through the Provision of e-Learning Services

Jeff B. Nyoka

Abstract

The City of Johannesburg Library and Information Services introduced e-learning services and technologies into the library environment to ensure the inclusion of the City of Johannesburg (COJ) communities in the digital society. Since the expansion of e-learning services in 2016, there have been a lot of successes amid challenges such as staffing, connectivity and budget cuts. COJ e-learning services have played a role in improving digital literacy, assisting in reducing unemployment, providing access to digital information and general internet usage.

The COVID-19 crisis has impacted on provision of library services in South Africa, Johannesburg. Librarians had to revisit the way library services are provided, by focusing on improving the use of information and communications technology and access to online content. This was to ensure that the Johannesburg communities are not left behind, especially considering that e-learning is being introduced to more sectors and for school learners and university students as a way of learning a wide range of disciplines. The COJ public libraries e-learning services can be viewed as an example of ongoing digital transformation of libraries, before and post the COVID-19 pandemic. This chapter documents the journey of COJ libraries since the introduction of e-learning services, including successes, failures and challenges faced.

Keywords: Digital transformation, e-learning in libraries, innovations in libraries, Sustainable Development Goals.

Introduction

The City of Johannesburg (COJ) is a metropolitan municipality within Gauteng Province in South Africa, with a population of more than four million citizens. COJ Library and Information Services (LIS), under Community Development, introduced e-learning services in libraries as part of the 'Smart City' project initiated by the City in 2013, focusing on rethinking existing structures to fully grasp the potential of information and communications technologies (ICTs), to deliver services and improve efficiencies (Ericsson, 2016).

e-Learning services were introduced to libraries in all seven Johannesburg regions, in 87 branch libraries. 'Smart community' is a term that has been used to characterize efforts to transform communities and make them more sustainable, efficient and transparent, and where citizen participation is the norm. COJ municipality has already made considerable progress in implementing Smart City measures, including the expansion of the Johannesburg broadband network; the roll-out of free Wi-Fi points around the city, including Wi-Fi spots within libraries, piloting e-health and e-learning programmes in libraries as part of the digital transformation process (City of Johannesburg, 2020).

Digital transformation involves the 'integration of digital technology into all areas of a business', to enhance business processes and services offered, which should lead to improved customer experience and retention (The Enterprisers Project, 2020). For public libraries, it is important to emphasize that digital transformation is not only about technology, but also about change management in terms of the organizational culture. While technology is the necessary tool, digital transformation must be focused on the customers, who are fast becoming part of a digital economy, and on addressing the performance and satisfaction of the employees who serve the customers. The main organizational strategy and vision should influence the digital transformation strategy. This process requires organizations to challenge how they operate, how they provide services, the skills of their employees and the value they bring to their customers. Different organizations have different needs for digital transformation.

Digital transformation strategy in COJ libraries

The digital transformation strategy in COJ libraries is influenced by the following areas of focus.

The people

Improving customer experiences through technology: Introduction of e-learning services was part of the Smart City vision of developing a smart citizenry within Johannesburg, where citizens are technologically savvy and can access information and knowledge to make informed choices as part of a smart society.

Improving employee performance: COJ librarians had to respond to the Smart City vision of a City that prioritizes efficient service delivery using technologies. Introducing digital technologies into any business has a potential for improving employee performance, work collaboration and skills advancement. This requires an organization to invest in ICT tools for communication, collaboration and connectivity to improve service delivery. COJ LIS has over 400 employees in library branches across seven regions and the head office. These consist of heads of departments, assistant directors, regional managers, senior librarians in selected branches, librarians, senior library assistants, library assistants and general workers. COJ LIS, also provides internship opportunities where possible. Reskilling and upskilling of employees plays an important role in enabling digital transformation in libraries.

The Smart City committee for COJ envisions Johannesburg being a city digitally transforming to be citizen-centric, innovative and inclusive; a city that innovatively uses technology to engage with citizens who have universal access to services and information for socio-economic development, and to provide efficient service delivery that makes the city safe, sustainable, liveable and resilient (City of Johannesburg, 2020).

Data science

Libraries exist in a data-heavy environment, and the ability to collect and analyse data can provide libraries an opportunity to re-engineer certain operations, improve services and invest in new resources. Like most organizations that collect data, COJ libraries have not taken steps to combine and analyse that data for improving decision making and service delivery. Libraries engage with citizens on different programmes and activities, including use of social media and electronic resources, in addition to circulation of library materials. Data available in the digital space has also evolved to reflect the kind of society that is participating in the digital economy and information made available to the Public (IFLA, 2018). COJ libraries have not fully explored big data available within library spaces and online, using data assessment tools and techniques to improve services. It is also an area where there is a skill gap in terms of librarians who understand data science.

Competitive advantage

Public libraries are in a unique position of providing free access to services in spaces that are accessible to communities. However, the emerging technologies and the digital economy have put a lot of pressure on libraries to find innovative methods of attracting and retaining customers, and also improving customer experiences, including outside the library walls. Libraries, for their own survival, cannot afford to rely on legacy systems of information service provision, because communities are exposed to more options and have become more demanding.

Johannesburg is regarded as the financial heart of South Africa and the economic powerhouse of sub-Saharan Africa, with the headquarters of more than 70% of South African companies. The city is also located within a province that attracts the largest inflow of migrants. More than 40% of the population is youth. However, by 2019 more than 60% of communities did not have access to ICT tools, and half of the COJ municipality population does not have access to the internet (STATSA, 2018).

Through digital transformation and the introduction of e-learning services, COJ libraries have begun the journey of addressing these challenges, to enable libraries to remain relevant and agile and to grow their customer base.

e-Learning services in COJ libraries

The concept of e-learning is generally defined as the use of electronic technologies to support learning and teaching. Several terms are used interchangeably, such as e-learning, blended learning, virtual learning, online learning or distance learning, among others. The complexity of electronic technologies and the use of different terminologies make it difficult to develop a clear and coherent conceptual framework for e-learning research (Guri-Rosenblit and Gros, 2011, 6). In COJ libraries, e-learning services are defined as the support and access provided by the libraries through availability of ICT tools such as laptops, tablets, free Wi-Fi and training on how to utilize these tools and access digital content.

COJ libraries e-learning services support lifelong learning for all age groups from different backgrounds, such as children from early childhood to adolescence, youth in high schools and tertiary-level institutions, adult recipients of basic education and senior citizens. COJ libraries' provision of e-learning services is aimed at increasing employability, strengthening entrepreneurship, promoting career and personal development and supporting academic needs, for all COJ communities.

The objectives of e-learning services are:

(a) to create platforms of learning and information sharing, with an emphasis on digital literacy;
(b) to enable access to ICT tools and digital content, particularly for the disadvantaged communities.

e-Learning services are also part of the digital transformation of libraries, challenging perceptions of how library services are provided, introducing new ways of delivering library services to allow communities, particularly youth, to be part of the fourth industrial revolution (4IR). This includes continuously transforming existing physical library spaces to accommodate new technologies and the needs of a community that is slowly becoming part of the digital economy. e-Learning services in the COJ libraries can be accessed within the library spaces or remotely. This includes using the internet (online), e.g. for accessing digital content, or online training, accessing e-books and journal articles, or using technology without the internet (offline), e.g. viewing downloaded content, or using ICT tools to type, read, play games, etc.

COJ e-learning services were formally introduced in 2015. These services consisted of free Wi-Fi, e-learning classrooms with laptops in selected libraries, desktop computers with public access to the internet (introduced in 2016 in 60% of libraries and phased out in 2019), access to e-resources and digital literacy training for staff and the public. More than 400,000 library users accessed the e-learning between 2016 and 2020.

Having learned from international libraries, particularly within the European, American and African continents, through collaborations, international conferences and research, there have been efforts by the COJ libraries e-learning unit to redesign library services through the introduction of innovative e-learning programmes such as mobile literacy, e-learning classroom digital literacy and the introduction of online courses as a means of enabling digital transformation in libraries. These efforts have been strongly supported by collaborations and partnerships.

Introducing e-learning services for a Smart City vision: the journey

As part of the Smart City vision, in 2013 the COJ introduced the PAIL (Public Access to Internet in Libraries) computers, with the aim of providing community access to digital content. This project was exciting for communities who also wanted to utilize these computers to improve digital literacy. One of the major barriers to access is digital illiteracy. Some community members still require digital skills training, and others fear technology, so there needed to be awareness of the value of these new e-learning services and technologies and the benefits released by the digital economy. The e-learning unit viewed users as both library staff and the public. This required efforts first to improve public digital literacy internally, before conducting any major awareness campaigns on the availability of computers and Wi-Fi in libraries.

Digital literacy training for library staff, 2015

COJ LIS department entered into a collaboration with the Goethe Institut, the German cultural institute with offices in Johannesburg, whose mandate is to also support information services professionals by offering train-the-trainer opportunities, aimed at empowering libraries in the regions with various skills in order to support cultural exchange. Thirty librarians were selected to represent their regions and attend a training on digital literacy. This training focused on (re)introducing librarians to computer skills such as Microsoft Office packages, producing documents, internet searches, etc.

Introduction of e-learning classrooms through the MOOV project, 2015

As part of measures to ensure the success of the Smart City vision, the City entered into another partnership with COJ Core Group & Think Ahead educational company, who introduced an e-learning concept called MOOV (Massive Open Online Varsity). This was a MOOC (Massive Open Online Courses) based, free, blended e-learning programme that provided access to selected course content from the MOOC partner institutions (Massachusetts Institute of Technology, Harvard University, Wharton School of the University of Pennsylvania, etc.). The City funded the creation of 12 fully equipped e-learning classrooms in 12 selected public libraries.

The programme was managed and co-ordinated by the Think-Ahead education specialist, who introduced it with minimum input and involvement of library staff. Communities were introduced to appropriate courses selected according to market skills demands, student skill levels and the needs of youth. Specially trained youth facilitators and subject tutors provided support to the learners. These were contracted staff, who were not qualified librarians. The first e-learning classroom, in Sandton Library, was opened in March 2015 as part of the launch of the COJ LIS e-learning programme. The introduction of this MOOV programme created employment opportunities for the facilitators who worked in the 12 classrooms. It introduced communities to online learning and online courses which they would have had to pay for, and these were subsidized by City funding. The market value of the two-year pilot was R5 million (about USD336,000+), and it included certification, connectivity, equipment such as servers, network equipment, iPads, laptops and printers and furniture for the classrooms.

The introduction of MOOV also resulted in more collaborations, such as the City's Youth Empowerment initiative (Vulindlel'eJozi) project, which was a collaboration between City libraries MOOV and a non-governmental organization (NGO) called Harambee. More than 100 youth were contracted in a two-year learnership programme. Over 15,000 youth registered for various programmes during a period of approximately 18 months. In addition to the cost of running the MOOV programme over two years there were other costs of more than R10 million (USD671,500+), spent on expanding classrooms to other regions, including the start-up infrastructure and equipment, as each e-learning classroom had to be designed according to the selected library infrastructure and community profile.

Training plan, 2016–17

When the e-learning office was fully operational, with an assistant director for e-learning and an e-learning manager for libraries, there was a need to assess the digital skills and competencies of the library staff. The 'super trainers' – librarians (renamed as e-learning champions) who had been trained by the Goethe Institut – were mandated to assist in coming up with ideas on programmes and activities to be implemented as part of 'ICT-based library services', now referred to as e-learning services. A survey was conducted among all library staff members to the level of senior librarian, to evaluate their competencies in Microsoft Office packages and other intermediate digital skills. The survey findings were submitted to a separate COJ libraries training unit that is responsible for sourcing training providers to organize training for staff on soft skills.

The e-learning unit drafted a specific training plan that outlined the objectives of e-learning services, training needs, strategy for training and curriculum to be addressed when training COJ library staff and users on the e-learning programmes and technologies that were being introduced. The plan presented the activities needed to support development of training manuals, coordination of training schedules, reservation of personnel and facilities, planning for training needs and other training-related tasks. Training manuals and activities were developed to train library users and library staff on the use of different e-learning-related programmes and systems as specified in the training criteria.

This plan for both staff and user training was introduced in the 2016/17 financial year to ensure the success of e-learning initiatives. By end of 2018, all library branches had formally introduced most of the e-learning services as part of the library service's offering. This was achieved through region-to-region in-person training conducted by the e-learning manager with a group of library staff over a period of six months, and through the e-learning 'champions', who communicated with their regions on all new e-learning programmes introduced. Over 70% of the 400+ library staff attended these workshops on 'understanding e-learning in libraries'.

For library staff, a forum (e-learning Champions) was established to identify support and training needs in the regions. The plan outlines basic digital literary and mobile literacy training to be given to staff to enable them to provide training to library users when necessary.

For library users, the plan encourages formal short training sessions for individuals, on request, on various matters related to the electronic services provided. Other organized training sessions can be provided for groups on selected topics on which the library staff is competent. The training plan is to ensure that librarians are trained and competent to train the users on e-learning services and related concepts.

The COJ e-learning unit developed the training content, focusing on e-learning programmes. The first module was 'Understanding e-learning in libraries'. The naming of the training module was important, to emphasize that e-learning services in libraries mean more than the generic definition of e-learning, which refers to online learning. The training content focused on the types of services offered under e-learning, the programmes and activities that one can introduce in libraries, the various tools to use and how to segment the target audience. Training material was developed from multiple sources, some of which were:

- Input from e-learning champions during brainstorming workshops, where training areas were classified under 'training for staff' or 'training for users'. Within these categories, training areas were separated into computer skills, social media skills, office technology and basic internet usage.
- Available digital content from existing partnerships and external online sources, identified by the e-learning unit. One of the first partnerships that provided content was the Microsoft for Digital Skills curriculum or other Microsoft products. Other learning content was carefully selected, downloaded and customized for staff and user training.

Collaborations and partnerships supporting digital literacy, 2017–19

Collaboration is necessary to achieve a common purpose when individuals or groups work together, especially where they share some resources and skills. Collaborations tend to be informal and occasional, without any interference in each other's businesses, but focusing on a specific project and goal. Partnerships are created through an expressed or implied and sometimes formalized commitment between two or more parties, to achieve a common goal over a certain period. This can involve combining assets or sharing infrastructure. Benefits for both parties must be clearly defined, with good governance practices applied. Partnerships can be complex, and not suitable for all situations; however, they can bring opportunities for libraries to reach a different type of user (Gatiti and Law, 2014, 4).

As part of the digital transformation process, COJ's e-learning services saw the value of establishing relationships with varied stakeholders such as NGOs, private companies, educational institutions and local leadership whose purposes align with the library services, especially in the ICT sector. This approach has been a major influence in the success of e-learning services in COJ libraries, particularly contributing to improving digital literacy.

While the Municipal Structure Act in South Africa does not prevent a municipality from funding library services, municipalities are not required to fund functions that have not been explicitly allocated to them by the Constitution or other national or provincial legislation (Department of Arts and Culture, 2013). This is a dilemma that affected e-learning services in COJ as a newly introduced library service.

Changes in any municipality administration usually have an impact in any municipal department, in terms of budget allocation and the municipality's vision on services to be delivered. COJ municipality administration also went through political changes in 2017, which saw library services funding for the e-learning programme withdrawn.

One of the e-learning services that was negatively affected by the withdrawal of funding was the MOOV e-learning classrooms, which required payment of facilitators, maintenance and upgrading of laptops and reliable connectivity. More than 16,000 youth relied on these classrooms and were in the middle of completing different online courses for certification. The libraries did not have any budget allocated for the classrooms. For more than four months while the Think-Ahead organization was renegotiating the extension of the pilot with the new administration, the communities were in limbo, the library department had no answers and the library staff in the 12 centres had to address community enquiries almost daily. By the 2017/18 financial year, e-learning services usage numbers had decreased from more than 140,000 to less than 50,000 per year because of budget cuts. The e-learning unit had introduced the Mobile Literacy programme, which also included re-engineering the use of e-learning classrooms as mobile classrooms.

In response to public library funding deficiencies, many people both inside and outside the field of librarianship have suggested that public libraries need to rely less on traditional government funding and more on alternative funding sources (Agosto, 2008). Collaborations and partnerships are not only about funding, but libraries also benefit from information sharing and skills development. In response to the challenges that were brought by the exclusion of library staff in management and ownership of the classrooms, the e-learning manager focused on exploring various opportunities outside the City administration that can benefit e-learning programmes without reliance on e-learning classroom funding. One of those was the Electronic Information for Libraries (EIFL) 2017 scholarship award, which he applied for and won, to attend an international conference called Next Library in Denmark, which is focused on innovations in libraries. This opportunity exposed the e-learning manager to various networks and ideas for how to enhance e-learning services, particularly the Mobile Literacy programme.

Gatiti and Law (2014, 4) highlight how building strategic partnerships presents libraries with new tools that can bring the most effective services to library users at affordable costs. Partnerships are necessary, as they provide libraries with opportunities to access new skills and technologies to enable digital transformation. At the Denmark conference, the first formal partnership was established between COJ e-learning services and a South African NGO called FunDza Literacy Trust, who had developed an app called FunDza.Mobi. They had won the 2017 Joy of Reading Award at the Next Library conference. FunDza Literacy Trust has been working in collaboration with COJ libraries since 2017, assisting libraries to introduce digital creative writing and reading for the teens using their mobile devices, working with libraries on reading development competitions and training librarians on creative writing.

Mobile Literacy programme for digital literacy

This programme was introduced in 2017, firstly as a response to the lack of mobile ICT tools in all libraries except the 12 with e-learning classrooms, and secondly to address a lack of skills among library users and staff in the productive use of mobile devices. While most literature and library services view mobile literacy as any service that involves portable and movable educational tools and programmes, in COJ libraries this refers specifically to the productive use of mobile electronic devices such as laptops, tablets, smartphones, both within library spaces and outside library walls. Productive use of such devices requires skills in identifying relevant online information for education, business, career or personal development or job hunting. This necessitates digital literacy. The Mobile Literacy programme is aimed at providing such skills to library staff and communities.

The key concepts driving the Mobile Literacy programme, are:

(a) *Edutainment*, where library users are introduced to mobile devices and other technologies to learn new skills and access relevant digital content while being entertained in some way and socializing with other library users.

(b) *Gamification*, which involves introducing library users to mobile devices with selected apps that have game-playing functionalities and engaging library users in competitions or playing as groups or solving puzzles. This stimulates their brains and development as well as reducing fear of technology. The starting point was the availability of 30 donated tablets, which were the first tools to be distributed to two selected libraries. These libraries were guided on how to find relevant digital content for the school learners.

The collaboration with Goethe Institut was the next step in formalizing the Mobile Literacy programme. The Goethe Institut offered to provide training of librarians on mobile literacy conducted by their contracted facilitator who runs a programme called MLiteracy. The MLiteracy programme defines mobile literacy in South Africa as an ecosystem of projects and initiatives by a variety of stakeholders that promote, support and enable access to literature and literacy projects on mobile devices, especially mobile phones, in the context of informal education (Mobile Literacy in South Africa, 2021).

The Goethe Institut facilitated the training of library staff in all regions on mobile literacy over a period of six months. Library staff were introduced to topics such as online identity, how to find digital content for library activities, gamification and the use of apps for reading development.

Immediately after these training sessions, libraries with donated tablets started implementing the ideas they had learned from the training. Libraries were encouraged to also share these 30 tablets with other branches who are interested in introducing the Mobile Literacy programme. One of the most popular activities libraries introduced to users was how to use QR codes and how to read downloaded e-books.

Introducing mobile e-learning classrooms as part of mobile literacy

The withdrawal of funding for e-learning classrooms forced the COJ libraries e-learning unit to find new ways of using the e-learning classrooms. The mobile e-learning classrooms concept was introduced as a solution to address the lack of mobile devices in most libraries, and to ensure that these ICT resources in classrooms would not remain under-utilized due to a lack of connectivity or adequate staffing. The e-learning classrooms' opening times and days were reduced to address staffing issues. Some laptops were redistributed to selected libraries that were keen on introducing their own mini classrooms with less than six laptops for mobile literacy programmes.

Mobile e-learning classrooms were also instrumental as a means of delivering services to underserved communities and libraries with insufficient resources.

One of the most successful digital literacy programmes that benefitted from this concept was a Senior Citizens Digital Skills and Creative Writing project, where more than 20 senior citizens were trained on basic computer skills and guided on how to write their own life stories using the computer skills they had gained. More than 20 stories were typed on the computers by these senior citizens aged from 50 to 65, between 2018 and 2019 in two different libraries that participated. This project required a mini mobile classroom to be set up every time a training was to be conducted by the e-learning manager at these libraries. Laptops were collected from the classroom and assembled inside the library on study desks for participants to be trained for an hour.

The mobile e-learning classroom concept has also been implemented through outreach programmes to venues such as book fairs where school learners are introduced to digital content for creative writing and school work, among other needs. Schools are also invited to library spaces for digital literacy competition programmes, such as e-learning quizzes conducted using the mobile e-learning classroom set up in any library space.

Introducing coding as a digital literacy programme in COJ libraries

COJ library services have always played a supportive role and worked with schools and educational institutions in their curriculums. In 2018, the South African Department of Basic Education announced that coding would be among the new subjects to be introduced in schools. Through e-learning services, COJ libraries had to be at the forefront in preparing communities and educators for this change. Most township schools in Johannesburg, South Africa are under-resourced and do not have electronic resources such as laptops, tablets or computer rooms. e-Learning services in libraries provide this support by collaborating with NGOs and corporations that can provide ICT skills, assistance in implementing the coding activities in all libraries and encouragement to youth to embrace computer science through coding after school, on weekends or during school holidays. The popularity of coding in conversations, while it was not well understood, challenged the e-learning unit to research the subject and find ways of introducing coding as a digital literacy activity within libraries.

Collaboration with Microsoft SA and an NGO – Siyafunda ICT – resulted in the training of 72 library staff on coding basics so that they can introduce the youth to coding in their libraries, working with schools. In the e-learning classrooms, 'Hour of Code' activities with content generated from the Code.org website were introduced where children learned 'Minecraft' and 'Scratch coding' every Saturday. The interest in coding in libraries increased from the Hour of Code activities, and in 2018 the e-learning unit engaged with Nelson Mandela University Computer Science Department, where an undergraduate student invented a puzzle-based coding programme called 'Tanks Coding Game'. 'Tanks Coding Game' is a mobile app-based educational puzzle that is aimed at teaching school learners basic computer programming principles through coding at primary school level. It is designed for pupils between the ages of 10 and 14. In 'Tanks', pupils in teams competing against each other must piece together puzzle-piece instructions to guide a tank through obstacles to a predetermined destination. They then take a picture of their puzzle-piece pattern using a tablet or mobile phone with the free 'Tanks' app installed (available at Google Play stores). The app uses photo-recognition to execute the path they have coded and determine whether their steps were correct. Once they have found the solution, they can proceed to the next level of difficulty. This uniquely South African coding game was presented as part of the UNESCO Mobile Learning Week in March 2019, in Paris. By collaborating with schools to introduce this game as part of library mobile literacy e-learning activities, COJ libraries intended to contribute to producing the next generation of software developers or computer programmers in the rural and township areas.

The success of this coding programme, which was piloted in three libraries with donated 'Tanks' puzzles, led to the purchase and distribution of more puzzles to all regions. Furthermore, this coding game was expanded through the introduction of a coding competition among regions, which culminated in a coding final during Africa Code Week in October 2019 where more than 60 learners from all regions of Johannesburg attended to compete. More than 1,500 youth and children have been introduced to coding activities and content in COJ libraries since 2018.

Collaborations focused on online content for digital skills development

The biggest and most impactful digital skills training collaboration was introduced in 2018, between Google SA and COJ libraries e-learning services. This two-year collaboration was aimed at providing communities with access to online Digital Skills for Africa courses. Google SA agreed to support e-learning programmes in the 12 libraries with classrooms, by providing free Wi-Fi for the public to access free Google Digital skills courses using the classrooms or their smart devices. These courses focus on employability, digital presence for entrepreneurship and other intermediate and advanced digital skills (coding, robotics, big data). Within a few months, more than 3,000 youth had been introduced to the Google Digital Skills curriculum, through self-paced learning in libraries or organized group training by a Google-appointed trainer. The portable plug-and-play Wi-Fi routers played a major role in supplementing the City's Wi-Fi, particularly whenever there were connectivity issues or during mobile literacy outreach programmes where mobile e-learning classrooms were introduced.

Another additional collaboration for digital skills was with IBM for their IBM Digital Nation Africa programme. COJ libraries also identified IBM as a partner that can bring digital skills to COJ communities using the e-learning classrooms. IBM Digital Nation Africa is a digital skills programme that aims to provide advanced digital skills on emerging technologies (artificial intelligence, coding, robotics, cybersecurity) and provide users with links to relevant jobs. Users earn badges for every module completed. Both platforms contributed to improving digital skills and employability for disadvantaged youth.

Notable successes

International exposure of library services, especially ICT-based services, is vital to ensure recognition of the work that libraries do in introducing communities to electronic technologies and digital content. This exposure also assists in sourcing support and collaboration and it enables digital transformation.

The e-learning unit submitted the e-learning classrooms programme to the United Nations' 2018 and 2019 World Summit on the Information Society (WSIS) Stocktaking Database, to ensure recognition of COJ libraries for their contribution to Sustainable Development Goals. The database is a publicly accessible system providing information on ICT-related initiatives and projects carried out by governments, international organizations, the business sector, civil society and other entities with reference to the 11 WSIS Action

Lines outlined in the Geneva Plan of Action. Both submissions were nominated for the WSIS prize.

In 2020 COJ libraries were short-listed for the London Book Fair International Library of the Year Award for the e-learning programmes that promote access to digital content. In January 2021, COJ libraries won the 2020 (14th) EIFL Public Library Innovation Award for libraries' response to COVID-19, where the e-learning unit used Facebook as an immediate solution to provide library services through a lockdown video series that attracted more than 50,000 views in 2020.

Notable e-learning services and programmes with Sustainable Development Goals (SDGs)

e-Learning classrooms service

Twelve e-learning classrooms were introduced in 2015, located within 12 libraries in eight regions of COJ. The classrooms open on selected days, depending on staffing. They are used for typing and printing, and – where there is connectivity – for internet searches, access to Google Digital Skills, Microsoft Digital Skills, IBM Digital Nation courses, other MOOCs and workshops with NGOs for digital skills training and for adult-based education classes. COVID-19 lockdown regulations interrupted the use of these e-learning classrooms. They were closed in March 2022, until libraries can come up with Standard Operating Procedures for facilities and computer usage. This service addresses Sustainable Development Goal (SDG) no. 9, which is to build resilient infrastructure, promote inclusive and sustainable industrialization and foster innovation.

Senior citizens digital literacy and creative writing

This programme started in 2018. The target audience is senior citizens aged 55+ and unemployed adults aged over 35, who are introduced to basic computer skills and creative writing of indigenous stories using computers. From these classes, 20 senior citizens have gained basic computer skills and learned to type 20 life stories using those skills. This is aimed towards the attainment of Sustainable Development Goal (SDG) no. 4, which is to ensure inclusive and equitable quality education and promote life-long learning opportunities for all, and to achieve gender equality and empower all women and girls.

e-Learning quiz programme

This is a digital literacy programme introduced in 2018 and aimed at children and youth from ages 6 to 18. It can be organized through schools or informally among children visiting libraries. It is an online or offline quiz competition testing knowledge of ICT, e-learning and other topics. Schools, working with libraries, select learners who will participate in regional competitions at the library. Using online quiz software or downloaded content, learners are assembled in a classroom setting and given laptops either in e-learning classrooms or through a mobile classroom in library sections, and they must answer the quiz questions based on ICT and social issues. This not only tests their knowledge of ICT and social issues but also improves their computer skills.

Mobile literacy

The mobile literacy programme promotes constructive and educational use of the free COJ Wi-Fi and personal mobile devices. The programme involves use of tablets, personal smartphones, e-readers and Wi-Fi or downloaded content, and mobile e-learning classrooms. Examples of gamification activities are digital storytelling activities using QR codes, e-learning quizzes and creative writing workshops (these include using reading and writing apps, treasure hunt apps, coding apps, science and physics apps).

The provision of free internet accessible via mobile devices and introducing communities to a range of content on mobile devices has resulted in COJ library users using mobile devices to improve their education or that of their children. Importantly, women are more likely than men to use mobile devices for educational purposes, showing that these devices can help reduce gender inequality. Quality of life improves as people gain access to skills in utilizing mobile technology.

Ongoing digital literacy for digital transformation in COJ libraries

The World Economic Forum highlights that, according to a study conducted by the International Finance Corporation, by 2030 Africa will have created more than 200 million jobs that will require digital skills, resulting in almost 600 million training opportunities (World Economic Forum, 2020). These jobs will require citizens who are skilled in accessing online opportunities and content. IFLA mentions the other dimensions that promote digital inclusion: are access to reliable connectivity infrastructure, digital devices and digital content, affordability and relevant skills to use technology to improve one's life.

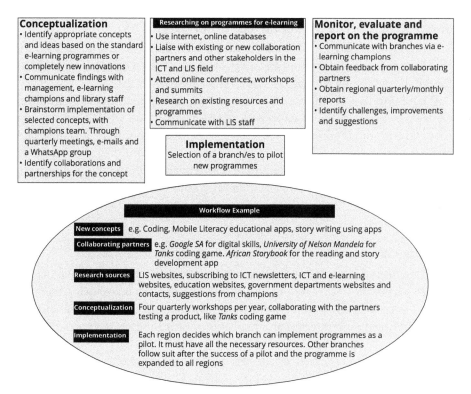

Figure 4.1 *Delivery of e-learning services: workflow*

The World Bank's 2018 assessment of South Africa's digital economy emphasized the importance of support organizations such as innovation hubs, co-working spaces and organized programmes for digital entrepreneurship (World Bank Group, 2018). COJ public libraries are community-centred spaces which have introduced programmes focused on entrepreneurship, such as business workshops, short videos on business topics and making available relevant e-resources for entrepreneurs. COJ libraries have a decades-long relationship with communities and their free offering of services positions them best to address these digital inclusion issues.

The digital transformation strategy for COJ libraries aims to contribute to addressing digital inclusion through various interventions using technology, by 2025. The 4IR (digital) economy presents new risks in society, from fake news to cybersecurity, protection of data and online identity. Libraries are the best resources and facilities to help communities to navigate the online space, to select, interpose and use online information responsibly. Librarians require new skills to assist communities that also need new skills relevant to the digital economy.

The digital literacy model for COJ libraries

The digital literacy programmes model for COJ libraries was influenced by the International Telecommunication Union's (ITU) Digital Insight 2020 toolkit model (International Telecommunication Union, 2020).

Public libraries, by their nature, are not academic institutions or training centres, but they provide support to these institutions while also serving communities of all backgrounds. This model focuses on basic, intermediate and advanced digital skills. It allows libraries to segment their communities according to their competencies and needs while providing them with access to digital literacy programmes that are suitable for their educational backgrounds, both informally and through organized settings.

Basic digital skills

Since the introduction of e-learning services, basic digital skills have been a bigger part of digital literacy in libraries. These include introducing users to computer parts and software, how to type and create documents or download apps and how to use internet or e-mail and transact online. Methods include:

- basic computer classes in e-learning classrooms, conducted by a competent library staff member or inviting a partner to provide training;
- promoting and providing access to the Microsoft Digital Skills curriculum for self-paced learning through classrooms.

Intermediate digital skills

The ITU defines these as digital skills that empower the beneficiary to learn how to use technology and digital tools to produce content or consume content that enhances livelihoods (International Telecommunication Union, 2020). These include skills such as coding, learning basic programming tools, desktop publishing, digital marketing, social media influencing and blogging, among others. COJ libraries promote the acquisition of such skills through various methods, including:

- organizing creativity competitions where users need to explore apps or technologies to produce content or create something on their own;
- promoting access to relevant online courses for intermediate digital skills;
- inviting partners who are experts in certain digital skills to train the public in groups.

Advanced digital skills

These are skills involving the use of emerging technologies, and are predominately found among professions such as computer programming, software development, data science and network management. Some of the 4IR technologies that communities need to learn about, include artificial intelligence, big data, cybersecurity, Internet of Things, augmented and virtual reality. These concepts are introduced to communities through various methods, namely:

- COJ libraries, as part of digital transformation, identified the introduction of makerspaces as one of the best ways of introducing communities to advanced digital skills and emerging technologies within the library environment. Makerspaces allow communities to conveniently access a safe space where they can learn to create technology on their own and produce items that they can sell or use for personal development and self-employment.
- Partnerships with innovation hubs allow libraries to organize staff and users to visit these hubs where they can learn about new technologies, particularly those used for entrepreneurship.
- Users are guided to specific online courses that focus on emerging technologies, such as the IBM Digital Nation courses and Google Digital Skills courses, which include robotics, data science, digital business and coding.
- Internships.

The future of COJ libraries and the digital transformation strategy

Focus on digital literacy programmes

The COVID-19 crisis has influenced most industries to explore the benefits of technologies in business processes and improving customer services in order to stay relevant. For public libraries, there is a need for an increased focus on supporting communities in developing relevant digital skills, guiding communities to relevant information sources online and on how to participate in the digital economy. Investing in new technologies will be a fruitless exercise if both staff and the communities do not possess the skills to utilize those tools productively.

Strengthening collaborations and partnerships

Collaborations and partnerships with NGOs and private companies have been instrumental in the success of e-learning programmes. However, internal collaborations with different COJ units will be necessary to pool resources and share skills for the purpose of community development.

Exploring the introduction of a learning management system

The COVID-19 pandemic challenges have forced most industries to engage in e-learning for employees and students. The learning management system has become a standard part of the higher education infrastructure, both for online and face-to-face courses and for some industries as well for employee training. Libraries are support structures for academic institutions, business and the general public. Provision of digital content in libraries such as e-books and e-resources should extend to providing access to carefully selected online learning content for different sectors of the community. This can be another support tool for library users of different categories to access a variety of approved materials for learning, with the assistance of skilled librarians, thus achieving the goal of delivering services equally to all types of public users. Collaborations and partnerships with different academic institutions will be instrumental in assisting COJ public libraries to enter the online learning industry.

Challenges

Funding and supportive procurement processes

Sometimes, when funds are available, challenges arise through the allocation of funds for certain functions, the processes of accessing certain funds and the availability of supportive procurement processes. Acquisition of ICT-related tools such as apps, software and other digital content is largely subscription based, and ICT is constantly changing. This requires the supply chain unit to be educated about these kinds of changes and the importance of these types of resources to the library environment, particularly in view of enabling digital transformation.

Leadership support and awareness

When leaders understand and appreciate the need to transform libraries using technologies, they are most likely to influence others and create awareness. This also includes local community leaders such as ward councillors and youth leaders. In the COJ some of the social ills people face include lack of housing and unemployment. Some communities do not believe that connectivity is also a priority if they do not have job opportunities and decent housing or running water. When the City introduced free Wi-Fi, social media comments lamented a lack of service delivery in other areas that communities deemed to be essential.

Lack of robust marketing on e-learning programmes

COJ libraries have done several impactful programmes; however, these programmes could have had a much bigger impact if there were stronger marketing tools and promotional exercises.

Connectivity

This a major hindrance to advancement of the digital transformation dream and the Smart City vision. A robust and successful digital economy is dependent on healthy, universal access to broadband and a connected and digitally literate society. COJ libraries have had many bumps along the way due to inconsistent internet connectivity, caused by delays in implementation and distribution, tender contracts issues, change of administration, cable theft and crime among other issues.

Conclusion

When e-learning services were introduced, there was a stronger focus and excitement from communities about introducing the ICT services and technologies, but not enough staff consultation and community involvement, due to time constraints and pressure to implement. This would have ensured that communities and staff felt a sense of ownership of the e-learning programmes and resources. Digital transformation works best if there is continuous engagement with library staff and consultation with all stakeholders, internally and externally, to ensure buy-in on the digital transition strategy and vision before investing in technologies.

When organizations start by digitizing, they run a risk of investing in technologies that will not be used, and thereby wasting funds that could have been utilized better elsewhere. Change management within the organization is a necessary and vital exercise to engage in, and a much more important element of digital transformation. Digital literacy alone is not enough; staff need to be convinced of the need to transform the library services and to change business processes, and of the value of ICT in library services. Change management planning is also necessary to prepare libraries for organizational change, such as the change in municipality administration, which affected library funding of e-learning programmes. This experience presented an opportunity for COJ libraries to learn to strengthen partnerships and collaborations so that programmes are sustained in any eventuality.

The introduction of innovative concepts in libraries using City funding for communities served by libraries should not be administered or managed by external partners, but libraries should take full ownership of the programmes and implementation thereof, as long as these programmes are within library spaces, for communities that utilize the library. The terms and conditions of partnerships should favour communities and the libraries that serve them, in order to increase the chances of sustainability and trust. Measuring the impact of e-learning services has also proven to be a challenge, due to lack of appropriate tools. COJ libraries will need to utilize relevant technologies for data analysis to make better decisions regarding customer experiences and all library services provided.

The digital transformation strategic focus for COJ libraries from 2021 to 2025 envisions library services that provide:

- community-centred library *spaces* that enable smart citizenry;
- libraries with library *personnel* that are digitally literate and understand the needs of smart citizens in a digital economy;
- library *collections* that are both global and Afrocentric;
- community-centred interactive *services* where technologies enable productivity and service delivery.

The digital transformation journey is an ongoing one for COJ libraries, because it is not a project of digitalizing, but of the willingness of libraries and leadership to change or modify existing processes in order to improve customer experiences and to remain relevant through the use of digital technologies in relevant situations. Some library services do not require digitalization. With lessons learned from the past, and innovations introduced through collaborations and partnerships, libraries can become the backbone of a digital economy, providing access to reliable, speedy information services to smart communities.

References

Agosto, D. E. (2008) Alternative Funding for Public Libraries: Trends, Sources, and the Heated Arguments that Surround It, *Advances in Librarianship*, **31**, 115–40.

City of Johannesburg (2020) *Joburg Smart City Strategy, Revised 2020–2025*, www.africanconstructionexpo.com/wp-content/uploads/2019/07/Monique.pdf.

Department of Arts and Culture (2013) *Project Report: Costing the South African Public Library and Information Services Bill*,

www.dac.gov.za/sites/default/files/Legislations%20Files/South%20African%20pu
blic%20library%20and%20information%20service%20bill.pdf.

Ericsson (2016) *Ericsson Networked Society City Index, 2016 edition*,
www.ericsson.com/en/trends-and-insights/networked-society-insights/city-
index.

Gatiti, P. and Law, M. (2014) *Better Together: Building Strategic Library Partnerships*,
http://ecommons.aku.edu/libraries/16.

Guri-Rosenblit, S. and Gros, B. (2011) E-learning: Confusing Terminology, Research
Gaps and Inherent Challenges, *International Journal of E-Learning & Distance
Education/Revue internationale du e-learning et la formation à distance*, **25** (1),
www.ijede.ca/index.php/jde/article/view/729.

IFLA (International Federation of Library Associations and Institutions) (2018) *IFLA
Big Data Special Interest Group October 2018: A Concept Data Science Framework for
Libraries*, www.ifla.org/wp-content/uploads/2019/05/assets/big-
data/publications/a_concept_data_science_framework_for_libraries.pdf.

International Telecommunication Union (2020) *Digital Skills Insights 2020*,
https://academy.itu.int/digital-skills-insights-2020.

STATSA (Statistics South Africa) (2018) *General Household Survey 2018*,
www.statssa.gov.za/publications/P0318/P03182018.pdf.

The Enterprisers Project (2020) *What Is Digital Transformation?*
https://enterprisersproject.com/what-is-digital-transformation.

World Bank Group (2018) *South Africa Digital Economy Assessment*, Background
Paper series, Digital Entrepreneurship Pillar,
https://openknowledge.worldbank.org/bitstream/handle/10986/33632/South-
Africa-Digital-Economy-Assessment-Digital-Entrepreneurship-Pillar.pdf?sequen
ce=1&isAllowed=y.

World Economic Forum (2020) *Africa Needs Digital Skills across the Economy – Not Just
the Tech Sector*, www.weforum.org/agenda/2020/10/africa-needs-digital-skills-
across-the-economy-not-just-tech-sector.

5

National Library of Nigeria and the Promotion of Digital Equity

Glory O. Okeagu, Okwuoma Chidumebi Chijioke,
Na'angap Daship and Solape Oshile

Abstract

Inclusivity and literacy are core areas that undergird the United Nations Sustainable Development Goals 2030 and African Union 2063 goals. They aim at bridging all the gaps and divides that breed inequalities, especially in Africa. Digital equity engenders digital inclusion and social justice. A large number of Africans are still not adequately included to access and utilize digital technologies. Libraries are spaces that promote inclusivity, as they offer programmes that imbue the citizenry with digital skills and access to digital infrastructure. This creates equity in access to information. This chapter examines the efforts of National Library of Nigeria in promoting digital equity to its user communities across the country. Perception, educational level, technology acceptance and user support are identified as the major challenges, while community engagement and leadership are some of the strategies that enhance the thrust of the institution in promoting digital equity all over the country.

Keywords: National Library of Nigeria, digital equity, digital inclusion, digital literacy, community engagement, leadership, technologies, ICT, IT.

Introduction

Information and communication technology (ICT) is a major contributor to the socio-economic well-being of any nation, and has become a non-negotiable enabler for engagements and transactions in all facets of life. The presence and use of technology can significantly impact on a person's ability to engage fully and inclusively in society. There have been rapid advances in

ICT, with new technologies continuously evolving and changing how people interact individually, as groups, and likewise access the services provided by government organizations and private workplaces.

New technologies have also been touted as the precursor for the fourth industrial revolution. It is for these reasons that individuals, organizations and nations are investing heavily in digital infrastructure and matching skills. Digital technologies have become critical for service delivery in the operation(s) of almost all government agencies, including libraries. Libraries are taking advantage of the numerous opportunities that ICT offers in meeting the information needs of users, and they have become intermediaries in helping community members to overcome digital divide, develop digital skills and promote digital inclusion (Sanders, 2020).

Libraries drive digital equity by providing access to computers and the internet in the provision of services, thereby equipping their user communities to make the most use of library resources in meeting their information needs. Digital equity is a condition in which all individuals and communities have the digital literacy capacity, no matter how basic, needed for full participation in our society, democracy and economy (Huffman, 2018). Digital literacy enables human and social systems which must change in order for technology to make a difference.

Digital literacy capacity entails that all individuals have access to computers, internet access and the necessary skills to participate in the information society. Information plays a major role in the economic, social, political and cultural life of society, and one of its key components is technology. Abdullahi (cited in Elebeke, 2020) points out that focusing on digital literacy skills rather than university and college degrees will fast-track digital inclusion and gradually increase the contribution of digital technologies to the Nigerian economy.

Skill is the art of possessing the ability, power, authority or competency to do the tasks required of an individual on the job, and these are facilitated by conditions that promote acquisition and the change that occurs when the skill is acquired (Bolt Lee and Foster, 2003; Okoro and Ursula, 2002, both cited in Ezeani, 2012). Digital literacy requires individuals to use a range of skills to perform tasks and solve problems in the digital environment. These include the access, use and analysis of texts, as well as their creation and distribution. Digital skills have been transformed into a precondition for benefiting from any technology across all sectors of the economy, and a digitally literate workforce is needed to build digital economies. Digital literacy has also become a requirement for social inclusion and an indicator of professional competence, digital citizenship and social skills (Milenkova and Lendzhova, 2021). Technology is taking the lead in everything since the onset of the

COVID-19 pandemic. The lockdown experienced during the COVID-19 pandemic pushed learning, teaching, research, religious activities and communication to online spaces. There has also been an extensive and far-reaching digital revolution in everyday life and practices. Governments, businesses and individuals employed new ways of meeting their obligations; teleworking, teleconferencing, remote learning, e-commerce, e-governance, online health services and digital payments were adopted to continue serving clients and to interact with citizens for public service and representation, while individuals explored new means of social interaction and consumption (Strusani and Houngbonon, 2021).

The closure of library spaces in Nigeria and globally during the COVID-19 crisis highlighted their inadequacies or lack of infrastructure for engendering digital inclusion. Some libraries responded creatively to the closure by offering digital services (e-lending, investment in content/licences, e-books, support for remote learning, digital story times and promoting services through their websites, etc.), while the entire library system closed for many others (IFLA, 2020). The post-COVID-19 pandemic library setting means that librarians have to take cognizance of differences in digital access, devices and skills among users so as to serve them better (Shuck et al., 2017, cited in Aguilar, 2020).

Digital technologies play a fundamental role in global and regional agendas, from information creation and dissemination to storage. Digital equity is therefore necessary for the achievement of the United Nations 2030 Sustainable Development Goals both as an end and as a means to the policy of leaving no one behind. Corroborating the importance of digital equity to the global agenda, Willems, Farley and Campbell (2019) defined digital equity as a modern-era civil right, taking their cue from the World Summit on the Information Society (WSIS, 2003) Declaration of Principles which states: 'everyone, everywhere should have the opportunity to participate and no one should be excluded from the benefits information society offers', which includes the digital world. The African Union (AU) digital transformation strategy for Africa (2020–30) envisions a digitally transformed continent for prosperity and inclusivity.

Botha (2016), citing Solomon, Allen and Resta (2003), defined digital equity as processes that ensure everyone, irrespective of socio-economic status, language, race, geography, physical restriction, cultural background, gender or other attributes historically associated with inequities, has equitable access to advanced technologies, communication and information resources and the experiences they provide. Digital equity also means that individuals have equal opportunity and capacity to be producers and consumers of current and future technologies, communication and information resources. Digital equity seeks to ensure that all residents and neighbourhoods have the information technology capacity needed for civic and cultural participation, employment, lifelong learning and access to essential services. The fundamental areas are access, digital literacy, content and services (Seattle Digital Equity Initiative Action Plan, 2015). All the descriptions above highlight inclusion and empowerment through connection with technologies.

Digital inclusion requires intentional strategies and investments to reduce and eliminate historical, institutional and structural barriers to access and use technology. According to Huffman (2018), the five (5) core elements of digital inclusion are:

- affordable, robust broadband internet service;
- internet-enabled devices that meet the needs of the user;
- access to digital literacy training;
- quality technical support; and
- applications and online content designed to enable and encourage self-sufficiency, participation and collaboration.

Middleton and Chambers (2010) averred that recent reports on digital divide indicate that the shape and size of the digital divide has changed greatly over the years depending on demographic and situational variables. Their study suggested that Wi-Fi access and use could help immensely to reduce the digital divide, with increased sales of computers, laptops and mobile devices. Although technologies may have become pervasive in our world today, their spread of access and use is uneven, with new technologies exacerbating inequity in use (Sanders, 2020; Katz and Levine, 2015). The gap between those with digital skills and those who struggle to overcome barriers to access and use was strengthened during the COVID-19 pandemic. Furthermore, the pandemic has convinced individuals to rethink or revise expected competencies, abilities and skills to maintain relevance. Workplace demands, expectations and circumstances have dramatically changed; digital literacy and skills have become a prerequisite for employment; the workforce are expected to be flexible in their work practices, operating when and where required as opposed to working from a particular location. The work from home policy during the lockdown exposed the vulnerabilities of many organizations, as they could not respond appropriately to meet their obligations. Increased access to ICT and the internet does not necessarily translate into increased usage. According to Nemer (2015), increasing access to technologies may give the impression that digital equity has been achieved, and many policy makers resort to the provision of digital technologies such as computers and internet without enabling the skills to use them. The aim of digital inclusion is to close the gaps in access to and adoption of dynamic ICTs and services. They need to address socio-economic inequalities and provide appropriate platforms that make it easier for people to acquire the skills they need to take advantage of digital tools for communication, teaching, learning, research, economic, social and religious activities in the modern world.

In many African communities, a lot of people are still underserved, unreached and most times digitally excluded, due to distance and poor or lack of digital literacy. Technologies are in the main located in the urban areas, while rural areas are often left out in the digital transition. Individuals with little disposable income, time, literacy or awareness of digital technologies have few incentives to spend the time and money to gain access. Digital equity is further constrained by limited local efforts to support parents, educators and other community stakeholders. The economically disadvantaged are more likely than the socially isolated to try to seek out access to internet-based services in libraries or places of education, and also to make use of the limited resources that they do have (Kuroda et al., 2019; Katz and Levine, 2015; Helsper, 2008).

Consequently, libraries are creating programmes and services that help to inculcate digital skills and literacy in communities where they exist. Libraries are working to provide free and equitable access to knowledge and information and this aligns with Article 19 of the Universal Declaration of Human Rights, which specifies the freedom to receive and impact of information without barriers (IFLA, 2019). The Nigerian 2011 Freedom of Information Act gives every one of its citizens the right of access to information, records and documents held by government bodies and private bodies carrying out public functions (Osuigwe, 2011).

The National Library of Nigeria (NLN), the apex library of Nigeria, was established over 50 years ago, in 1964, with the mandate to serve as the intellectual storehouse of the nation's memory. It is required to serve the general public and maintain branches in all the 36 states of the federation, including the Federal Capital Territory (FCT), and currently has 27 branches. It is, then, crucial that policies, programmes, capacity development and practices on ICT(s) are geared and tailored towards everyone considered as a member of the community, irrespective of their peculiar needs. The NLN, in line with this, carries out services and programmes to promote digital equity in its vast constituency of more than 180 million people. Improved ICT systems have enhanced and strengthened organizational infrastructure and capacity by increasing employees' efficiency and service coordination, especially between the headquarters and branches and information sharing between departments. Some of the branch libraries carry out digital literacy programmes and services periodically, both onsite and offsite, to empower their user communities and to enable ease of access to their services. This has led to increased patronage.

Digital equity programmes designed to address the challenges of the disadvantaged in the community, including economic and workforce development and training, are imperative to maintain relevance. Evaluation and feedback mechanisms are needed to track the impact and success of such programmes. It is possible to give individuals access and skills, but continuity in the exploitation of ICTs depends on their everyday circumstances. Low-income families, for example, will not prioritize spending money on transport, often to a distant access location. Many factors (e.g. demographic, geographical, gender, age, psychological, attitude, educational, economic, sociological, labour, cultural, disabilities, political, lack of technical infrastructure, lack of affordability of technologies, lack of digital literacies) may contribute to the disparity in people's ability to access web-based information and ICTs (Willems, Farley and Campbell, 2019).

The NLN has made significant efforts to promote digital equity to its staff, from the deployment of Wi-Fi across the entire organization, to investments in hardware and software, automation of some functions, digital literacy for staff and users and the development of digital collections.

Digital services and programmes in the National Library of Nigeria

Some of the NLN's digital services and programmes are described in the following sub-sections.

Provision of e-library services in 18 state branch libraries

The National Information Technology and Development Agency (NITDA), through the Universal Service Provision Fund, donated the e-libraries in both the NLN (Table 5.1 opposite) and other libraries in the country. The NLN needs adequate funding for the sustainability of this project, and under the leadership of Professor L. O. Aina it has made great efforts to resuscitate some of these e-libraries. Each e-library has 50 working computer systems and a server. The e-libraries provide internet services to readers as well as access to a good number of e-books that have been downloaded and provided offline on various subjects.

Table 5.1 *Location of e-libraries within the National Library system*

S/N	E-library location	Geographical zone	Total no. in zone
1	NLN, Abia State Branch, Umuahia	South East	3
2	NLN, Enugu State Branch, Enugu	South East	
3	NLN, Imo State Branch, Owerri	South East	
4	NLN, Cross River State Branch, Calabar	South South	2
5	NLN, Edo State Branch, Benin	South South	
6	NLN, Lagos State Branch, Alagomeji	South West	4
7	NLN, Ogun State Branch, Abeokuta	South West	
8	NLN, Ondo State Branch, Akure	South West	
9	NLN, Oyo State Branch, Ibadan	South West	
10	NLN, Taraba State Branch, Jalingo	North East	1
11	NLN, Kaduna State Branch, Kaduna	North West	3
12	NLN, Kano State Branch, Kano	North West	
13	NLN, Sokoto State Branch, Sokoto	North West	
14	NLN, Kwara State Branch, Ilorin	North Central	5
15	NLN, Nasarawa State Branch, Lafia	North Central	
16	NLN, Niger State Branch, Minna	North Central	
17	NLN, Plateau State Branch, Jos	North Central	
18	NLN, FCT Branch, Area 2, Abuja	North Central	

Digital literacy training

Some of these branch libraries use the e-libraries to carry out digital programmes to improve the lives of their users and staff. Some of the programmes and services provided include Microsoft Office, website creation, coding, drone and basic robotics, financial literacy, technology utilization in business, library automation training (library software), electronic learning management system and computer-based testing (CBT) training, database management for teachers, internet proficiency course, internet browsing and others.

Adult users

There are 18 e-libraries in the 27 branches of the NLN. These e-libraries serve as intervention platforms to address digital equity in their various communities, and the branches partner with stakeholders to carry out digital literacy support programmes for users. The users are mostly young people (students, applicants), researchers and the general public. The stakeholders provide the skills and the technical support to facilitate digital literacy training. In addition, some branches also have a staff person who is technology proficient and whose major task is to provide information technology (IT) assistance to users. For many users, the acquisition of digital skills is a means to an end – to get a job, prepare and write the Joint Admissions Matriculation Board (JAMB) Unified Tertiary Matriculation Examination (UTME) and projects, perform their assignments in work settings, expand their horizons by exploring the online environment or others. IT trainings have been conducted for retirees, teachers, children and business people in some of the branches. Some branches average two to four programmes a year with 25 to 50 participants in each one.

These programmes are primarily targeted at enhancing digital equity among the various user communities. From 2018 to the present, the statistics vary from one branch to another; some branches are more proactive than others and are creatively promoting digital equity in the community. The statistics range from as high as four hundred (400) and as low as twenty-five (25). On average, in one of the branches 60 users visit the e-library to browse the internet monthly, apart from the programmes organized. The Kwara State branch has been actively involved in partnering with a non-governmental organization, Women in Technology, in training young secondary school girls on basic digital literacy and in training the trainers on electronic learning management systems for digital classrooms and wiki library updates.

Similarly, the FCT branch partnered with the founder of <codeIT>, Mrs Damilola Anwo-Ade, to train children and teenagers on coding and drone programme. The teaching of coding was done in the electronic library and the resource centre concurrently. Fifty children were trained in a class split into junior (5–9 years) and senior (10–18 years) groups to aid understanding

Table 5.2 *Adult participants in the programmes*

Branch	Participants
Ogun (Abeokuta)	20
Abuja (FCT, Area 2)	200
Abia (Umuahia)	76
Gombe (Gombe)	250
Plateau (Jos)	25
Sokoto (Sokoto)	25
Kwara (Ilorin)	400
Kaduna (Kaduna)	50
Lagos (Alagomeji)	120

and control. This was a vacation programme held over three weeks from 7 to 25 August 2017. The children were introduced to HTML. The high point of the programme was selecting the best coders in the different categories. Awards were given to the children courtesy of the sponsor, the American Embassy. The closing ceremony was held in the Embassy and the children were awarded certificates of attendance. The essence of the programme was to give the children hands-on digital experience to sharpen their individual creativity. More children started coming to the library, as their parents wanted more.

Children's vacation programme

Six librarians from NLN who participated in the African Library & Information Associations and Institutions (AfLIA) Cohort 2 training of the International Network of Emerging Library Innovators Sub-Saharan Africa (INELI SSAf) organized a one-week digital literacy empowerment programme for children. Eighty children, including teenagers, participated. The FCT branch e-library was used to teach the children website design and basic computer appreciation, among other things.

Website design

The children were taught website design. The training was hands-on, as the 50 computers in the electronic library were used for the training. Most of the children were able to create their own website at the end of the programme.

Basic computer appreciation

Another resource person taught the children basic knowledge of the computer. This included the hardware components of the computer and their uses. They also learned how to boot and shut down the computer and open and save files. Certificates of attendance were also issued to the children. This enhanced digital equity among the children, as some coming from the satellite towns and the villages were able to learn the basics of computer use. It also increased the number of children using the library facility.

Table 5.3 *Programmes for digital skills acquisition*

Type of programme	Location	Participants
Computer appreciation	Abuja (FCT, Area 2)	80
Website design	Abuja (FCT, Area 2)	50
Coding	Abuja (FCT, Area 2)	50

One-month computer training in Jos branch for the youth

Another librarian who was trained in the AfLIA Leadership Academy (AfLAc) cohort 2 organized digital skills training for the youths using the e-library of the Plateau State Branch of NLN. Twenty youths from Anglo-Jos, a community close to the library, were trained on computer appreciation (word processing, MS Excel and MS PowerPoint presentations). A series of discussions and meetings with Anglo-Jos youths identified the kind of digital literacy training they desired. They asked to be trained on MS Office, which would give them basic computer skills to navigate the employment market and to create, share and exchange information. The AfLIA leader engaged an IT expert who provided the skills for the training. The training lasted for one month. Table 5.4 shows the details of the programme.

Table 5.4 *Digital skills training, National Library Plateau State branch*

Computer package	Modules	Participants
Word processing	Typing of words using MS Word, creating, saving, opening, closing files	20
Microsoft Excel	Creating spreadsheet	20
PowerPoint	Creating presentation slides	20

Two of the participants got jobs as a result of the skills acquired in the training.

Financial literacy in Ketti

A librarian in the NLN who participated in the International Network of Emerging Library Innovators, sub-Saharan African (INELI SSAf) programme, run by AfLIA as an initiative of the now ended Global Libraries, funded by the Bill and Melinda Gates Foundation, also carried out an outreach programme at Ketti, a suburb in the Abuja Municipal Area Council. The people were underserved and almost excluded digitally. The programme, tagged 'Banking the unbanked', was carried out in partnership with Access Bank, Central Business District, Federal Capital Territory, Abuja, and aimed to bring banking services to the grassroots. The training included financial literacy for money-making ventures they could engage in, introduction to agency banking and account opening.

Fourteen local community members were in attendance, and staff from Access Bank demonstrated how to use the Point of Sale (POS) facility and ATM cards to open a bank account and withdraw or transfer money. This they called agency or mobile banking. Five people opened individual accounts and a participant indicated an interest to start a mobile banking service in the village as an agent for Access Bank. The service would save the inhabitants the cost and stress of travelling a long distance just to access banking services in town.

Staff

The NLN annually circulates questionnaires to capture the technology training needs of staff and plan accordingly. Staff are trained on their areas of interest, leading to staff buy-in which ensures a successful digital inclusion. Training in skills specifically needed for their work is compulsory. The benefit here is that as computers and systems become pervasive in the organization, the requisite skills to use them are also available. Some staff receive training on matters as simple as attaching documents to e-mails and other skills.

Online issuance of ISBN

To encourage authors and the publishing industry, the NLN has made possible the issuance of ISBNs online so that community members can apply for an ISBN at their convenience. The International Standard Book Number (ISBN) and International Standard Serial Number (ISSN) are some of the basic tools use by the NLN to ensure bibliographic control. Over the years, applications for ISBN and ISSN have been made manually. This is both cumbersome and time consuming. The online service that the NLN has developed has reduced the stress which publishers go through when applying for numbers. Also, to encourage compliance of legal deposit obligations, authors and publishers are given free CD-ROM copies of the published National Bibliography of Nigeria. The NLN has been organizing a series of training workshops for publishers and authors on how to access and use the application, and also to create awareness.

Digital content development

NLN is digitizing documents of historical importance for learning and research. Digitization of information resources has created new means of storage, conservation, preservation and access for information resources. The creation of computerized representations of printed analogue materials (Swain and Panda, 2009) is a great effort which most libraries are undertaking in an attempt to make them available to users. Digital content development in libraries is very necessary to enable library resources to be accessible either offline or online, and library users need digital skills in order to access them.

This is even more imperative in the post-COVID-19 period, with NLN's continuous efforts to support education.

Another dimension of digital equity is access to content that is of high quality, meaningful and culturally relevant, and opportunities to create, share and exchange new content (Resta et al., 2018; Judge, Puckett and Cabuk, 2004). The digitized documents will be available in the National Virtual Library of Nigeria database on its website. To facilitate this, robotic scanners and other types of equipment have been procured; three staff were also sent on training abroad to learn the intricacies of handling and maintaining some of the scanners.

Challenges

Perception

There are still individuals (users and staff) who are technophobic, and so the benefit of ICT is coloured by their perception of its ease of use and usefulness. The cost of accessing NLN digital training programmes may be too high for many users to bother, since the branch libraries of the NLN are situated in the city centres (State capitals). Unless they are in a setting where ICT access and use is mandatory, many would prefer the status quo. The NLN is sometimes viewed by some as elitist and not for everyone and therefore constant advocacy and awareness raising is needed to encourage people to avail themselves of the programmes provided.

Technology acceptance

There are different levels of prejudice against technology use. For many older users and staff who are already set in their ways, change is somehow resisted, while for others a lack of confidence that they can use technology hinders their acceptance of it. Many people are digitally illiterate because they are not aware of the huge potentials technologies can offer. According to Kuroda et al. (2019), many internet users in the developing countries equate the internet with social media services like Facebook, rather than the many benefits and services it offers.

Educational level

Different categories of users with varying levels of education use the NLN facilities. The objectives for usage also differ. During computer test examinations like the JAMB UTME, more users come in, and when the examinations are over they may not return. Levels of education also determine the speed of understanding and development of ICT skills and benefits.

User support

NLN branches help to reach a wider audience in the community, but unfortunately many of the branches do not have the necessary skills to support users' needs. Digital literacy support in the branches is low, as there are few NLN staff in the branches who are ICT proficient.

Funding

The high cost of ICT infrastructure, capacity building and maintenance requires adequate funding to be in place. The NLN has experienced dwindling funding in recent years. Some of the e-libraries are in dire need of repair, revamping and replacement of equipment.

Strategies

As already noted, NLN has encountered some challenges in the quest to propagate digital equity in the community. Some of the strategies that could enhance digital equity are suggested in the following sub-sections.

Community engagement

Community engagement involves working with the community to understand and solve community needs. It is also the processes of establishing and maintaining relationships with your stakeholders. In designing and customizing digital literacy programmes it is important for the library to know its community very well – who they are, what they do and what they need. This is called profiling, understanding the demographics of the community. Interviews, questionnaires, etc. help to identify and understand IT needs and skills and the potential impact on people's lives. According to the American Library Association, community engagement is the process of working collaboratively with community members, who might be library users, residents, education faculty, students or partner organizations, to address issues for the benefit of the community. The NLN must engage with its communities from time to time and continuously re-evaluate relationships with them. The NLN's community comprises its stakeholders, users, federal and state governments and partners.

Leadership

The transformation of libraries is powered by the vision, creativity, willingness and abilities of their leaders. For example, a leader who does not believe in the efficacy and value of technologies will find it difficult to encourage and push for their deployment in an organization. The funding might be there, but it will be channelled in a different direction, and we have seen this happen until recent times in the NLN. The improvement in IT infrastructure is obvious in the following ICT systems: hardware, software, power systems, general technical and matching professional competencies and managerial skills (expansion of the internet bandwidth, provision of computers, repairs, networking of the e-libraries in the branches and role-specific IT training, for example). A leader who stimulates technology plans and shares a common vision of their benefit for organizational goals and mandates can stimulate the staff to embrace IT. There has been much research on library leadership, but for the purposes of this chapter we prefer to define leadership in the library as more of a relationship between people than the characteristics of a single individual (Mech, cited in Wong, 2017). A leader may be visionary and willing, but if the people around him or her do not respond positively to the desire for digital equity, then there will be a lot of frustration along the way, from sabotage to outright refusal to join the digital train. There must be therefore a strategic move to ensure that community members' buy-in to digital equity. Leadership and concerted efforts and drive will determine the success of digital inclusion and equity.

Partnerships and collaborations

Amid dwindling funding, it has become imperative for libraries, including the NLN, to look outwards for partnerships and collaborations in pushing their digital programmes. These partnerships and collaborations may be across diverse private and public sectors, including both financial and technical support for digital literacy. Many of the branches are already exploring such support with IT businesses to train individuals. Many librarians who received leadership and professional development training from AfLIA through the AfLAc and INELI SSAf programmes have delivered IT training programmes for members of the community. NLN and AfLIA provided the partnerships platform on which these projects were carried out.

Awareness/sensitization

Sustained and robust awareness/sensitization campaigns are crucial for successful digital equity processes. If people are not aware of what you have, or of the importance of ICTs in their lives, they may not make the effort to avail themselves of them. Members of the community must know about the digital programmes and opportunities provided in the library. It is necessary to involve multiple stakeholders in creating awareness and in the development of digital literacy training programmes. These would help to overcome people's individual prejudices and perceptions of ICT.

Upskilling NLN staff on IT applications and courses

The training and professional development of NLN staff will provide the skills they need to facilitate user support, and is necessary for the NLN to adequately meet the demands of the times. Determined and sustained, continuous training and retraining of the staff on ICT applications is needed. The ICT capacity of NLN branch staff should be enhanced to deliver digital inclusion programmes in the community.

Continuous reassessment of IT programmes and policies

The provision of a germane environment that will engender excitement and interest is important for IT programmes and policies to succeed. Take the workplace, for example. What measures have been put in place for the staff who will use and man these systems, to increase their acceptance and use of technology and reduce any negative effects on their health and well-being? Every impediment that would discourage people from utilizing digital programmes in the library should be removed, and conditions that facilitate their sustained use should be implemented and maintained.

Conclusion

Technology usage has become necessary, as shown with the recent lockdown because of the COVID-19 pandemic. There is a need for all to embrace it, from the top organizational level down to individual level. It may not be mandatory, but it is a vital tool for survival. Libraries, including the NLN, are making deliberate efforts to transform more of their traditional services to the online environment. Time and location should no longer be barriers to accessing the NLN's library programmes and services. The e-libraries should be enhanced, sustained and extended to other branches that are yet to benefit. This would propel the branch libraries to carry out programmes that would promote and deepen grassroots digital equity in the NLN library community. Maintaining digital libraries and carrying out digital equity services requires adequate funding. Procuring equipment like computers, computer accessories, power-generating facilities, technical assistance, providing adequate internet accessibility etc. involve a lot of money. Libraries that cling to the traditional services model in the era of new IT, rising costs and flat budgets, cannot thrive (Dahl, Banerjee and Spalti, cited in Gbaje, 2007). Where government funding is decreasing rather than increasing, partnerships and collaborations become the saving grace. Consequently, digital equity must be systematic, holistic and community driven.

References

Aguilar, S. J. (2020) Guidelines and Tools for Promoting Digital Equity, *Information and Learning Sciences*, **121** (5/6), 285–99.

Botha, J. (2016) Digital Equity and Social Justice: Whose Reality? In Bavker, S., Dawson, S., Pardo, A. and Colvin, C. (eds), *Show Me the Learning – Proceedings ASCILITE 2016, Adelaide*, 76–85, https://ascilite.org/past-proceedings.

Elebeke, E. (2020) Digital Inclusion Gateway to Digital Nigeria – NITDA – DG *Vanguard*, 5 November, www.vanguardngr.com/2020/11/digital-inclusion-gateway-to-digital-nigeria.

Ezeani, N. S. (2012) The Teacher and Skills Acquisition at Business Education: From the Perspective of Accounting Skills, *Arabian Journal of Business Management Review (OMAN Chapter)*, **2** (4), 25–36.

Gbaje, E. (2007) Provision of Online Information Services in Nigerian Academic Libraries, *Nigerian Libraries*, **40**, 1–16, https://core.ac.uk/reader/11884100.

Helsper, E. J. (2008) *Digital Inclusion: An Analysis of Social Disadvantage and the Inform-ation Society*, Department for Communities and Local Government, London, UK.

Huffman, A. (2018) *Broadband and Adoption, Digital Equity and Inclusion*, www.ucpcog.org/Digital%20Equity%20&%20Why%20Is%20Broadband%20Important.pdf.

IFLA (2019) *Submissions for the Third Cycle of the Universal Periodic Review in the United States of America*, www.ifla.org/wp-content/uploads/2019/05/assets/faife/ifla_submission_for_the_u.s._universal_periodic_review_3rd_cycle.pdf.

IFLA (2020) *COVID-19 and the Global Library Field*, www.ifla.org/covid-19-and-the-global-library-field.

Judge, S., Puckett, K. and Cabuk, B. (2004) Digital Equity: New Findings from Early Childhood Longitudinal Study, *Journal of Research on Technology in Education*, **36** (4), 383–96, doi: 10/1080/15391523.2004.10782421.

Katz V. S and Levine, M. H. (2015) *Connecting to Learn: Promoting Digital Equity Among America Hispanic Families*, The Joan Ganz Cooney Center at Sesame Workshop, https://joanganzcooneycenter.org/wp-content/uploads/2015/03/jgcc_connectingtolearn.pdf.

Kuroda, R., Lopez, M., Sasaki, J. and Settecase, M. (2019) *The Digital Gender Gap*, Policy Brief, GSMA.

Middleton, K. L. and Chambers, V. (2010) Approaching Digital Equity: Is Wifi the New Leveler? *Information Technology & People*, **23** (1), 4–22, doi: 10.1108/09593841011022528.

Milenkova, V. and Lendzhova, V. (2021) Digital Citizenship and Digital Literacy in the Conditions of Social Crisis, *Computers*, **10** (4), 40: 1–14, doi: 10.3390/computers10040040.

Nemer, D. (2015) From Digital Divide to Digital Inclusion and Beyond: A Positional Review, *The Journal of Community Informatics*, **11** (1), doi: 10.15353/joci.v11i12857.

Osuigwe, N. E. (2011) Freedom of Information Act in Nigeria: Its Relevance and Challenges to National Development, *Journal of Applied Information Science and Technology*, **5** (1), 58–65, www.jaistal/org/Osuigwe_2k11pdf.

Resta, P., Laferrière, T., McLaughlin, R. and Kouraogo, A. (2018) Issues and Challenges Related to Digital Equity: An Overview. In Voogt, J., Knezek, G., Christensen, R. and Lai, K. W. (eds), *Second Handbook of Information Technology in Primary and Secondary Education*, Springer International Handbooks of Education.

Sanders, R. (2020) *Digital Inclusion, Exclusion and Participation*, Iriss, doi: 10.31583/esss.20200911.

Seattle Digital Equity Initiative Action Plan (2015) *Phase One-Building the Foundation, Progress Report*, www.seattle.gov/documents/Departments/Tech/DigitalEquity_PhaseII.pdf.

Strusani, D. and Houngbonon, G. V. (2021) *The Impact of COVID-19 on Disruptive Technology Adoption in Emerging Markets*, IFC, https://www.ifc.org/wps/wcm/connect/537b9b66-a35c-40cf-bed8-6f618c4f63d8/202009-COVID-19-Impact-Disruptive-Tech-EM.pdf?MOD=AJPERES&CVID=njn5xG9.

Swain, D. K. and Panda, K. C. (2009) Use of Electronic Resources in Business School Libraries of an Indian State: A Study of Librarians' Opinion, *The Electronic Library*, **27** (1), 74–85, doi: 10.1108/02640470910934605.

Willems, J., Farley, H. and Campbell, C. (2019) The Increasing Significance of Digital Equity in Higher Education: An Introduction to the Digital Equity Special Issue [editorial], *Australasian Journal of Educational Technology*, **35** (6), 1–8.

Wong, G. K. W. (2017) Leadership and Leadership Development in Academic Libraries: A Review, *Library Management*, **38** (2–3), 153–66.

WSIS (World Summit on the Information Society) (2003) Declaration of Principles, www.itu.int/net/wsis/docs/geneva/official/dop.html.

6

Driving Digital Literacy: An Assessment of Ghana Library Authority's Interventions against the COVID-19 Impact on Library Services

Hayford Siaw

Abstract

With the unforeseen challenges the novel coronavirus (COVID-19) posed to library services, libraries around the world have transformed the modes by which services are provided to maximize the usage of library resources and services and libraries' overall contribution to the improvement of literacy. The Ghana Library Authority, in pursuit of its digital literacy drive, introduced literacy initiatives such as Read2Skill, Edmodo, the Digital Library App, automation of the issuing of ISBNs and ISSNs and many others to ensure that access to information goes on through online platforms. The sudden shift of all engagements and interactions to online spaces raised concerns about the preparedness of libraries that have not yet explored the world of digitization in the provision of services, and the challenges associated with working with underserved communities. However, libraries have risen above these concerns to ensure continuity of services to mitigate the effects of the crisis on education. This chapter provides an overview of the impact of the pandemic on library services in Ghana and of the innovative approaches employed to support dissemination of information and opportunities to access reading materials, as well as online teaching and learning, since March 2020.

Keywords: Digital literacy, innovative services, COVID-19.

Introduction

Ghana Library Authority (GhLA) is a state agency under the Ministry of Education with oversight responsibility for public libraries in Ghana. The agency is mandated to establish, equip, manage and maintain public libraries across the country. One of the major responsibilities of GhLA is to provide access to reading and learning materials to inculcate lifelong learning habits among citizens that will help to improve the country's learning outcomes. The organization does this by working jointly with other state actors.

In the space of three years (2017–20) GhLA has increased its library footprint in Ghana from 61 to 90. As part of its core functions, it provides services such as book lending, research support, mobile library, book box, bindery, cataloguing and processing of books, acquisition and distribution of books, software development, a digital library service, conference venue hiring, issuance of International Standard Book Numbers (ISBN), International Standard Serial Numbers (ISSN) and International Standard Music Numbers (ISMN) and many other functions.

As the novel coronavirus continued to hinder normal human engagement, including travelling and gathering for different purposes across the world, the next fight was to stop its spread. Upon its declaration as a pandemic by the World Health Organization, it became mandatory for every country to do its best to fight and contain the virus from spreading further. In light of this, multiple nations worldwide, including the most developed ones, attempted to limit and slow the spread of the virus.

Like any other institution, the GhLA also had its fair share of virus 'impact', as the majority of its planned activities, including a membership drive to schools, library visits, commissioning of new libraries, and commemoration of the Authority's 70th anniversary, among others, were stalled. However, strategic measures were adopted to ensure the safe usage of public libraries in Ghana and the availability of teaching, learning, and research materials through easily accessible online platforms that require mostly simple basic digital skills.

Digital literacy in Ghana

The meaning of the term 'literacy' has evolved from just the 'ability to read and write' to involve concepts such as 'information literacy, multimedia literacy, and digital literacy' (Darkwa, 2020). According to Hall (2007), not only has the term literacy evolved, but the content that frames the standard of literacy has also evolved to include the peculiar ways in which the meanings of words are connoted positively or negatively, and 'how mass communication works to promulgate ideas and values' (Hall, 2007, 40).

Digital literacy, which has become a common phenomenon in recent times, can be referred to as the 'ability to use information and communication technologies to find, evaluate, create, and communicate information, requiring both cognitive and technical' abilities (American Library Association Digital Literacy Task Force, 2013). It is seen as one of the most valued skill sets for living and working in today's world (Burton, 2021). Digital literacy therefore is in play when people have knowledge about how to use digital technology, can engage with multimedia to read and interpret text, sounds and images and can manipulate and evaluate data to construct their own meanings.

Elsewhere in the world, digital technologies have become indispensable tools in contributing to people's digital literacy rates. Several factors are expected to be in place before a country can be marked as digitally literate. The entire population of Ghana is approximately 31,428,257, as of 20 January 2021, based on World Meter elaboration of the latest United Nations data (World Meter, 2020); and according to Statista.com, the rate of adult (15 years and above) literacy in Ghana stood at 79% in 2018. The total adult literacy rate had previously increased from 57.9% to 71.5% in 2000 and 2010, respectively (Statista, 2020).

If, indeed, 79% of the country's population are considered literate, then Ghana is on the right literacy promotion journey. The problem lies, however, in the percentage of the population considered to be digitally literate, as real disparities have been found to exist in developing countries, including Ghana, in relation to access to and the use of technology (Do4Africa, 2020). In the global context, digital divide can be referred to as the gap between individuals, households, businesses and geographical areas with regard to opportunities to access and use information and communications technology (ICT) (Darkwa, 2020). In simpler terms, it refers to the unequal access people have to digital technology. In Ghana, challenges such as low levels of education and literacy among the population, lack of internet access, irregular or non-existent electricity supply and lack of network coverage, among others, continue to remain factors impeding efforts made by the government to bridge the digital divide (Yawson, 2003).

Identified gaps in digital literacy

Digital literacy revolves around one's ability to use technology to find, assess, create, communicate, process and store information. When consuming or sharing digital content one must be knowledgeable about many aspects of technology (DKAP Framework for Education, 2019). This includes using a search engine, posting online and reading an electronic book (TeachHub, 2019). Yawson (2003) has identified four systemic factors that constitute challenges contributing to the digital literacy gaps. These are:

- lack of access to technological equipment;
- high cost of computers and their peripherals, making them less obtainable by individuals;
- inability on the part of both old and young to understand and operate ICT hardware and software/poor technical know-how and capabilities;
- irregular or non-existent electricity supply and high cost of internet access.

These challenges, if not addressed, are likely to thwart efforts geared toward bridging the digital divide in the country. However, since the use of digital technologies has become a necessity in the promotion of digital literacy in Ghana, pragmatic efforts have been/are being made by government to introduce interventions through the provision of financial resources for the establishment of universal service and universal access to all communities, as well as to facilitate the provision of access to basic telephony, internet services, multimedia broadband and broadcasting services. This signifies how Ghana is gradually working on its digital promotion agendas (Kubuga, Ayoung and Bekoe, 2021). However, the rural-urban disparities in education/literacy rates continue to widen, and the shift to the digitization of education services has worsened the situation, as rural communities continue to face challenges.

Statement of problem

The outbreak of COVID-19 revealed many lapses in the daily operations of public libraries in Ghana. After COVID-19 was declared a global pandemic there was a need for Ghana to put measures in place to curtail the spread of the virus. As a result, public libraries were closed, and patrons were left with no other option than to access the Ghana Library App for their educational needs (reading resources). The app did not have adequate resources on it to serve all levels of learners and other people from other professions. Thus, an immediate upgrade was needed. Moreover, although there are a considerable number of public libraries in the country, most of the libraries' operating systems had not been automated.

These omissions paved the way for the GhLA to work towards an agenda of digitizing its work processes to serve the growing needs of Ghanaians. This also meant that digital literacy activities had to be introduced to consciously engage patrons during their stay at home to ensure continuous learning. Some of these activities introduced included the National Short Story Writing Challenge, increased publicity for the use of the Ghana Library App to access e-books and other e-learning materials and increased scholarship opportunities to access online learning platforms for free through the Read2Skill programme, among others. These activities allowed individuals to build their digital literacy and tech skills in a real-world context, as exploring the digital resources on their own provided first-hand digital learning experience. There has also been training of ICT teachers who can attend virtually to various ICT-related requests addressed to them by library patrons.

Impact of COVID-19 on library services in Ghana

According to a UNESCO (2020) Global Education Coalition Report on COVID-19's impact on education 'from disruption to recovery', millions of students were affected due to the closure of schools globally. Reports captured as of 25 May 2020 indicated that 990,324,537 learners were involved globally, making 56.6% of total learners in 130 countries (IFLA, 2020).

As a result of the pandemic, the Government of Ghana had to put restrictions on large gatherings, close down education and learning centres, which included public libraries, and actively encourage people to take extra measures to protect themselves. Due to these restrictions, GhLA had to adapt to new measures in its daily operations to ensure continuity of services for patrons. GhLA's network across the country was initially faced with hard choices concerning the kinds of services to offer and how to offer them, as COVID-19 preventive measures ranged from minimal restrictions to full closure of libraries. This paved the way for GhLA libraries to reconsider going digital with most of their services to patrons.

When restrictions were eased, GhLA had to adopt new measures, which involved the removal of items that posed risks for transmission of the virus, such as toys in the children's library sections. Materials that were lent out had to go through a waiting or quarantine period before being shelved. In preparing for potential further restrictions, GhLA ensured that almost all the staff had the necessary skills and tools to work remotely (from home) to enable the provision of services digitally.

GhLA initiatives

With the advent of the COVID-19 pandemic, GhLA responded quickly to ensure continuity of service provision while protecting the safety of learners and its staff. This led to a swift inclination towards remote and digital approaches to learning and information/knowledge dissemination.

GhLA collaborated with the Commonwealth of Learning, the Ghana Education Service and the Ministry of Education to roll out the programmes described in the following sub-sections and upgraded the Ghana Library App with increased e-books, audio books and tutorial videos shown on a dedicated TV channel (Ghana Learning TV).

Read2Skill workforce recovery programme

The Read2Skill programme was successfully launched to help Ghanaians upgrade and regrade their skills through a platform that housed over 4,000 courses from several fields of study. Some of the activities that were undertaken to support the Read2Skill project were regional meetings (Coursera and Udemy learners) to educate stakeholders on the goals of the projects; international monthly project meetings with partners; international virtual conferencing among Commonwealth of Learning (CoL) countries/partners; GhLA–Coursera Helpdesk Enrolment of School Librarians; Open House with Commonwealth of Learning; and many others.

It was part of the 2020 Year of Learning strategy of GhLA to offer Ghanaians the opportunity to enrol on Udemy – one of the world's largest open learning platforms. The Authority received 31,574 applications from all 16 regions of Ghana to study through the Read2Skill initiative.

Edmodo learning management system (LMS)

The Edmodo learning management platform was also introduced to enhance the virtual learning that was necessitated by the closure of schools and public libraries. The platform was introduced to connect Ghanaian learners to their teachers to ensure continuity of their classroom learning. Edmodo LMS works by helping school administrators to create an online school for their teachers and students and gives access to parents who want to monitor their children's learning progress. On 5 November 2020, the Ministry of Education, together with GhLA and the Ghana Education Service, launched the Edmodo LMS and made it accessible to Ghanaians. GhLA played a technical role by creating a landing page for users and a support platform for ticketing. The Authority also led in the marketing of the LMS through TV and radio advertisements, to teachers' associations, media engagements and social media. GhLA also ensured that students and teachers easily understood the features of the platform by creating a user-friendly landing page which is suitable for the Ghana education system. On the landing page, various account types are clearly defined for users to understand. GhLA also added a 30-minute basic training on the landing page to orient new users.

Enhancement and promotion of the Digital Library App

The Digital Library App was enhanced for easy accessibility and navigation. Thousands of digital books were uploaded to the platform through a call for digital content requests that the Ghana library syndicated across the country. Learning video tutorials on the App have also been shown concurrently on a dedicated TV channel for distance learning. Promotion of the App also led to an increase in the number of downloaded resources.

The mobile App was also zero-rated on the Vodafone network. This meant that there were no data charges for anyone who accessed the App on the network. The GhLA undertook this role to ensure that it delivered on active digital inclusion for all.

Automation of the issuance of ISBNs, ISSNs and ISMNs

GhLA also made efforts to automate the issuance of ISSNs, ISBNs and ISMNs. The payment system was also set up and made fully functional. Training sessions were conducted for staff to equip them with the right skill set and knowledge for the system.

The impact of COVID-19 on GhLA's services

Membership/patronage

One of the several areas that was affected by the global pandemic was the patronage of public libraries. The closure of our physical libraries meant that GhLA recorded low direct patronage numbers in 2020. Combined statistics for direct patronage and visits to our libraries across the country before COVID-19 were 26,334 in 2019. However, during the COVID-19 period, as of November 2020, library membership reduced drastically, by 61.2%, to a total of just 10,221 members (Figure 6.1). In terms of patronage, the library recorded 1,074,275 visits in 2019. By November 2020, there was an 83.6% decrease, to a total number of 175,807 visits to the library (Figure 6.2 on the next page).

New Membership_2019 vs 2020   (*Before Covid*)
vs (*Covid, Library reopened*)

26,334

10,221

2019

2020 (as at Nov)

Figure 6.1 *New memberships in 2020* (61.2% decrease on 2019's figure)

Promotion of the Ghana Library App

The COVID-19 pandemic gave GhLA the opportunity to increase its activities for promotion of the digital App. As a result, the Authority recorded an increase in the number of downloads and registered online users. By the end of 2020, GhLA had recorded a total of 12,794 online registrations during the COVID-19 period, amounting to a 101.01% increase, with an additional 6,429 registrants (Figure 6.3). Inasmuch as the pandemic affected other aspects of our services, this was a positive impact for the library.

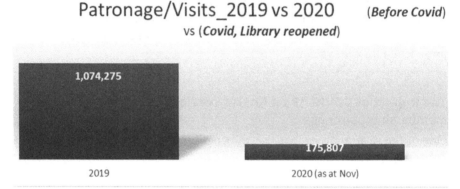

Patronage/Visits_2019 vs 2020   *(Before Covid)*
vs *(Covid, Library reopened)*

1,074,275

175,807

2019

2020 (as at Nov)

Figure 6.2 *Patronage/visits in 2020* (83.6% decrease on 2019's figure)

GhLA Mobile App Registrations_2019 vs 2020

12794

6365

2019

2020 (As at Nov.)

Figure 6.3 *Increase in mobile app registrations*

Increase of e-contents on the Ghana Library App

GhLA's quest for increased content on the library app heightened in 2020.

Prior to the pandemic, the Authority had below 5,000 e-content items on its App; however, as at the end of 2020, e-content numbers had increased to 20,887. The content comprises of 4,023 e-books, 15,889 audiobooks and 975 videos (Table 6.1). This increase was as a result of the establishment of strategic digital content partnerships.

Table 6.1 *e-Resources in Ghana Library Authority*

Digital format	Number of items
e-Books	4,023
Audiobooks	15,889
Videos	975
Total	20,887

Challenges

Promoting the culture of reading, inculcating and enhancing digital literacy skills is key to achieving sustainable development goals; however, in carrying out activities to promote digital literacy, we were faced with the following challenges:

- low levels of the public embracing contemporary trends in technology;
- insufficient budget allocated by the government for procuring e-content;
- limited access by patrons, especially in rural communities, although our mobile library van and ICT services were extended to rural areas;
- lack of trained librarians with adequate digital skills to provide digital library services (although efforts were made by GhLA to quickly equip them with the necessary skills);
- poor internet access;
- poor communication networks.

Conclusion

Just like any other country, organization or firm across the world, GhLA was affected by the pandemic, which caused some disruptions; however, in its bid to intensify provision of improved digital library services, the Authority forged ahead to rise above the effects of the pandemic and develop its online platforms in order to provide library services to the public. GhLA believes in lifelong learning and is ready to adapt and adjust in promoting digital literacy in Ghana.

References

American Library Association Digital Literacy Task Force (2013) Digital Literacy, https://literacy.ala.org/digital-literacy.

Burton, P. (2021) The Importance of Digital Skills in the Modern Workplace, www.skillsyouneed.com/rhubarb/digital-skills-modern-workplace.html.

Darkwa, O. (2020) Overcoming Barriers to Digital Literacy, www.ghanaiantimes.com.gh/overcoming-barriers-to-digital-literacy.

DKAP Framework for Education (2019) Digital Literacy in the Classroom: Gaps and Ways Forward, https://dkap.org/classroom-digital-literacy.

Do4Africa (2020) Digital Literacy in Africa, www.do4africa.org/en/digital-literacy-in-africa/8961.

Hall, S. (2007) The Uses of Literacy and the Cultural Turn, *International Journal of Cultural Studies*, **10** (1), 39–49.

IFLA (2020) Covid-19 and Libraries, www.ifla.org/covid-19-and-libraries.

Kubuga, K. K., Ayoung, D. A. and Bekoe, S. (2021) Ghana's ICT4AD Policy: Between Policy and Reality, *Digital Policy, Regulation and Governance*, **23** (2), 132–53, doi: 10.1108/DPRG-02-2020-0020.

Statista (2020) Adult Literacy Rate in Ghana 2000–2018, www.statista.com/statistics/1171920/adult-literacy-rate-in-ghana.

TeachHub (2019) Technology in the Classroom, www.teachhub.com/technology-in-the-classroom-what-is-digital-literacy.

UNESCO (2020) *Covid-19 Impact on Education from Disruption to Recovery*, https://en.unesco.org/covid19/educationresponse.

World Meter (2020) World Population – Ghana Population, www.worldometers.info/world-population/ghana-population.

Yawson, R. M. (2003) *Emerging Technologies and the Digital Divide – Bridging the Gap, the case of Ghana*, Food and Research Institute.

7

Impact of COVID-19 on Digital Divide: Perspectives of an Educator and a Librarian in Botswana

Lynn Jibril and Priti Jain

Abstract

The COVID-19 pandemic has affected every walk of life: business, government, daily wage earners, hawkers, academia and librarians. As the disease sweeps the globe, homebound workers, students, teachers everywhere are turning to digital platforms such as video-conferencing, online teaching and self-services. One effect of this is that the digital divide is widening in developing countries, particularly in Africa. It is a challenge and a cause of anxiety for educators and librarians to shift to online teaching, learning and dissemination of information. An educator's mandates are teaching, learning and research and a librarian's first and foremost duty to society is to make authentic and reliable knowledge available to the community. As the COVID-19 crisis rages on, it has become critical to enable those who have limited access to knowledge to access the relevant information so that they can safeguard themselves against harm. This chapter gives an educator's and a librarian's perspective of the impact of pandemic-related measures on the digital divides in Africa, with particular emphasis on Botswana.

Keywords: Digital divide, Africa, COVID-19, pandemic, University of Botswana, librarians, digital literacy, library school.

Introduction

The COVID-19 pandemic has imposed extreme hardships on humankind in various facets of our lives, changing virtually every aspect of our lives ranging from the way we shop, learn, teach or communicate to how we offer services.

It is a whole new paradigm shift in human relations and interactions. In libraries, the pandemic has proved to us that change is inevitable and that without change we can never be challenged to be innovative and serve our clients better. It has therefore become imperative for libraries and librarians to be the agents and drivers of change and offer services to their patrons that will ensure safe and equitable access to information. Open educational resources, open access to information, fair use of information and open institutional repositories have become familiar terms meant to encourage the free use and openness of resources without the many barriers brought on by copyright and licensing restrictions. The use of Creative Commons rights for licensing information resources for openness and sharing of information is now considered more than ever before, as the 'new normal' continues to widen further the already existing gap between the haves and the have-nots.

For some (especially those used to remote working), this may not be much of a change from normal; but for those who are used to working in person, great adjustments have had to be made. Digital services, software tools and content have become a part of nearly every aspect of our life. Our lives have become highly dependent on our ability to connect across professions, nations, regions and globally using digital skills. As much as the pandemic has necessitated great shifts from face-to-face encounters to the current norm of working from home, many of the world's citizens, especially in Africa, have been left out by this global wind of change. COVID-19 has led to increased demand for internet connectivity (O'Halloran, 2020). Yet only 53% of the world is connected to the internet. In Africa, less than 39% of Africans have internet access and a large population living in rural areas find it expensive to connect with others via current cable or satellite technologies, due to the high cost of data and/or lack of appropriate or sufficient digital skills. As a result, only a few jobs can be done from home, and only a few people were privileged to have access to online education during the lockdown (Lashitew, 2020).

Consequently, issues of inequality, lack of access to critical information on health and other social matters, lack of access to the internet, exclusion of minority groups have risen high on the national development agendas of African countries. An International Telecommunications Union (ITU, 2019) report estimated that around 3.6 billion people remain offline. It further states that the situation is much worse in the least developed countries, where an average of just two out of every ten people are online at any given point in time. As mentioned earlier, COVID-19 has intensified the digital divide. It affects everyone's work, from the small retailer to institutions of higher learning, and affects all aspects of our lives. It has impacted on the economy, development, education, society and information centres. As a result, most tasks/activities are online and working from home is a 'new normal'. There is a close relationship between COVID-19 and the digital divide.

Like other developing countries, Botswana has been hard hit by the digital divide, as *The Voice Newspaper* (TheVoiceBW, 2020) writes, 'The digital divide is actually widening under the new normal caused by the COVID-19 pandemic. As people migrate more work and study online, the digitally disadvantaged people are hit harder.'

In the above context, the purpose of this chapter is to explore the impact of COVID-19 on the digital divide in Africa with specific attention on Botswana from an educator's and a librarian's perspectives. To this end, this chapter seeks to:

- underscore the impact of COVID-19 on the digital divide in Africa and in Botswana;
- review the initiatives of the Government of Botswana towards bridging the digital divide;
- highlight the perspectives of an educator and a librarian towards the digital divide in Botswana;
- identify the major challenges in fulfilling the responsibilities of an educator and a librarian towards bridging the digital divide; and
- recommend strategies to reduce the impact of COVID-19 on the digital divide.

Research methodology

This chapter is based on an in-depth and recent literature review on digital divide and COVID-19 and, most importantly, the personal experiences and observations of the authors.

Concept of digital divide

Unlike before the 1990s, digital divide as a concept has a wide-spectrum meaning in current times. This gap can be between rural and urban residents, developing and developed countries, between the rich and the poor who cannot afford digital technologies, between educated and uneducated, between the literate and the illiterate, between digitally literate and digitally illiterate, and so on. The COVID-19 crisis has changed how we define the digital divide. It is no more a resource or a skills issue but a human right (Wilson, 2021). Gartner Glossary (2021) defines digital divide as the gap in opportunities experienced by those with limited accessibility to technology, especially the internet and skills to successfully navigate online spaces. The digital divide is also described as the gap that exists between individuals who have access to modern information and communication technology (ICT) and those who lack access (Steele, 2019).

Globalization and digitization have made the world to be as small as a village, many thanks to the connectivity offered by the internet. The internet has become a very critical part of human life without which many human activities and engagements would be stifled. As much as the internet offers huge opportunities for individuals and, indeed, nations alike to connect, interact and collaborate for socio-economic prosperity and development, it can also be viewed as a divisive tool that draws a line between the rich and the poor, the haves and have nots, the literate and the illiterate. The lack of good network and bandwidth creates a digital divide that can be attributed to many societal ills such as poverty, ill-health, low literacy levels and more. The digital divide presents itself as a roadblock to socio-economic development in different regions and countries. With the presence of the divide, many opportunities offered by the digital revolution, such as online job search, efficient information management (IM), online social networks and electronic mail systems cannot be accessed (Sedimo, Bwalya and Du Plessis, 2011). All of these call for a digital literacy framework to guide librarians in assisting members of their user communities to access the internet and develop digital literacy skills that would help them to be participants and creators of content in the information society.

Digital literacy and policy framework

Digital literacy affects digital divide. 'Digital literacy builds upon the concept of digital divide to indicate the ability not just to access digital infrastructure, but also to utilize it' (Jaeger et al., 2012). The term digital literacy gained popularity in the mid-1990s, as it became clear that simple access to ICTs was not enough to obtain needed information or services; one needed knowledge, skills and abilities as well (Jaeger et al., 2012). The concept of digital literacy has evolved over time because of changes in the digital environment resulting in new thinking. In the context of this study, digital literacy is the 'ability to understand information, data, media literacies, digital learning and self-development, communication, collaboration, participation in digital creation, innovation, scholarship and digital identity' (Joint Information System Committee, 2016, 2). It is also defined as the ability to understand and use information in multiple formats from a wide variety of sources when it is presented via computers and, particularly, through the medium of the internet (Gilster, 1997, 6).

With the advent of ICTs, online education and online services, digital literacy has become a necessary survival skill that imbues one with the requisite advantage to compete equally in the global arena. Digital literacy has become a critical life skill, and can be an object of power or exclusion. It is more than just the ability to use and handle computers, it is being able to adroitly navigate the digital space, whether one is creating, using, adapting or storing and processing information.

The digital divide presents significant opportunities for libraries to equip their patrons with skills that will enable them to use technology productively as they enter virtual spaces. For academic libraries, this new turn of events may nudge them into exploring meaningful ways to introduce digital literacy into university curricula. Furthermore, the shift in education from teacher-based methods of instruction to student-based methods also supports the introduction of digital literacy, as it prepares learners to actively and effectively participate in online learning platforms such as Moodle and Microsoft Teams.

As more libraries transition to technologically centred digital media/services, students will need to have digital literacy skills in order to effectively engage with diverse perspectives found available online, and to critically assess and analyse information sources. To achieve this type of a learner, deliberate efforts have to be made to teach digital literacy and information skills, thereby contributing to the producing of 21st-century lifelong learners, who will in turn contribute to the creation of knowledge for the growth of the knowledge-based economy.

The lack of a clear framework to guide the activities of academic librarians in developing digital literacy is still a challenge. It has been established that there is still a wide gap between developed and developing countries in designing a policy framework for librarians to operate in an environment driven by digital technology (Raju, 2017).

Impact of COVID-19 on digital divide in Africa

The African continent faces many challenges, ranging from a high level of illiteracy, poverty and uneven distribution of resources to underdeveloped economies, and the global pandemic did not spare it. In fact, the already existing gap between the developed and developing worlds widened further in Africa. Turianskyi (2020) posits that COVID-19 has emphasized the digital divide, a term referring to the uneven access to/distribution of ICTs in societies, which is a global problem. He goes on further to state that the digital divide is even more pronounced on the African continent. A number of factors can be adduced for this state of affairs and these are socio-economic, weak infrastructure, access to ICT and internet shutdowns.

Socio-economic factors

The COVID-19 pandemic is not only a health issue: it extends far into other facets of lives. The several lockdowns instituted by governments as measures to contain the virus had far-reaching implications on the socio-economic lives of multitudes on the African continent. For many countries it has affected numerous social activities, including business. Its impact can be felt far and wide, more especially in rural areas. The United Nations (UN) framework for immediate socio-economic response to the COVID-19 crisis warns that 'it will most likely increase poverty and inequalities at global scale making the achievement of sustainable development goals even more urgent' (United Nations Botswana, 2020).

According to the Global System for Mobile Communications, the mobile operators' trade body, approximately three-quarters of the population in sub-Saharan Africa – 747 million people – have a mobile connection. However, only a third of these – 250 million – are smartphone users (Turianskyi, 2020). This means that only a small proportion are able to connect to the internet and use the applications that enable them to join and participate in social networks, work from home and do business, including buying and selling through online platforms. Many people in the informal sector, including artisans, are most likely to have been adversely affected by the lockdowns as business came to a standstill. Unemployment in Africa has risen drastically, as companies in the private sector could not keep employees on their payroll while they stayed at home. International Labor Report (2020) points out that the economic consequences of the COVID-19 pandemic have not fallen with equal severity on all shoulders, and that existing vulnerabilities have been exposed and inequalities entrenched. The report further claims that many of those affected are those in the informal sector, with more being women.

Gender-based violence (GBV) also saw a sharp increase during the COVID-19 lockdown clearly marking a huge gap in gender parity the world over. Mittal and Singh (2020) are of the opinion that, as much as quarantines and lockdowns were necessary to mitigate the impact of the novel coronavirus, they also had negative outcomes, including a surge in GBV. They further argue that, despite its global prevalence, GBV has been one of the most neglected outcomes of the pandemic.

Weak infrastructure

It is difficult to imagine development without the internet, which plays a major role in universal connectivity. In support of this, Johnson (2021) acknowledges the critical role of the internet in socio-economic development and writes that, connecting billions of people worldwide, the internet is a core pillar of the modern information society. However, statistics reveal that less than 39% of Africans have internet access, due to a combination of supply and demand constraints. This could be a major setback for Africa's economic development.

According to Internet World Stats (2020) at the end of 2019, Africa had an internet penetration rate of 39.3%, which was the lowest figure among all continents, with Asia being the second-lowest at 53.6%, as compared with Europe and North America with the highest penetration rates of 87.2% and 94.6%, respectively. As of January 2021, the internet penetration rate in Botswana stood at 47% (Faria, 2021). With the given statistics, there is indeed a lot that governments in Africa ought to do to help their citizens to be able to afford cheap and affordable internet so that, as in other countries of the world, they can participate equitably in the digital economy.

Internet shutdowns

In the aftermath of COVID-19 shutdowns, there is a great need for African countries to accelerate the provision of affordable internet for both businesses and social purposes. However, with the many internet shutdowns imposed by African countries, this may be a great challenge for the sustainable development of many countries in Africa. Shutdowns cost African economies over USD2 billion in 2019. A report by ICT Policy Centre for Eastern and Southern Africa (CIPESA, 2019) reiterates that internet disruptions, however short lived, affect many facets of the national economy and tend to persist far beyond the days on which access is disrupted.

An analysis by CIPESA notes that 77% of African countries that ordered internet shutdowns in the past five years are classified as 'authoritarian regimes' by the democracy index, produced by the Economist Intelligence Unit. These shutdowns add political challenges to socio-economic ones, especially for those living in closed, oppressive societies. According to the ITU (2019), only 28% of Africans used the internet, and online shoppers are still relatively few.

Impact of COVID-19 on digital divide in Botswana

When countries around the world went into lockdown, Botswana was no exception. All library services had to be closed down, schools, universities and offices were shut down and people had to stay home under lockdown. These were unprecedented times and, as such, they caught most librarians and educators by surprise, as no one was prepared for it. Libraries had to rethink how they would return to offering their very crucial service of information provision without compromising the health of both their staff and patrons. Consequently, services had to be shifted to virtual platforms and intensive training of both librarians and their patrons had to be done in order for them to key in. A lot of collaborative efforts between libraries and service providers like publishers had to come into play to ensure that no gap was left unclosed and that librarians were ready to step into the 'new normal' with confidence. Many opportunities came out of this seemingly unpleasant situation. However, the more opportunities there were for those with access, the more the gap widened between those with access and those without electricity and technological gadgets like computers and laptops. As countries moved fast to recover from the crisis using all the strategies of going virtual, a huge population without internet access was left behind.

Government of Botswana initiatives towards bridging the digital divide

Long before the periods of lockdown came in, people across nations, regions and globally were communicating and connecting with each other through various social media platforms such as Facebook, Twitter and others. This, however, was not at the same scale as we have seen during the crisis of managing a pandemic like COVID-19, which has made the internet a necessity in our everyday life without which very little can be achieved. In recognition of the status quo, governments the world over are increasing efforts to put in place measures that will reduce the already wide gap caused by the digital divide. Guermazi (2020) asserts this and states that governments in the Middle East and North Africa (MENA) region have acted fast to respond to the need for improved broadband networks and enhanced internet services. The Internet Society (2020) also supports this, saying that 'to ensure the internet functioned smoothly, governments and service providers launched numerous emergency initiatives, including flexible spectrum use, additional spectrum release, increased international and domestic capacity, subsidized broadband services, and free access to online resources'.

Botswana too has realized the need for and importance of developing and improving the already existing infrastructure to facilitate catching up with what exists globally in order to be inclusive and not leave anyone behind when it comes to access to information. This can be seen in a recent development where Gaborone City Council partnered with BoFinet to offer free internet to all citizens in the capital city within certain selected Wi-Fi hotspots for one hour daily (Magang, 2020). Indeed, this is a welcome initiative that affords citizens the opportunity to connect with the rest of the world. The Thuto.Net is another project that strives to have enough computers linked to the internet for all junior secondary and senior schools in the country, and later in primary schools.

The Ministry of Communication, Science and Technology launched a project known as i-Partnership aiming to empower government employees and unemployed youth to buy computers through government schemes (Sedimo, Bwalya and Du Plessis, 2011). The Sesigo project, which was implemented by African Comprehensive HIV/AIDS Partnerships (ACHAP) together with co-operating partners to introduce the use of ICTs in public libraries, is another project aimed at improving access to ICT and information for all in the country. All these projects are aimed at enhancing broadband connectivity and internet penetration and thereby directly contributing to bridging the digital divide in all facets of society. The Nteletsa I & II project by Botswana Telecommunications Corporation (BTC) aims to supply, install, commission and carry out the operation and maintenance of network infrastructure in rural areas of Botswana. Tele-centres such as Community Access Centers (CAC) popularly, known as Kitsong centres – were initiated to serve as gateways to the internet and access to other services in rural areas (Sedimo, Bwalya and Du Plessis, 2011).

BTC also successfully completed the multi-million pula Trans Kalahari fibre-optic project (approximately 2,000 km) for data, voice and electrical signal transmission – all this in a bid to improve the speed and manner in which the population receives internet services. The BTC also runs a rural communication programme that aims to connect 62 villages. The Universal Access (UA) and Universal Service (US) Policy aim to allow all citizens access to ICT opportunities on an equal basis (Sedimo, Bwalya and Du Plessis, 2011).

Mascom e-school project

This project is a partnership between two entities, Mascom and BoFinet, where they install internet in all government schools, covering primary, junior secondary and senior schools. To date, 623 schools have been connected to ensure continued learning on online platforms, even when schools are closed. Further, free SMS to students and access to an e-learning platform with Botswana General Certificate of Secondary Education and Junior Certificate content has been made available.

Orange Botswana

A telecommunications mobile service provider has a programme that aims to bridge the digital divide by leveraging technology to improve access to education in primary schools in remote areas. Orange Foundation has signed a memorandum of understanding with the Ministry of Basic Education and the Ministry of Local Government and Rural Development to provide 1,600 tablets and 62 servers to 32 schools. In addition, the Foundation has diversified its offerings with ATLEGA (meaning 'succeed') and MPOTSA (meaning 'ask me') which serve as mobile education platforms.

The educator's perspective

Like other universities in the region, the University of Botswana (UB) started e-learning initiatives as far back as 2002 (Ntshwarang, Malinga and Losike-Sedimo, 2021). This started with a web course tool (WebCT), a web-based learning management system that is licensed to colleges and institutions for e-learning. It also regulates the management of online courses, including their design and delivery. WebCT is now owned by Blackboard. These tools evolved from relatively basic platforms to the current more contemporary and advanced forms such as Moodle, Microsoft Teams and the SMART classrooms.

When e-learning started at UB there were many challenges that hindered its immediate uptake and adoption. The challenges ranged from lack of training of lecturers and a consequent paucity of digital skills to inadequate infrastructure and negative attitudes on the part of both lecturers and students. However, when the global pandemic set in there was urgency for all stakeholders in the education sector to quickly transfer teaching and learning activities to online platforms. It goes without saying that all lives were disrupted, and more drastically so for students.

With a fifth of UB students living on campus, the real repercussions for digital inequity quickly came to the surface, as many could not afford devices or data. Furthermore, when the campus abruptly closed, it presented the huge challenge of moving back home. Students were faced with different kinds of difficulties, typically related to different malfunctions of the online platforms and poor internet connections. In 2020 during the COVID-19 pandemic, UB experienced two lockdowns between March and August. These lockdowns interrupted the academic calendar, teaching and learning, internships, the planned vacations and the annual end-of-year closure of the University. It became very clear that the University could no longer operate in the traditional way of having large classes under the traditional mode of teaching face to face. The COVID-19 protocols demanded that learners, and indeed everyone, should observe social distancing of at least 1–2 metres.

Consequently, UB had to step up its efforts to adopt and accept e-learning in order to offer students the opportunity to continue learning from home, and in the comfort of their own rooms for those staying on campus. Although both the lecturers and students were never ready for this sudden change, it was clear that change had come and that it had to be embraced by both. The University had to remodel (new) ways of offering teaching and learning without putting anyone at risk and without leaving anyone behind. As a result, UB entered into a contract with BTC to provide students with SIM cards loaded with internet data to access and download learning materials (UB, 2020). The University also adjusted the current and next semester almanacs as part of its response to the pandemic. The use of the internet has generally increased across the globe and in Botswana over time, but there are still some eventualities that show the digital divide. With the general population under lockdown, people were forced to work and study from home. Many of the students lived in communities with poor network coverage, and others in areas without electricity. This is because the University attracts students from various demographic areas, including rural and remote areas where students may lack digital fluency as they may not have prior exposure to ICT (Mbodila, 2020). Although students may be generally perceived as digital natives, not all students are fluent in navigating through the learning management system used by the University.

According to UNESCO, around 1.5 billion learners have been affected by school closures caused by COVID-19. This represents 89.4% of the total number of enrolled learners globally (Junio, 2020). As in other developing countries, many students in Botswana do not have internet connectivity and for most students the internet is an unfamiliar experience; they are more accustomed to the social and interactive side of education. An academic institution's main mandate is teaching, learning and research, which have been negatively affected by the pandemic, which had widened the digital divide. Students are confronted with several challenges.

Major challenges faced by an educator

Based on online teaching experience, the major challenges are those described in the following sub-sections.

Inadequate technological infrastructure

Some students do not have personal devices to use for online learning, and they depend on university computer labs, which are always overcrowded. Some of students have to share their laptops and computers with their parents, sisters/brothers. Due to the inadequacy of technological infrastructure, students have difficulty downloading the online teaching materials that are provided to cover for their missing lectures.

Insufficient digital literacy training

Inadequate training for both academic staff and students is another big challenge, which widens the digital divide between those who are adept in using technology and those who are not. It was discovered that it is hard for many academics and students to start using an online learning management system without additional training to understand the features and functionality of the platform. They become overwhelmed and frustrated by the amount of data they have to deal with and by having to teach and learn in an unfamiliar environment.

Students' access to the internet

Many times, access to the internet is a problem. However, while sometimes students do have other genuine problems, occasionally they may use poor network connection as an excuse for not attending their online lectures. It was also observed that sometimes a student would log in for a lecture to establish their presence and then disappear from the class after a few minutes to do their errands. One student observed that COVID-19 has widened the digital divide. Internet connectivity requires money, and because data is accessed through prepayment, some students do not have data to access the internet and some of them have no Wi-Fi access. The packages sold by internet providers are not affordable by many less-privileged students from low-income families. Internet costs are relatively expensive in Botswana, varying according to the internet service provider (ISP). The main ISPs, Mascom, Orange and BTC networks offer mobile internet connection plans that most students cannot afford.

Table 7.1 summarizes data and internet costs. For students, on average 5GB of data is sufficient to perform daily tasks that require an internet connection. The price per 1GB is the lower limit that a student will use per day; the price per 5GB is the upper limit that is sufficient for an average student workload for tasks requiring the internet.

Table 7.1 *Internet prices, cost per mobile network operator*

Mobile network	Price/1GB		Price/ 5GB		Monthly price for average student workload	
Mascom	P18	$1.64	P90	$8.21	P2700	$246.38
Orange	P20	$1.83	P100	$9.13	P3000	$273.76
BTC	P20	$1.83	P100	$9.13	P3000	$273.76

Poor network and low bandwidth

As in other developing countries, poor network and low bandwidth are serious issues in Botswana. Although, internet speed in Botswana is no longer as glacially slow as it was in the late 2010s, it is still among the slowest both in the world and on the African continent. At the download average of 1.92 megabytes per second (mbps), Botswana ranks 165th in the world and is 22nd in Africa, according to statistics furnished by cable.co.uk. This is quite significant, considering that the country trails behind even comparatively poorer countries such as Zambia, Zimbabwe, Mozambique and Sudan (Magang, 2020). Due to poor network and low bandwidth at the University of Botswana, sometimes it is difficult to start a lecture, other times only half of a lecture is delivered because of the network challenge. Educators and students can also be thrown out by the system. Due to the poor network, students also have difficulties in logging on for their online lectures, and many times receiving and downloading online teaching materials takes an inordinate amount of time.

Compromised quality of teaching and research

Owing to COVID-19, it is not possible to send students for practical attachments. Due to the digital divide, virtual attachments are not practical. This has an impact on the quality of teaching and learning. Similarly, collection of research data is affected. Conducting face-to-face interviews was more convenient than carrying out such exercises online. For example, in online video interviews, connectivity could suddenly become a challenge, and in voice-only interviews facial expressions that serve as cues cannot be observed. As one student observed, 'although online learning is proving helpful in safeguarding students' and faculty's health amid COVID-19 pandemic, it is not as effective as conventional learning. Online learning cannot produce desired results in developing countries like Botswana, where a vast majority of students are unable to access the internet due to technical as well as monetary issues.'

Emerging roles of the librarian

As the whole world makes a transition from the traditional face-to-face services to digital platforms, librarians need to upskill themselves to remain adaptable and relevant when offering competitive library services. They should be able to train their patrons on the use of the internet, internet-enabled devices, electronic databases and other electronic sources. Their roles have become diversified to include contemporary life skills, emotional intelligence skills, creativity, website development skills for communicating remotely with patrons, as well as critical thinking skills. The African Union 2063 agenda recognizes human capital as key to the progress and prosperity of Africa. Therefore, investing in the continuous professional development of librarians has become paramount. The African Library and Institutions Association (AfLIA, 2020) recognizes this and states that 'beyond the noted roles of libraries in inculcating and promoting literacy skills, libraries of all types perform significant and crucial functions in driving development through the provision of access to information and knowledge. The librarian's new role is to equip patrons with skills and competencies that will allow them to confidently and competently use digital platforms, by teaching digital literacy skills. Their role is to provide access to information that will promote the wellbeing of citizens, inclusivity, peaceful coexistence and justice, among others.

COVID-19 has offered golden opportunities for digital scholarship. By using such opportunities to develop professionally, librarians can take on new roles as diverse information specialists. Increasingly as countries, especially in Africa, adopt technology within their daily operations, librarians too have had to unlearn old skills and learn new ones that will enable them to cope with the demands of the networked world where services are offered way beyond the confines of the library buildings. These skills include, among others, media and information literacy skills, data management skills and digital literacy skills, to mention a few. It is the duty of the librarian to ensure that during this time of uncertainties posed by the pandemic, patrons can access credible information that will enable them to make decisions not only pertaining to their health but also pertaining to how they can relate with their environment for sustainability. With so much fake news in the media, patrons have to be taught how to assess and evaluate credible sources, and distinguish them from fake sources of information. Librarians need digital skills so as to support researchers and lecturers working from home to access online applications and information sources. They need to acquire data skills to assist researchers with the research process and to produce research that is findable, accessible, interoperable and reusable, and to accelerate the closing of the existing digital divide gap.

Librarian's perspective

From a librarian's perspective, the COVID-19 pandemic has been like none other, as it has presented both challenges and opportunities for the library profession and for library users, both of which have contributed significantly to the increase in the digital divide. Librarians have witnessed a shift from normal library service provision to virtual and online spaces. These have necessitated continuous professional development for librarians to be able to provide services on digital platforms to support online learning, remote work and research, and to reimagine library spaces, offer safe spaces for online learning and support safe teaching and learning for teachers and students in school libraries.

As a result, many webinars were offered locally, regionally and internationally for librarians to help them to cope with the challenges of opening up while the virus is still very much at large. Many ideas on how services could be redesigned, reimagined and re-engineered were shared through open and free platforms. Huge professional development opportunities existed openly and for free, all of which raised librarians' profile and boosted their confidence. AfLIA partnered with many other important stakeholders to ensure that libraries and librarians remained resilient and played important roles in providing excellent information services on the African continent during and post COVID-19 shutdowns.

The pandemic heightened more than ever the importance of access to credible information. Societies have been faced with challenges of misinformation, disinformation and infodemic. To be digitally literate through having the skills to search for current and credible information sources that will empower people to make the right decisions is critical. Digital literacy skills have become a survival tool that everyone should have. If we are to achieve our 2030 Sustainable Development Goals they need to be seen as a basic human right.

Librarians in Botswana were fortunate to enrol on a course organized by AfLIA on global media and information literacy, the main aim of which was to raise awareness of the importance of media and information literacy among librarians. This course was particularly important because of the many challenges of misinformation, disinformation and infodemic around COVID-19.

AfLIA came in to close this gap and empower librarians to help their library patrons assess and evaluate the quality, authenticity and credibility of information sources. In addition, AfLIA also entered into a memorandum of understanding with Wikipedia to further provide librarians with the skills to edit and contribute notable sources of information to the Wikipedia platform by adding citations and references and editing wiki sources. All these were efforts to keep librarians up to speed and ready to serve in digitally enhanced environments and to help them to remain relevant in the knowledge-based economy.

Numerous other professional development opportunities existed for free for librarians both regionally and nationally. Likewise, AfLIA, in partnership with Commonwealth of Learning, offered a workforce recovery programme fully sponsored online for African citizens, including librarians and library users. This course was designed in recognition of the catastrophic effects of the pandemic on millions of people who had become unemployed or were on the verge of losing their jobs (AfLIA, 2020).

Within the many roles played by library professionals, there is great potential for using digital services platforms for work efficiency and collaboration in the library workplace. These require efficient strategies and skills. Consequently, the Botswana Library Association organized a workshop on digital platforms and strategies for remote work for library professionals. The main aim of the training was to meet the ICT needs of librarians in sustaining best practices in the use of digital platforms in their day-to-day activities. However, these were not without challenges.

Major challenges faced by a librarian

In the midst of the pandemic, different kinds of libraries remained partially or completely closed, thereby limiting access to information resources needed by researchers, academia, students and the general public. This state of affairs created a huge gap between the various groups of library users, impacting on the already existing societal divide. Further, as most libraries have moved from the usual direct-contact service provision to digital platforms, many users in Africa, especially in Botswana, have been left out. This, could be attributed to various reasons ranging from poor connectivity to lack of digital skills, to low bandwidth, impacting further on the digital divide.

The COVID-19 pandemic is a completely new challenge for libraries, and indeed for everyone globally. It has challenged both educators and librarians and kept them alert, as they never knew what to expect from it. We were never prepared for it, in that, as we closed the library doors, no policy was in place to guide the closure, nor was there a policy on opening up or even on dealing with the crisis itself.

The matter of dealing with the handling of books returned by patrons was dealt with very haphazardly; questions regarding how many patrons to allow back in the library and how long they should be permitted to stay in the library were issues of great concern that were never given the attention they deserved. In addition, the library never had the COVID-19 mitigation protocols for dealing with positive cases, contact tracing and probable cases.

Many of our students, though, were eager to use the library space for assignments and research even though they were not using the physical resources of the library. This presented many challenges for our patrons, as almost always the network was poor, library operating hours were limited and so not much study could be done within the limited hours. Many of our off-campus students relied on the library's desktop computers and the library's opening hours were never favourable for them. BTC could not cope with the online traffic, and therefore connectivity was very slow and sometimes completely down, making it very difficult for our patrons to access library resources online. Apparently the 1GB worth of internet given to each student per day did not allow them to take all their lessons, as most of their time on the internet was wasted in trying to connect.

Conclusion

From the foregoing, it is clear that COVID-19 has widened the digital divide, which has a great impact on teaching, learning and librarianship, and the need to close the gap is urgent. One of the major policy implications of COVID-19 is universal connectivity for education and economic resilience. Internet access and speed have been identified by the World Bank as key drivers of economic growth, job creation and social inclusion (Pedroncelli, 2019). As the world transitions to a digital economy, countries should be mindful of the fact that they need to be inclusive in their strategies, without leaving anyone behind, so that we all can achieve the Africa We Want by 2063 and the UN 2030 Sustainable Development Goals. Although there are noticeable efforts by governments in developing countries to step up their efforts towards closing the digital divide, more can still be done to bring everyone on board across geographical boundaries so as to be truly inclusive in the digital economy.

Countries in Africa can take a leaf out of the book of developed countries and invest in providing affordable internet services to people even in remote areas, as well as in increasing the speed of the internet. As former IFLA President Donna Scheeder appropriately stated, 'there is no truly sustainable development without access to information, and no meaningful, inclusive access to information without libraries'. Development of people's livelihoods is highly dependent on their ability to access and use information effectively to guide their decision-making processes. Providing internet access as a basic service has become paramount in this kind of economy. Since the 2030 Sustainable Development Agenda is about people, planet, prosperity and partnerships, African countries more especially should channel their efforts towards ensuring that their people can prosper from what modernity offers and partnering with all relevant stakeholders for sustainability of resources.

Strategies to reduce the impact of COVID–19 on the digital divide

Based on the literature review and the authors' own observations, the following strategies are offered to reduce the impact of COVID-19 on the digital divide (Figure 7.1).

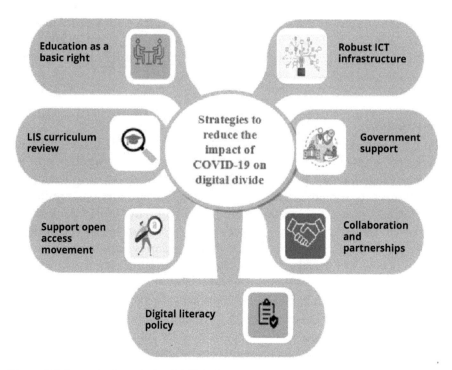

Figure 7.1 *Strategies for reducing COVID-19 impact*

Robust ICT infrastructure

A robust ICT infrastructure, including high-speed internet connection/bandwidth, high-performance computing facilities and data services, is indispensable for reducing the digital divide. It would help to disseminate and share knowledge more effectively through open access platforms at the global level. Like other countries of the world, policy makers in Botswana should invest in internet infrastructure to bring internet access and devices to every citizen for increased access to support the move to digital platforms. The need for government support in the realization of the Africa We Want, as well as the 2030 Sustainable Development Agenda, cannot be overemphasized. For countries to transition to inclusive knowledge and digital economies their respective governments must invest in supporting both the private and non-governmental sectors in their efforts to be creative and innovative in their use of the necessary socioeconomic, financial and cultural resources in online spaces. Governments have key roles to play in the development of their citizens and therefore they should be committed to the provision of adequate funding for a robust and functional ICT infrastructure and high-speed internet.

Collaboration and partnerships

There is a need for collaboration between national, regional and international library associations as the voice of information professionals. These professional bodies should actively advocate for free open access resources as well as for standards on digital services. Strong partnerships between the private sector and governments, regionally and globally, for the provision of digital connectivity, e-learning, e-commerce, teleworking and teleconferencing to close down the digital gap should be established. Indeed, the achievement of the Sustainable Development Goals is highly dependent on all the relevant stakeholders working together to ensure *innovative technological development, fair trade and market access, especially for developing countries.*

Support for the open access movement

Open access movement initiatives should be intensified in all African countries, including Botswana, to support and encourage the sharing of knowledge and to enable knowledge economies to thrive. Libraries should advocate for robust open access in order to achieve true development for our societies. Librarians must leverage digital platforms and strategies for working online, and stay ahead of the curve.

Library and information science curriculum review

Library and information science education/curricula should be reviewed to include media and information literacy as well as digital literacy skills, so as to empower learners with the appropriate skills to enable to them adapt and cope with the current digital environment.

Education as a basic right

The right to a basic education is a human right, and this pandemic has taught nations that in spite of all the challenges the pandemic posed to learners and teachers alike, no learner should be denied this right. Education should continue even when school doors are closed. This of course will empower learners with the right skills to seek employment in the future, to alleviate poverty, to uphold human dignity and to foster peaceful societies.

Digital literacy policy framework

In order for Africa to inspire its citizens to participate fully in the knowledge-based economy, digital literacy has to be a major focus of human endeavour. Africa as a continent has to accelerate its efforts towards a digital literacy framework which will serve as a guide towards bridging the digital divide.

References

AfLIA (African Library and Information Associations and Institutions) (2020) https://web.aflia.net/2020-global-media-and-information-literacy-week-short-course.

CIPESA (Collaboration on International ICT Policy for East and Southern Africa) (2019) *Despots and Disruptions: Five Dimensions of Internet Shutdowns in Africa,* https://cipesa.org/2019/03/despots-and-disruptions-five-dimensions-of-internet-shutdowns-in-africa.

Faria, J. (2021) Penetration Rate of Internet Users in Botswana 2017–2021, www.statista.com/statistics/1155039/internet-penetration-rate-botswana.

Gartner Glossary (2021) Digital Divide, www.gartner.com/en/information-technology/glossary/digital-divide.

Gilster, P. (1997) *Digital Literacy,* Wiley Computer Publications.

Guermazi, B. (2020) Digital Transformation in the Time of COVID-19: The Case of MENA, *World Bank Blogs,* https://blogs.worldbank.org/arabvoices/digital-transformation-time-covid-19-case-mena.

International Labor Report (2020) *The Impact of the COVID-19 Pandemic on Jobs and Incomes in G20 Economies,* ILO–OECD paper prepared at the request of G20 Leaders, Saudi Arabia's G20 Presidency 2020, www.ilo.org/wcmsp5/groups/public/—-dgreports/—-cabinet/documents/publication/wcms_756331.pdf.

ITU (International Telecommunications Union) (2019) New ITU Data Reveal Growing Internet Uptake but a Widening Digital Gender Divide, www.itu.int/en/mediacentre/Pages/2019-PR19.aspx.

Internet Society (2020) *COVID-19 Impact on Internet Performance: Case Study of Afghanistan, Nepal and Sri Lanka,* www.internetsociety.org/resources/doc/2020/the-impact-of-the-covid-19-pandemic-on-internet-performance-in-afghanistan-nepal-and-sri-lanka.

Internet World Stats (2020) Usage and Population Statistics, www.internetworldstats.com/stats1.htm.

Jaeger, P. T., Carlo Bertot, J., Thompson, K. M., Katz, S. M. and DeCoster, E. J. (2012) *Digital Divides, Digital Literacy, Digital Inclusion, and Public Libraries: The Intersection of Public Policy and Public Access,* https://researchoutput.csu.edu.au/ws/portalfiles/portal/8843534/PID40502manus cript.pdf.

Johnson, J. (2021) Worldwide Digital Population as of January 2021, www.statista.com.

Joint Information Systems Committee (2016) *Developing Digital Literacies*, www.jisc.ac.uk/guides/developing-digital-literacies.

Junio, D. R. (2020) Digital Divide in the Time of COVID-19, https://cs.unu.edu/news/news/digital-divide-covid-19.html.

Lashitew, A. (2020) COVID-19 Exposes Africa's Digital Divide, *African Business*, https://african.business/2020/09/technology-information/covid-19-exposes-africas-digital-divide/

Magang, D. (2020) Internet Connectivity in Botswana: Time to Narrow Digital Divide, *Weekend Post*, www.weekendpost.co.bw/29024/columns/internet-connectivity-in-botswana-time-to-narrow-digital-divide.

Mbodila, M. (2020) Online Learning – The Pandemic cannot Change Reality, *University World News: Africa Edition*, www.universityworldnews.com/post.php?story=2020042013022 2745.

Mittal, S. and Singh, T. (2020) Gender-Based Violence during COVID-19 Pandemic: A Mini-Review, *Frontiers in Global Women's Health*, 8 September, doi: 10.3389/fgwh.2020.00004.

Ntshwarang, P., Malinga, T. and Losike-Sedimo, N. (2021) e-Learning Tools at the University of Botswana: Relevance and Use under COVID-19 Crisis, *Higher Education for the Future*, doi: 10.1177/2347631120986281.

O'Halloran, D. (2020) 5 Ways to Protect Critical Digital Connectivity during COVID-19, *World Economic Forum/Forbes*, www.weforum.org/agenda/2020/04/covid-19–5-ways-to-protect-critical-digital-connectivity.

Pedroncelli, P. (2019) 10 African Countries with the Fastest Broadband Speeds, https://moguldom.com/220816/10-african-countries-with-the-fastest-broadband-speeds.

Raju, J. (2017) *LIS Professional Competency Index for the Higher Education Sector in South Africa*, https://openbooks.uct.ac.za/uct/catalog/download/LISindex/14/398-6?inline=1.

Sedimo, N. C., Bwalya, K. J. and Du Plessis, T. (2011) Conquering the Digital Divide: Botswana and South Korea Digital Divide Status and Interventions, *South African Journal of Information Management*, **13** (1), https://sajim.co.za/index.php/sajim/article/view/471/511.

Steele, C. (2019) *What Is the Digital Divide?* www.digitaldividecouncil.com/what-is-the-digital-divide.

TheVoiceBW (2020) *The Voice Newspaper*, Botswana,
    www.facebook.com/TheVoiceBW/posts/the-digital-divide-is-actually-widening-
    under-the-new-normal-caused-by-the-covid/10157991899369086.
Turianskyi, Y. (2020) COVID-19: Implications for the 'Digital Divide' in Africa, *Africa
    Portal*, www.africaportal.org/features/covid-19-implications-of-the-pandemic-for-
    the-digital-divide-in-africa.
United Nations Botswana (2020) *Socio-economic Impact Analysis of COVID-19 in
    Botswana*, Analysis Brief No. 1.
UB (University of Botswana) (2020), https://www.ub.bw/news/ub-adjusts-almanac-
    response-covid-19-pandemic#:~:text=The%20University%20of%20Botswana%20h
    as,to%20the%20COVID%2D19%20pandemic.
Wilson, F. (2021) COVID-19 Pandemic has Changed How we Define the Digital
    Divide, *Tennessean*, www.tennessean.com/story/opinion/2020/10/01/covid-19-
    pandemic-has-changed-how-we-define-digital-divide/5885668002.

8

Digital Literacy Skills Investigation among Third-Year Bachelor of Library and Information Science Students of Makerere University

Faridah Muzaki, Sarah Kaddu and Eric Nelson Haumba

Abstract

This chapter investigates the digital literacy skills among Bachelor of Library and Information Science (BLIS) Students at the East African School of Library and Information Science (EASLIS), Makerere University. Objectives were to establish: the level of digital literacy among third-year students and attempts made by EASLIS to impart digital literacy skills to students; to identify challenges affecting digital literacy skills acquisition among students; and to recommend strategies for promoting digital literacy skills acquisition among the students. Qualitative and quantitative research approaches were used with a case study research design. Challenges affecting digital literacy skills acquisition that were identified by students and academic staff who participated in the study. The study proposed several strategies for improving digital literacy skills acquisition among BLIS students. It concluded that digital literacy skills among third-year BLIS students are inadequate in areas that require advanced skills in computing.

Keywords: Digital literacy, information science, EASLIS, Makerere University.

Introduction

The use of information and communication technologies (ICTs) has increased globally since the late 1980s, with computers playing an important role in different aspects of life. Today, computers are found in homes, offices, schools and in business. This has made people realize that in the information society, knowing how to use computers and other digital devices is an important life skill required by professionals for effective delivery of services in organizations worldwide.

The advancement of ICT has also provided information institutions with a variety of ways for collecting, organizing, storing, retrieving and disseminating information (Gunjal and Dhamdhere, 2013, 9). ICT facilitates global interconnectivity and faster exchange of information, hence the ability of organizations to use digital technology and communication networks appropriately to solve information problems for effective service delivery is important. These include being able to use ICT to research, collect, organize, evaluate and communicate information and the possession of a fundamental understanding of issues related to the access and ethical use of information (Haneefa and Abdul Shukkoor, 2010, 57).

As computers and the internet become more available, digital literacy skills have become important in all sectors. Digital literacy refers to the ability by individuals to understand and use information in a variety of formats from different sources presented in electronic form (Brown et al., 2016; JISC, 2015). This definition has evolved over the years to include the ability by individuals to access, manage, integrate, evaluate and communicate information that is in electronic form so that they are able to function effectively in the knowledge society (Aaron, 2012, 17). However, Belshaw (2011, 201, 230), argued that digital literacy is a complex term that is used ambiguously both consciously and unconsciously with a multitude of different backgrounds and intentions. According to Bawden (2001, 230) because of the contradicting definitions, it is better to adopt a perspective of describing rather than defining what digital literacy is. He further argues that the name given to the terms does not matter, it is the concepts themselves and their relevance for practice that matters. Bawden (2001, 233) observed that it is too restrictive to express ideas focusing on a given set of particular skills to be learned and competencies that should be demonstrated. Eshet-Alkalai (2004, 97) opined that digital literacy is much more than the ability to use software or hardware. From the above, it can be inferred that there are diverse views on what is entailed in digital literacy. This can be attributed to the fact that digital technology is changing rapidly, making it difficult to have a common inventory of digital skills and expected outcomes.

ICT has become a valuable tool that needs to be promoted to facilitate work in the information society (National Development Plan, 2010, 27). This realization has spurred countries worldwide to harness the potential of ICT through policy formulation, development of infrastructure and human resource training to support its exploitation for increased productivity and better service delivery. However, studies conducted on digital literacy in developing countries, such as those by Andema, Kendrick and Norton (2013,

27) and Ameen and Gorman (2008, 110) show that educational institutions face numerous challenges in implementing digital literacy programmes. These include the challenges of infrastructure, inadequate skills among staff responsible for training and minimal support from policy makers affecting digital literacy training initiatives.

Uganda developed its first National ICT Policy in 2003, with a major objective of integrating ICT into educational curricula as well as other literacy programmes to provide for equitable access for all students, regardless of academic level (Farrell, 2007, 13). When the Ministry of ICT was established in Uganda in 2006, a number of policies that facilitate ICT training and access to infrastructure were developed in collaboration with the Ministry of Education and Sports (MoES); for example, ICT policy on education for primary and secondary schools, which aims at training teachers in ICT skills. According to Twinomujuni (2011, 9) for the tertiary education subsector in Uganda, the ICT policy is not particularly integrated and initiatives are taken on by individual universities. The Ministry and other stakeholders such as the National Council for Higher Education (NCHE) and development partners provide support in terms of providing guidelines, best practices and identifying baseline requirements.

In line with global commitments to improve digital inclusion and to realize the UN Sustainable Development Goals for 2030, the Government of Uganda has committed the country to developing a digital vision for Uganda. It aims to 'build a digitally-enabled society that is secure, sustainable, innovative, and transformative to create a positive social and economic impact through technology-based empowerment'. The Digital Uganda Vision provides an overarching framework that responds to the national Vision 2040 by providing a unified ICT policy direction. It further provides the Government's integrated policy and strategic framework to show how ICT can empower Ugandan citizens and achieve the goals of universal inclusion, sustainable development, economic progress and poverty eradication through digital innovation.

Theoretical perspective

Digital literacy in this context is treated as an example of skills acquisition and therefore invokes one of the skills-acquisition models – Dreyfus' (2004, 179) five-stage model of skill acquisition. This model postulates that disciplines combine formal and informal competencies in terms of rational thinking, professional skills and experiential knowledge construction which are acquired through written or verbal instruction – that is, what students are taught – and through experience – that is, doing what they have been taught.

It is argued that, to achieve this, students pass through five stages: novice, advanced beginner, competent, proficient and expert.

These stages were formulated based on research and Piaget's constructivist theory of learning, where each stage describes the phenomenological characteristics of learning strategies for developing expertise.

The novice performs trial-and-error strategies without reflection. The advanced beginner depends on rules but reflects within learning by doing. The competent may act independently and deliberately plan and change strategies. However, the competent does not question the basic assumptions. The novices, advanced beginners and competent assimilate and accumulate new knowledge. They are to a certain level dependent on rules and instruction and they prefer to react rather than to be proactive. In contrast, the proficient and the experts act in a way that is independent, reflective and proactive. The proficient may question basic assumptions and radically change their strategy due to reflection and experience, while the expert deals with challenges by intuitively drawing on tacit knowledge and thought experiments (Levinsen, 2011, 53). Hall-Ellis and Grealy (2013, 589), in their application of Dreyfus and Dreyfus' model (1986, 179) to library and information science career development, propose that, to maximize human capital development, trainers need to determine skill development levels among students so that they can identify skill gaps and address them. Digital literacy, just like any other skill training, must be based on a skills acquisition model so that it can address the pertinent issues involved in facilitating the advancement of skills at each stage of training (Dreyfus and Dreyfus, 1986, 130). Other studies that have used this model in assessing knowledge include Cope and Phillips (2006). By adopting the Dreyfus and Dreyfus' (1986) five-stage model of skill acquisition, this chapter considers the level of digital literacy, current attempts to address digital literacy skills, challenges affecting digital literacy and strategies for promoting digital literacy among third-year Bachelor of Library and Information Science (BLIS) students at the East African School of Library and Information Science (EASLIS), Makerere University.

Conceptual perspective

Digital literacy is the ability of individuals to access, manage, integrate, evaluate and communicate information that is in electronic form so that they are able to function effectively in the knowledge society (Aaron, 2012, 17). The California Emerging Technology Fund (CETF) (2008) proposed a standardized approach to assessment, diagnosis and continuous improvement of digital literacy skills for students and the workforce. The CETF approach proposes elements similar to those of other international and national digital literacy frameworks, and these elements are summarized in Table 8.1.

Table 8.1 *Basic elements of digital literacy*

Element	Definition	Competencies
Access	Knowing about and knowing how to collect and/or retrieve information.	Search, find and retrieve information in digital environments.
Manage	Applying an existing organizational or classification scheme.	Conduct a rudimentary and preliminary organization of accessed information for retrieval and future application.
Integrate	Interpreting and representing information – summarizing, comparing and contrasting.	Interpret and represent information by using ICT tools to synthesize, summarize, compare and contrast information from multiple sources.
Evaluate	Making judgements about the quality, relevance, usefulness or efficiency of information.	Judge the currency, appropriateness and adequacy of information and information sources for a specific purpose.
Create	Generating information by adapting, applying, designing, inventing or authoring information.	Adapt, apply, design or invent information in ICT environments (to describe an event, express an opinion or support a basic argument, viewpoint or position).
Communicate	Communicating information persuasively to meet the needs of various audiences through the use of an appropriate medium.	Communicate, adapt and present information properly in its context (audience, media) in ICT environments and for a peer audience.

Source: CETF (2008).

The Association of College and Research Libraries, a division of the American Library Association (ALA), is a key source for standards and performance indicators of digital literacy. The ALA proposes five key areas with specific indicators of digital literacy, focusing on the need for cognitive, ethical and technical skills. These are summarized in Table 8.2.

Table 8.2 *Digital literacy indicators*

Standard	Indicator
Know	Define and articulate the need.
Access	Access the information, service or activity effectively and efficiently.
Evaluate	Critically evaluate and incorporate information into personal knowledge base and value system.
Use	Use information effectively to accomplish a specific purpose.
Ethical/Legal	Understand many of the ethical legal, and social issues surrounding the use of information, and access and use it ethically and legally.

Source: ALA (2012).

From Table 8.2 it can be observed that digital literacy involves knowledge and skills of recognizing a need for information, using ICT to find the information and evaluating information that has been found for personal use while taking into consideration the ethical and legal aspects of using information, such as copyright and intellectual property rights.

In the Ugandan education system, students start learning ICT at Ordinary level (forms 1 to 4 of the secondary school) and continue at Advanced level (forms 5 to 6 of the higher secondary level), where ICT is taught as one of the optional and subsidiary subjects, respectively. Given the fact that at Advanced level ICT is offered as a subsidiary subject, many students who go on to university do not get a chance to take it. Secondary schools face challenges such as inadequately skilled teachers, power outages, inadequate computers and internet connectivity that hinder the learning process. The integration of ICT into university study programmes as a priority would enable students who did not take ICT as a subject at the secondary school level to get another chance to acquire the ICT skills required to support their learning at the university and their progression in the workplace upon graduation.

Contextual background

Makerere University is a public university, the oldest and largest university in East and Central Africa (Makerere University, 2022). Established in 1922 from the Uganda Technical College, Makerere University was affiliated to the University of London until 1963, when it became one of the three constituent colleges of the University of East Africa. It became an independent university in 1970 by an Act of Parliament.

EASLIS is one of the schools at Makerere University in the College of Computing and Information Sciences that started as a regional training centre in 1963 with initial financial assistance from the United Nations Education and Scientific Organization (UNESCO). Currently the school offers the following programmes: Bachelor of Library and Information Science (BLIS), Bachelor of Records and Archives Management, Master of Science in Information Science, Master of Science in Records and Archives Management and Doctor of Philosophy in Information Science. This chapter investigates the digital literacy skills among third-year BLIS students at EASLIS.

Statement of the problem

Universities worldwide are responsible for training to enable students to gain the critical skills and knowledge necessary for the labour market. However, universities in Uganda still face challenges in terms of inadequate ICT facilities, high student numbers and lack of ICT expertise among the staff (Twinomujuni, 2011, 16). These challenges affect the quality of digital literacy training at universities, even with an up-to-date curriculum, hence affecting the level of digital literacy skills acquired by students. Digital literacy skills are important in the library and information activities of retrieval, processing, managing and storage of information. It is therefore important for LIS students to be equipped with the necessary digital literacy skills to use both at the university and when they start employment after completing their studies. However, a number of studies such as Magara, Bukirwa and Kayiki (2011, 32) and Twikirize (2011, 17) have reported that digital literacy skills among BLIS students at EASLIS are inadequate. Therefore, if the current situation at EASLIS continues, the quality of BLIS graduates may be low and the future of LIS graduates from Makerere University will be at stake. While many factors may be responsible for this situation, inadequate ICT facilities, inadequate academic staff, inadequate practical training, and inadequate integration of ICT into the BLIS curriculum could be the cause (Twikirize, 2011, 18). Murray and Pérez (2014, 95) recommend that universities should assess the digital literacy skills of students as they are about to graduate because these skills are essential not only in the workplace but in all spheres of life. Therefore, it was necessary to investigate digital literacy skills among BLIS students at EASLIS to establish their level of digital literacy skills and propose strategies that may help to improve the situation among third-year students.

Objectives

1 To establish the level of digital literacy among third-year BLIS students at EASLIS.
2 To examine attempts made by EASLIS to impart digital literacy skills to BLIS students.
3 To identify challenges affecting digital literacy skills acquisition by BLIS students at EASLIS.
4 To propose strategies for promoting digital literacy skills acquisition among BLIS students at EASLIS if the situation was found wanting.

Literature review
Overview of digital literacy

According to Bawden (2001, 230), literacy refers to the ability to read and write; it also requires some skills or competence and an element of learning. Bawden (2001, 230) further asserts that over time the definition of literacy has taken on a more than ordinary meaning of being able to effectively use information gained from written materials. However, UNESCO (2006, 3) defines literacy as the ability to identify, understand, interpret, create, communicate, compute and use printed and written materials associated with varying contexts. Literacy involves a continuum of learning to enable an individual to achieve his or her goals, to develop his or her knowledge and potential and to participate fully in the wider society. ACRL (2015) asserts that information literacy refers to a set of abilities that are needed by individuals to recognize when there is a need for information and to find, evaluate and use information effectively. Nalumaga (2005, 29) argues that information literacy may have different meanings to different people, but it is one of the skills that are vital for the information age. Tilvawala, Myers and Andrade (2009, 7) state that information literacy is the ability of individuals to recognize the need for information, find and evaluate, store and retrieve information and use that information ethically to create and communicate knowledge.

Importance of digital literacy in university education

Countries worldwide have invested heavily in university education as a means for the economic and social development of their human resources. Universities have the primary role of training students to enable them to acquire advanced skills required in the workplace. According to Kavulya (2007, 213), traditionally, universities produce new knowledge through research and act as channels for the transfer and dissemination of knowledge generated elsewhere in the world. Digital literacy is increasingly being recognized by universities throughout the world as an important skill that can increase students' chances of employment after completing their studies. This is because digital literacy enables individuals to acquire skills required to function effectively in the knowledge and information society and to adapt to changing skills requirements in the job market. In the work environment, digital literacy is important for being productive citizens in a knowledge-driven society, and employers want their employees to have these skills for effective service delivery in organizations. As a result, universities are beginning to require digital literacy as one of the competencies for graduation (Katz and Mackline, 2007, 708).

Digital literacy in the context of library and information science education

The library of the 21st century is different in terms of users, forms of information materials and user expectations, due to advances in ICT that have led to the rapid dissemination of information and have revolutionized how information is handled in libraries and other information institutions. ICTs have provided new avenues of collecting, organizing and disseminating information. This has compelled libraries to adapt specific library functions and operations by innovatively using ICTs to enhance service delivery (Mathew, 2011, 82). This necessitates new skills to meet the ever-changing needs of users and the widespread use of the internet and worldwide web. Digital libraries and institutional repositories have made the role of information professionals based on the five laws of library science postulated by Ranganathan more evident than ever. The five laws provide us with a way of thinking about how information institutions work and therefore give us a framework through which to examine the LIS professional training that is offered by universities.

Methodology

The study used both qualitative and quantitative research approaches with a case study research design. Data was collected using questionnaires distributed to 124 BLIS students who were randomly selected; interviews were conducted with four members of staff responsible for teaching digital literacy courses and the head of the Department of Library and Information Science. In addition, relevant documents such as the BLIS curriculum, Makerere University quality assurance framework, Makerere University Strategic Plan 2007/08–2017/18 and field attachment reports, among, others were also reviewed.

Key findings

Level of digital literacy skills among third-year BLIS students

Third-year BLIS students were asked to rate their level of digital literacy skills, as shown in Table 8.3.

Table 8.3 *Level of digital literacy skills among third-year BLIS students at EASLIS*

	Frequency	Percentage
Proficient	28	23
Intermediate	72	58
Beginner	24	19
Total	124	100

Source: Field data (2020).

Table 8.3 shows that 58% of third-year BLIS students rated their digital literacy skills as intermediate, 23% of respondents indicated that they were proficient and 19% revealed that they were at the beginner level. This means that not all third-year BLIS students are proficient in digital literacy. Academic staff who were interviewed also rated the level of digital literacy skills among third-year BLIS students at EASLIS as intermediate. One academic staff member who was interviewed said: 'BLIS third-year students have intermediate digital literacy skills.'

Students suggested that:

EASLIS should improve on existing courses and make them more practical ...

[P]rovision of the required software, increase access to computers through the provision of more computers in the labs.

There should be adequate support by Lecturers ... because some students do not know anything.

Mohagheghzadeh et al. (2014, 275) observed that most university students have intermediate digital literacy skills, and this implies that it is the responsibility of the university to ensure that students get adequate training in order to improve their digital literacy skills. Buarki (2010, 139) focused specifically on LIS students and established that by the time of graduation LIS students possess only 50% of the digital literacy skills required by the job market.

Attempts made by EASLIS to impart digital literacy skills to BLIS students

In 2002 Makerere University, with support of Delft University of Technology in the Netherlands, started the integration of ICT into teaching and learning through the use of electronic learning to enhance and support learning and teaching. The aim of the electronic learning project was to enhance traditional teaching methods and create learning flexibility for students. Makerere University Electronic Learning Environment (MUELE) enables academic staff to make lecture notes and assessments available to students online (Makerere University, 2022, 32). Interviews with academic staff revealed that EASLIS has organized several training workshops for academic staff to equip them with the skills needed to use MUELE. However, although Makerere University has implemented e-learning, according to one student, 'the university should emphasize the use of online blogs and chats as a way of teaching'. The head of department recommended: 'We need to strengthen the use of e-learning by all academic staff and this will eventually force students to use it.'

From this study it was established that Makerere University has not fully realized the benefits of using e-learning. According to the head of department of LIS, currently MUELE is hosting partly developed courses and serving mainly as a repository for course materials. Academic staff said that a number of challenges have affected the use of MUELE by students and academic staff, such as the limited number of computers, slow internet connectivity, inadequate ICT skills among students and inadequate skills among academic staff on the integration of ICT into teaching and learning. Adetimirin (2011, 391) suggests that one of the strategies universities can use to improve the digital literacy skills of the students is to encourage academic staff to use ICT in teaching and learning.

Making use of the college computer laboratories

In 2011, EASLIS and Faculty of Computing were merged to form the College of Computing and Information Sciences. This meant that the two schools had to share their facilities. Before the merger, EASLIS did not have a strong ICT infrastructure. Availability of computers and access to the internet greatly influence the acquisition of digital literacy skills. Interviews conducted with head of department of LIS established that EASLIS uses computer laboratories at the School of Computing and Informatics Technology (SCIT), College of Computing and Information Sciences (CoCIS) for purposes of teaching in an effort to improve digital literacy skills among BLIS students. This finding is in line with what is echoed by Okello-Obura (2012, 90) as one of the benefits EASLIS has derived from the collegiate system. However, one student recommended that 'EASLIS should ensure that students have enough access to computers to improve on their digital literacy skills'.
Another student said:

> EASLIS should put in place a strategy to ensure that all students have laptops because the computers in the computer lab are not enough. This can be done through the College by appealing to the government or donors or including it on the fees paid so that it is paid in portions every semester and by the end of the three years the amount will be completed.

Due to high student numbers, the student to computer ratio (5:1) remains high. This means that students have to queue in order to use the computers at the College (Makerere University, 2014, 18).

Curriculum review

Kigongo-Bukenya and Musoke (2011) argued that change brought about by ICT is one of the reasons that normally necessitates a curriculum review. To address this change, EASLIS reviewed the BLIS curriculum to focus on projects, so that students who have ideas that are implementable using ICT tools can put their digital literacy skills to use. According to the National Council for Higher Education (2014) guidelines, universities have to review the curricula of their programmes after a cohort has passed. This allows enhancement of the curriculum and addresses any gaps that may have been identified during training. Academic staff interviewed and documents reviewed revealed that the current BLIS programme at EASLIS was revised in 2009 and more digital literacy courses were incorporated, such as Multimedia Librarianship, Information Literacy and Management of Electronic Resources.

Field attachment

Field attachment is a training method that enables students to apply what they have learned in class in a work environment. According to Kigongo-Bukenya and Musoke (2011), field attachment is undertaken by BLIS students at the end of their second year of study in the recess term, with the intention of providing students with practical LIS skills. The aim of field attachment is to help students to become familiar with the work environment, apply the knowledge acquired in class and gain practical skills in library and information work. Students on the BLIS programme are attached to established organizations with libraries, registries, records centres, archival institutions, information service centres and publishing houses. It is important to note that although EASLIS has implemented field attachment, one student suggested: 'EASLIS students should always be given a full year in the field to practise what has been taught in class …'.

Indeed, this is also affirmed by a similar study by Bukaliya (2012) who pointed out that the duration of field attachment is not adequate to enable students to derive maximum benefit from the exercise.

Encouraging students to use electronic information resources

From the documents reviewed it was established that Makerere University Library, with support from different stakeholders, has embraced the use of ICT in library services. This includes through subscription to electronic information resources such as journals and electronic books, which are intended to be used by students and staff. The aim of providing these electronic resources is to enable students and staff to have timely access to information via the internet. However, interviews with academic staff at EASLIS who participated in this study revealed that while students are normally required to use electronic information resources for their coursework assignments and research projects, many students do not use them. One academic member lamented: 'We need a policy to enforce use and citation of online resources, especially journal articles.'

This implies that there is a need for a deliberate effort and strategy to encourage students to use electronic information resources. Thanuskodi (2012, 4) observes that electronic information resources are vital in academic institutions, as they provide students with wider access to information that is vital for their academic success.

Challenges
Inadequate ICT facilities

Although EASLIS has made use of the College computer labs, findings indicated that ICT facilities are still inadequate (80%). Third-year BLIS students identified three aspects of inadequate ICT facilities: these included limited access to computers, absence of some of the required software, intermittent and slow internet speed. While EASLIS enabled students to have greater access to computers by making use of the College computer laboratories, due to the large number of students in the College (4,255 registered students as of 2014) the student to computer ratio was high (5:1), making it difficult for students to have access to computers any time they would wish to use them (Makerere University, 2014). It was established from interviews with academic staff that for practical courses they would like to have one computer per student. Academic staff also indicated that the different practical courses they teach have different software requirements. Some of the software is commercial and sometimes the College cannot purchase it when it is required. The implication of this is that students end up not having enough time for hands-on practice. One academic staff member said: 'The ratio of students to computers is high. Students cannot use computers anytime they wish, they found them occupied, use is on first come, first served basis.'

Students revealed that the internet connection is sometimes slow and intermittent, making it difficult for them to use it for study purposes. This finding is consistent with Qureshi et al. (2012) and Danner and Pessu (2013), who argued that access to ICT facilities is about availability of adequate ICT equipment, internet and software.

Power outages

According to Ikwaba and Uhomoibhi (2013), the availability and reliability of electricity is a prerequisite for the use of ICT devices and a crucial aspect in acquisition of digital literacy skills. The study established that power outages (76%) was one of the challenges affecting digital literacy skills acquisition among third-year BLIS students at EASLIS. Power outages have a negative impact on students' acquisition of digital literacy skills. CoCIS block A and B have standby generators, while block C has no generator. One student said: 'Sometimes power goes off in block C and classes have to stop because there is no other alternative …'.

Rugumayo (2010, 23) observed that power outages are caused by the inadequate capacity of the power generation company to meet the growing power demand in the country. Because of the challenges faced by the power supply sector, such as the poor infrastructure that necessitates rationing of power, the power supply company was compelled to introduce a load-shedding programme to ensure equitable supply of power to consumers. This finding is similar to that of Opati (2013, 38), who observed that frequent power outages affect teaching and learning at Makerere University.

Inadequate digital literacy and pedagogy skills among academic staff

Academic staff are expected to support students' learning by being accessible to students, motivating them and guiding them in solving their learning problems. MacGregor (2003, 17) suggested that, ideally, support can be in the form of counselling, mentoring, career advice and support for student learning focusing on the development of certain abilities in the students. Students indicated in the study findings that they do not receive the necessary support from the academic staff for them to be able to effectively acquire digital literacy skills because some academic staff do not have digital literacy and pedagogy skills. One academic staff member lamented: 'There is over-reliance on old professors who are out of touch with new trends in digital and information technology advancements.'

This implies that some of the academic staff do not have up-to-date skills and therefore cannot effectively support students' learning. This in turn affects students in acquiring digital literacy skills. Qureshi et al. (2012) suggested in their studies that it is important that knowledgeable people such as academic staff are available to assist and motivate students to enable them to learn. They argued that academic staff's support to students greatly contributes to students' academic success. Buarki (2010) observed that support from academic staff is important in helping students to improve their digital literacy skills.

Few digital literacy courses offered in the BLIS curriculum

The digital literacy courses offered on the BLIS programme include: Information Technology I and II, Analysis of Information Systems, Database Management and Information Retrieval, Web Document Management, Automation of Library and Information Systems, Web Design, Publication Design and Production, Multimedia Librarianship, Information Literacy and Management of Electronic Resources. Students as respondents indicated that the digital literacy courses offered by EASLIS are not adequate (76%). In the BLIS curriculum ten (27%) courses related to digital literacy are offered out of the total 37 course units. Academic staff revealed that the digital literacy courses offered within the BLIS curriculum are inadequate because they focus more on teaching students to use but not to develop information systems, as the head of department pointed out in the interview: 'BLIS students possess the skills to use ICTs but not to develop automated information systems, they are trained to be users of automated information systems but not to design information systems.'

Hashim and Mokhtar (2012) highlighted one of the professional competencies of the librarian as being able to use appropriate ICT to acquire, organize and disseminate information. It is therefore the role of library science training schools to ensure that they design the curriculum in such a way that the skills required to meet the changing job market are imparted.

Challenges identified by academic staff

High student to academic staff ratio

Findings from the interviews with academic staff indicated that a high student to academic staff ratio (250:1) is one of the challenges affecting digital literacy skills acquisition among third-year BLIS students at EASLIS. From documents reviewed it was established that in the academic year 2012/13 EASLIS increased its student enrolment figure from approximately 800 to 1,500, but unfortunately the number of staff and ICT facilities has not increased. There has been a drastic increase in student enrolments as a result of increased demand for university education in Uganda (National Council for Higher Education, 2014, 89). One academic staff member interviewed lamented that 'The high student to lecturer ratio of 1:250 is worsened by the pre-university education system that seems to be affecting the general performance of students. They come to the university with generally low levels of digital literacy ...'

This finding contrasts the view of Okello-Obura (2012, 90) that the formation of the CoCIS that saw the merger of SCIT and EASLIS has made it possible to have more academic staff available to teach digital literacy courses.

Negative attitude of the students towards independent learning

Academic staff who were interviewed mentioned the poor attitude of students towards independent learning as one of the challenges that affect digital literacy skills acquisition among BLIS students. As one academic staff member lamented: 'Students have a spoon-feeding attitude; they cannot do independent work unless marks are attached to it ...'

This means there is a need to train academic staff in teaching strategies such as group-based instruction that makes use of scaffolding. This allows students who are novices to be assisted at the beginning and then left to learn on their own. It is therefore imperative that academic staff engaged in teaching digital literacy courses design teaching and learning strategies that motivate students and foster positive attitudes, such as emphasizing the attainment of mastery through independent study. Moreira (2010) stated that students should be able to construct knowledge and learn independently, especially when they have access to different ICT facilities. Togia, Korobili and Malliari (2012) suggested that LIS education institutions should devise learning strategies that motivate students and promote active learning through the use of authentic tasks and problem-solving activities that are linked to students' interests.

Inadequate information literacy skills among students

Through interviews with academic staff it was established that students have inadequate information literacy skills. One staff member lamented that 'our students have inadequate information literacy skills'. These skills are required to help LIS students to master content and extend their investigations, and to become more self-directed and assume more control over their own learning (Moreira, 2010). As indicated earlier, information literacy is one of the courses taught on the BLIS programme in the first semester of first year of study. It is therefore surprising to the researcher that academic staff at EASLIS rate the information literacy skills among BLIS students as inadequate. This finding is consistent with that of Kinengyere (2007, 330), who established that university students in Uganda have inadequate information literacy skills.

Conclusion

Based on the study findings and conclusions, the study was able to arrive at the following recommendations.

Digital literacy and pedagogy skills development among academic staff

Since effective teaching requires a good understanding of subject content and pedagogy for effective learning to take place, it is important for academic staff to renew their competencies in order to support student learning effectively. It is therefore recommended that academic staff undergo continuous training to help them acquire the skills necessary in a changing work environment that has rendered obsolete some of their original skills and knowledge as teachers in tertiary institutions.

Timely curriculum review

It is recommended that the Department of Library and Information Science should review the curriculum periodically to enable students to be offered core computing courses such as programming, advanced database and website design and computer networks and systems administration from SCIT.

Quality assurance in teaching and learning

Academic staff recommended that there is need for EASLIS to fully implement the University's quality assurance policy, especially in the area of monitoring teaching and learning to ensure that quality training is achieved. This can be done through implementing quality assurance controls, audit mechanisms and assessments.

Improve ICT facilities

It is important for EASLIS to improve existing ICT facilities such as computers, software and internet bandwidth. This can be achieved through regular repair, procurement of more ICT equipment and exploring the use of open source software to reduce the cost of software licences. EASLIS must try to find ways of obtaining funds from the University administration, exploring income-generating activities at the school and college level and collaborating with the private sector. Furthermore, television white space is being advocated for libraries in other parts of Africa in order to have regular access to the internet. Plans are under way to deploy this technology in universities in Kenya, Malawi, Ghana and Zambia. Regulators in Uganda can follow the example of those countries where this project is being implemented and adopt it in the Ugandan setting. This would make internet access more affordable for many students.

Strengthening the use of ICT in teaching and learning

It is recommended that the use of ICT in teaching and learning by all academic staff should be encouraged as one of the strategies to address the challenge of high student numbers.

Focus on practical and learner-centred teaching of digital literacy courses

To improve the level of digital literacy skills among BLIS students, it is recommended that EASLIS should encourage academic staff to focus on teaching methods that enable students to practise what has been taught as much as possible and to learn independently.

Use of alternative sources of energy

It is recommended that EASLIS should explore the possibility of using alternative sources of power such as generators and solar energy to deal with the current situation of power outages, especially in block C. This would ensure that when there is a power outage, teaching can go on as scheduled and students can use the computer laboratories for their revision and independent studies.

This study has revealed that significant progress is being made in the endeavour to incorporate ICTs into teaching and learning at all levels in Uganda. Uganda generally has clearly formulated policies and strategies in place to promote digital literacy in educational institutions at all levels. These policies are wide ranging but tend to focus on the curriculum and professional development in particular. Furthermore, there is a growing awareness that providing equipment is insufficient to promote educational change. As a result, government and non-governmental bodies are emphasizing the development of teachers' skills and pedagogy as the key to effectively implementing curricula, to using ICT to enhance teaching and learning and to raising educational standards. The embellishment of policies on integrating ICT into education has led to increased government investment in ICT in all public universities, and most prominently in Makerere University, where pioneering use of ICT is well established. Available data on ICT infrastructure and usage is limited, however, and in many cases outdated. This means that the true picture is hard to assemble and trends cannot easily be tracked. From what we can glean and in our experience, exposure to ICT in institutions of higher learning remains low, especially in poorer, rural institutions. While the policies are highly ambitious, the limited evidence available of their implementation indicates that their status remains largely at a basic level in some institutions and in some aspects.

References

Aaron, J. (2012) The Authors Guild v. Hathitrust: A Way Forward for Digital Access to Neglected Works in Libraries, *SSRN Electronic Journal*, doi: 10.2139/ssrn.2205374.

ACRL (2015) Framework for Information Literacy for Higher Education, www.ala.org/acrl/standards/ilframework.

Adetimirin, A. E. (2011) ICT Literacy among Undergraduates in Nigerian Universities, *Education Information Technology*, **17**, 381–97, doi: 10.1007/s10639-011-9163-y.

ALA (American Library Association) (2012) *Core Values of Librarianship*, www.ala.org/advocacy/intfreedom/corevalues.

Ameen, K. and Gorman, G. E. (2008) Information and Digital Literacy: A Stumbling Block to Development? A Pakistan Perspective, *Library Management*, **30** (1/2), 99–112. doi: 10.1108/01435120910927565.

Andema, S., Kendrick, M. and Norton, B. (2013) Digital Literacy in Ugandan Teacher Education: Insights from a Case Study, *Reading & Writing*, **4** (1), doi: 10.4102/rw.v4i1.27.

Bawden, D. (2001) Information and Digital Literacies: A Review of Concepts, *Journal of Documentation*, **57** (2), 218–59, doi: 10.1108/EUM0000000007083.

Belshaw, J. A. D. (2011) What is Digital Literacy? Doctor of Education thesis, Durham University.

Brown, C., Czerniewicz, L., Huang, C-W. and Mayisela, T. (2016) Curriculum for Digital Education Leadership: A Concept Paper, Commonwealth of Learning, http://oasis.col.org/handle/11599/2442.

Buarki, J. H. (2010) Towards an Improvement of LIS Graduates' ICT Skills and Employability Needs in Kuwait, PhD thesis, Loughborough University.

Bukaliya, R. (2012) The Potential Benefits and Challenges of Internship Programmes in an ODL Institution: A Case for the Zimbabwe Open University, www.ijonte.org/FileUpload/ks63207/File/13a.bukaliya.pdf.

CETF (2008) Digital Literacy Pathways in California: ICT Leadership Council Action Plan Report, www.cetfund.org/wp-content/uploads/2019/09/Digital_Literacy_Pathways.pdf.

Cope, B. and Phillips, A. (2006) *The Future of the Book in the Digital Age*, Chandos Publishing.

Danner, R. B. and Pessu, O. A. C. (2013) A Survey of ICT Competencies among Students in Teacher Preparation Programmes at the University of Benin, Benin City, Nigeria, *Journal of Information Technology Education: Research*, **12**, 33–49, doi: 10.28945/1762.

Dreyfus, H. and Dreyfus, S. (1986) *Mind over Machine: The Power of Human Intuitive Expertise in the Era of the Computer*, Free Press.

Dreyfus, S. E. (2004) The Five-Stage Model of Adult Skill Acquisition, *Bulletin of Science, Technology & Society*, **24** (3), 177–81, doi: 10.1177/0270467604264992.

Eshet-Alkalai, Y. (2004) Digital Literacy: A Conceptual Framework for Survival Skills in the Digital Era, *Journal of Educational Multimedia and Hypermedia*, **13** (1), 93–106.

Farrell, G. (2007) *Survey of ICT and Education in Africa: Uganda Country Report*, www.infodev.org 5/11/2008.

Gunjal, A. B. and Ddamdhere, S. N. (2013) Application of Information and Computer Technology in Libraries, *International Journal of Computing Communications and Networking*, **2** (1), 6–11.

Hall-Ellis, S. and Grealy, D. (2013) The Dreyfus Model of Skill Acquisition: A Career Development Framework for Succession Planning and Management in Academic Libraries, *College & Research Libraries*, **74** (6), 587–603, doi: 10.5860/crl12–349.

Haneefa, M. K. and Abdul Shukkoor, C. K. (2010) Information and Communication Technology Literacy among Library Professionals in Calicut University, Kerala, *DESIDOC, Journal of Library & Information Technology*, **30** (6), 55–63.

Hashim, L. and Mokhtar, W. N. (2012) Preparing New Era Librarians and Information Professionals: Trends and Issues, *International Journal of Humanities and Social Science*, **2** (7) 151–6.

Ikwaba, P. D. and Uhomoibhi, J. (2013) Solar Electricity Generation: Issues of Development and Impact on ICT Implementation in Africa, *Campus-Wide Information System*, **31** (1), 46–62, doi: 10.1108/CWIS-05-2013-0018.

JISC (2015) *Developing Students' Digital Literacy*, www.jisc.ac.uk/guides/developing-students-digital-literacy.

Katz, I. R. and Mackline, A. S. (2007) Information Literacy: Integration and Assessment in Higher Education, *Systemics, Cybernetics and Informatics*, **5** (4), 703–20.

Kavulya, J. M. (2007) Training of Library and Information Science (LIS) Professionals in Kenya: A Needs Assessment, *Library Review*, **56** (3), 208–23.

Kigongo-Bukenya, I. M. N. and Musoke, M. G. N. (2011) LIS Education and Training in Developing Countries: Developments and Challenges with Special Reference to Southern Sudan and Uganda, paper delivered at the Satellite Pre-Conference of SIG LIS Education in Developing Countries, IFLA Puerto Rico, San Juan, 11–12 August.

Kinengyere, A. A. (2007) The Effect of Information Literacy on the Utilization of Electronic Information Resources in Selected Academic and Research Institutions in Uganda, *The Electronic Library*, **25** (3), 328–41, doi: 10.1108/02640470710754832.

Levinsen, K. T. (2011) Fluidity in the Networked Society: Self-initiated Learning as a Digital Literacy Competence, *The Electronic Journal of e-Learning*, **9** (1), 52–62, www.ejel.org.

MacGregor, L. H. Y. (2003) Students' Perceptions of Quality in Higher Education, *Quality Assurance in Education*, **11** (1), 15–20.

Magara, E., Bukirwa, J. and Kayiki, R. (2011) Knowledge Transfer through Internship: The EASLIS Experience in Strengthening the Governance Decentralisation Programme in Uganda, *African Journal of Library, Archives & Information Science*, **21** (1), 29–40.

Makerere University (2014) *Makerere University Fact Book 2013/2014.*

Makerere University (2022) www.mak.ac.ug.

Mathew, S. K. (2011) Impact of Information Communication Technology (ICT) on Professional Development and Educational Needs of Library Professionals in the Universities of Kerala, PhD thesis: Universities of Kerala.

Mohagheghzadeh, M. S., Mortazavi, S. M. J., Ghasempour, M. and Jarideh, S. (2014) The Impact of Computer and Information Communication Technology Literacy on the Academic Achievement of Medical and Dental Students at Shiraz University of Medical Sciences, *European Scientific Journal*, **10** (9), https://eujournal.org/index.php/esj/article/view/3061.

Moreira, M. A. (2010) Why Offer Information and Digital Competency Training in Higher Education, *Universitat Oberta de Catalunya*, **7** (2), 2–6, doi: 10.7238/rusc.v7i2.976.

Murray, M. C. and Pérez, J. (2014) Unraveling the Digital Literacy Paradox: How Higher Education Fails at the Fourth Literacy, *Issues in Informing Science and Information Technology*, **11**, 85–100, http://iisit.org/Vol11/IISITv11p085-100Murray0507.pdf.

Nalumaga, R. E. (2005) From Library Skills to Information Literacy: Considerations for Makerere University Library and Faculty. In Tusubira, F. F. and Mulira, N. K. (eds), *Universities: Taking a Leading Role in ICT Enabled Human Development*, Phanton Solutions.

National Council for Higher Education (2014) *Quality Assurance Framework for Universities and the Licensing Process for Higher Education Institutions.*

National Development Plan (2010) *2010/2011–2014/15*, National Planning Authority, www.npa.go.ug/wp-content/uploads/2020/08/NDPIII-Finale_Compressed.pdf.

Okello-Obura, C. (2012) Reforms at Makerere University in Uganda: Implications for Information Science with a Focus on Records and Archives Management Education in the Digital Era, *ESARBICA Journal*, **3**, 83–98.

Opati, D. O. (2013) The Use of ICT in Teaching and Learning at Makerere University: The Case of College of Education and External Studies, MPhil dissertation, University of Oslo.

Qureshi, I. A., Ilyas, K., Yasmin, R. and Whitty, M. (2012) Challenges of Implementing e-Learning in a Pakistani University, *Knowledge Management & e-Learning: An International Journal*, **4** (3), 310–24.

Rugumayo, A. (2010) *The Electricity Supply Situation in Uganda and Future Direction*, http://public.ises.org/PREA/2_Presentations/1_KeyNote/4_Rugamayo_EnergySupply.pdf

Thanuskodi, T. (2012) Use of e-Resources by the Students and Researchers of
    Faculty of Arts, Annamalai University, *International Journal of Library Science*, **1**
    (1), 1–7, doi: 10.5923/j.library.20120101.01.

Tilvawala, K., Myers, D. M. and Andrade, D. A. (2009) Information Literacy in
    Kenya, *The Electronic Journal on Information Systems in Developing Countries*, **39** (1),
    1–11, https://onlinelibrary.wiley.com/doi/abs/10.1002/j.1681-4835.2009.tb00275.x.

Togia, T., Korobili, S. and Malliari, A. (2012) Motivation to Learn and Learning
    Strategies: IT Courses in a Library and Information Science Department, *Library
    Review*, **61** (1), 41–56, doi: 10.1108/00242531211207415.

Twikirize, M. (2011) Education and Training of Information Professionals in a
    Changing Information Management Environment: A Case of the East African
    School of Library and Information Science, Makerere University. Unpublished
    Master's dissertation, Makerere University.

Twinomujuni, J. A. (2011) Problems in ICT Implementation in Selected Institutions
    of Higher Learning in Kabale District. Unpublished Master's dissertation,
    Makerere University.

UNESCO (2006) *Education for All Global Monitoring Report*.

9

ICT Training for Children with Hearing Impairment
Rachel Andisi

Abstract

The world is in the midst of an information technology revolution that is fundamentally changing the way government offices, organizations, educational institutions and individuals conduct business and interact with others. It is now becoming necessary for everyone to acquire skills in ICT for everyday activities. Learners with hearing impairment (HI) have been discriminated in most fields, including instruction in ICT skills, due to their limitations in spoken language. On the other hand, very few people have acquired sign language for communicating with hearing-impaired persons. As stated by Laurillard, Derrick and Doel (2016), developments in ICT necessitate the acquisition of digital skills by people with HI in order for them to be fully included in society. This calls for introduction of ICT programmes in schools, libraries and other learning institutions that include learners with HI. Kenya National Library Service Lusumu is endeavouring to bridge the gap of the digital divide and has carried out digital literacy training for learners with HI.

Keywords: Hearing impaired, inclusion, public libraries, digital literacy.

Introduction

Children with hearing impairment are part of the community and their inclusion in digital literacy programmes is important so that they will not be shut out. Digital literacy has taken the world by storm and anyone without the skills is left a thousand miles behind in development. The embracing of ICT in education has changed the way learning is done and has created a barrier to learners with hearing impairment (HI), who in most cases are not able to acquire the digital skills due to the oral communication barrier. Very few people have acquired sign language skills that enable direct communication to deaf people in the giving of instruction. In this respect, sign language emerges as a more dynamic language that removes barriers between deaf and hearing people. To bridge the gap between the hearing and the hearing impaired, there has to be a medium of communication, and ICT plays this role successfully (Lerslip, 2019, 2–4).

ICT training for children with HI is basically empowered by Kenya's policy on ICT mainstreaming, the main aim of which is to help citizens acquire technology skills through education and other training. This will give Kenyans the competitive edge that will enable them to compete globally in all sectors. Kenya's Vision 2030 identified eight sectors that require drastic reforms. One of these sectors is ICT. The sector has undergone tremendous growth, due to the fact that it is perceived to be the foundation enabler or booster of the social and economic development pillar. ICT, together with five other sectors, has contributed to Kenya's GDP by 57% (Ministry of Information, Communication and Technology, Kenya, 2016, 8–9). There is a great need and demand to develop human resource skills in ICT to support the socio-economic development (Etta and Aligula, 2006, 225–30). This is why ICT should be embraced and adopted by everyone, including learners with HI, globally.

Background

The population of Navakholo Constituency is approximately 137,165. It has an area of 257.9 sq km (KNBS, 2019). Navakholo sub-county has five wards, 54 primary schools, 13 secondary schools and one technical college. Lusumu area in Navakholo sub-county is inhabited by a farming community that practises sugar cane farming, maize farming and the rearing of domestic animals. Sugar cane is the main cash crop in the area and hence this crop has dominated most farms. This crop takes almost 24 months to be harvested, which in the end increases hunger and poverty levels, since farms are not big enough to accommodate other, short-term crops. Despite the poverty in the community, families strive to educate their children, with discrimination against girls and children who may have disabilities and/or who are slow in learning. In times when resources are limited, these categories of people are left out. It has been generally observed that in Lusumu community, boys are given priority for education. However, as is evidenced in a report by the Kenya Ministry of Education (2020), while there is a slightly higher enrolment of boys than girls in primary schools, in secondary schools the disparity is in favour of girls. The literacy level is high, as can be seen from the operations and activities they are involved in. The schools in the community are mixed (boys and girls) and are densely populated, which could be adduced as evidence of the high literacy level of the community (Ministry of Education, 2020).

People with HI in Lusumu community are given the least priority in terms of education. They are perceived as simple-minded people, with no consideration of the fact that this group of people have at some time in their lives lost the ability to perceive sounds and communicate through oral language. According to Baker (2006), hearing loss has a continual impact on the daily learning experience. This tends to be one of the greatest barriers to knowledge acquisition and utilization, hence leading to poor living standards for people with this condition. According to UNESCO (2009, 23), access to education should be universal for all children, including those with HI. All means should be use to advocate for inclusive education, as this will help to identify the individual needs of learners and help them to overcome barriers that in many respects prevent them from reaching their full potential (BECTa, 2000a).

Kenya National Library Service (KNLS) Board is a statutory body of the Government of Kenya, established by an Act of Parliament, Cap 225 of the Laws of Kenya, in April 1965. The Board is currently under the Ministry of Sports, Culture and Arts. The Board is also subject to the provisions of the State Corporations Act, Cap 446 of the Laws of Kenya. KNLS is mandated to promote, establish, equip, manage and maintain libraries in Kenya. It is through this mandate that KNLS Lusumu was established. This community library is situated in Kakamega County, Navakholo sub-county, and Bunyala community of the larger Luhya community in the western part of Kenya. There are five secondary schools and five primary schools within a radius of ten kilometres of the library. The library currently serves a population of over 20,000, adults and children included. The library also serves children in the neighbourhood school for hearing-impaired children. This school is an ordinary public primary school for normal learners but it has accommodated children with HI, providing them with special education. They follow the curriculum provided by the Ministry of Education to ensure that they receive a mainstream education, as against the use of a special curriculum for those with special needs.

The provision of information for development through the national and public library service network enables people to fight poverty, deprivation and illiteracy and thus supports the Government's reading and recovery programme. Through various reading campaigns, KNLS provides opportunities for communities to enhance their reading and information-seeking habits, therefore building and sustaining literacy as well as lifelong learning. In its endeavour to serve communities in Kenya satisfactorily, KNLS has collaborated with different organizations such as Communication Authority of Kenya (CAK), BAI, World Reader, Microsoft, Digital Opportunity Trust (DOT Kenya) and EIFL, among others, to achieve efficiency and reliability in the provision of information using modern technologies. ICT strategically drives, fortifies and supports information provision. This marks out the literacy training that is necessary for the achievement of the national and global agenda.

Digital literacy training

Digital training is becoming paramount to individuals in all sectors as the world embraces the digital era. According to Bhattacharjee and Deb (2016, 1–6), it has been observed that most teachers of 35 years and older lack digital skills, due to lack of exposure in their initial career training. This has resulted in a shortage of teachers with digital training in learning institutions, hence slowing down the whole process of digital growth. Research conducted by Wakhaya (2010) reports that 32.1% of teachers of learners with HI are computer literate, while 67.9% are computer illiterate, which is a hindrance to digital development in schools. The Government of Kenya initiated a project on digital literacy which comprised ICT integration in primary education. The main aim of this project was to align the use of ICT with teaching and learning for lower primary pupils from Grade 1 to Grade 3. The project was initiated to ensure improvement in ICT infrastructure, develop available digital content and help to build teachers' ICT skills in teachers. The project also helped to ensure that all primary schools in the Republic of Kenya acquired ICT devices for online learning (Ministry of Education, 2016). The project was not fully implemented as envisaged by the Ministry of Education, due to some internal barriers. This gave some public libraries room to explore how to fill the gap in digital training for teachers and students.

According to the statistics report given by KNBS (2019) on ICT literacy among citizens and people residing in the country, it is assumed that there is a high level of digital training in Kenya, which emerged due to the mushrooming of training facilities in various places. Some of these facilities are government institutions, individual institutions and cyber cafés that have flooded the country. Kenya's national ICT policy also addresses development gaps related to women, youth, rural and other disadvantaged groups, including people with HI. However, none of these development thrusts and policies have played a positive role in running training on digital skills for persons with HI. This may be due to lack of skills in communication with the deaf community. Through the KNLS Board initiative to train its staff in ICT and sign language, communication with the deaf community is now easy, and hence ICT training for the hearing impaired has been introduced. In Kenya there are institutions that train individuals in sign language and KNLS has taken advantage of this to train at least one or two staff from each library branch to ensure that inclusive library and information services are provided to all.

KNLS Lusumu community library took its cue from this and is committed to providing its user community with high-quality accessible services and sustainable programmes as permitted by the available resources. The library strives to provide access to information in response to the expressed and observable needs of the community. To this end, the availability of adequate and relevant information and communication technologies is an integral part of KNLS's service delivery.

New and advanced technologies that have been incorporated into service provision have changed the demands and expectations of library users, and hence improved service delivery in most library institutions. The Internet of Things, cloud computing and advanced mobile technologies have completely changed the way libraries operate. This has resulted in more innovations and new, interactive, customer-focused services. Among these innovations is the ICT training that is ongoing for pupils with HI.

ICT is providing first-hand experience that supplements and extends students' work without them being dependent on text to formulate their ideas. Technology provides solutions, supports learners' performance and achievement, and hence leads them to be independent in day-to-day living. Masson (2000) states that learners who have access to appropriate information technology are more likely to be successful in their education programmes. Modern technologies are used to develop the language experiences of learners with HI without necessarily depending on the spoken word. They develop descriptive language that helps them to describe, compare and contrast objects (Egaga and Aderibigbe, 2015). This encourages them to extend their use of language and their understanding of concepts as they plan and carry out their work. Communication between teacher and learner is facilitated through digital platforms. Some of these platforms enable class assessment, tutoring, management of assignments and many more activities within the school environment (Richards, 2004, 43).

In an effort to train learners with HI on how to use modern technologies to improve their learning experience, KNLS Lusumu community library identified pathways for equipping them with digital skills. The skills acquired through the digital training came in handy for all our library learners during the COVID-19 lockdown, which affected normal learning. Following recommendations from UNESCO, schools, universities and colleges were closed throughout Kenya, with the aim of curbing the further spread of the coronavirus. The Government of Kenya, like other countries, initiated alternative learning pathways whereby teaching was done remotely on digital platforms sponsored by the Kenya Ministry of Education (Gichuhi and Kalista, 2022, 16–19).

Some of the digital training conducted at KNLS Lusumu community library includes:

- basic computer applications
- multimedia such as text, graphics, animations, video
- whiteboards
- data logging
- control software
- CD-ROM
- Microsoft Academy.

Most of the training is conducted Monday to Friday from 3pm to 5pm by library staff together with a class teacher from the school that is in charge of special education. Currently, this training has been done for 20 learners and three teachers from the library's neighbouring school. The training has exposed learners to suitable technology applications and how to use them, opening up opportunities for being creative and innovative with technology. Learners are equipped with the skills to create, access, save and manage documents by themselves and those with HI are given an equal opportunity to communicate with friends and family members with ease, like other people.

Basic computer training

This entails an introduction to computer applications and concepts. It covers the basics of computer hardware, software and networking and learners develop skills in Windows, Microsoft Office and web page creation (Sinha and Sinha, 2011). They learn about the safety of computers and ethical issues pertaining to usage and access to sites. The basic training is provided to anyone with an interest in digital literacy, but first priority is given to those with HI. There is greater take-up of training during school holidays, since learners have more time then to attend training sessions. Positive outcomes have been experienced; for example, one male with HI has opened a cyber café, with support from an area Member of Parliament, while another male with HI has found employment. The training is described in the following sub-sections.

Computer hardware

In order for learners to master or relate well to the training, it is essential first to learn about all the computer hardware and peripherals and their functions. This helps learners understand the input and output devices that they will be working with during training. Training is given about monitors, mouse, central processing unit (CPU), keyboard, computer data storage, sound card, speakers, graphics card and motherboard, among others (Sinha and Sinha, 2011). HI learners are also taken through a set of simple computer maintenance skills so as to extend the life span of the computers used for training. Training is given on how to install antivirus software, run computer maintenance, backup files, keeping keyboards clean, cleaning the screen, removing dust from vents and fans and covering the computers, among other things.

System software

This is the operating system that controls the hardware and all other software. It is essential for learners to know how operating systems work, how to boot the computer, utility software, device drivers and firmware. One of the common operating systems is Microsoft Windows. This course is very short, but complicated for hearing impaired learners due to their disability.

Windows

Learners are taught how to navigate from one program to another. All of the training is delivered in the Windows environment.

Communication and information literacy

ICT has created new platforms for communication and users are coming up with new information demands that require access to the internet and other ICT services. The present challenge is how to identify needs and locate, evaluate and effectively use information to solve daily problems as stated by Sinha and Sinha, (2011). According to BECTa (2001), using ICT and accessing digital information is a lifelong learning process, as systems are continually being upgraded and information is updated regularly. This aspect raises a need for consistency in training activities so as to build a knowledgeable and skilled workforce that can handle the growth in technology. Henceforth, ICT has made it easy for students with HI to communicate with others through e-mail, WhatsApp, Facebook, Twitter, Telegram and so on – the list is endless. Further in BECTa's observation, it is posted that clicking on a digital link on a website gives a student with HI equal access to information and thus empowers them to be independent in information seeking. This also enables them to access employment advertisements, sponsorship programmes and, most importantly, to become information literate.

Computer ethics

It is important for users to learn and understand the ethics of computer use (Onunga and Shah, 2005). The computer ethics training includes:

- privacy concerns such as computer hacking, malware, data protection and anonymity of use;
- intellectual property rights, which includes copyright, plagiarism, cracking and software licences;
- effects on society, including avoiding harm to other users, honesty and trustworthiness, contributing positively to society and ensuring human wellbeing.

Networks and security

Training is given on physical security to protect hardware, access security to control use of the network and data security to prevent loss of data. The instructors take the learners through this course in order to equip them with basic online detective skills. Learners are trained on how to create strong passwords and install anti-virus software on computers and laptops so as to minimize computer hacking.

Logging onto the internet creates a data history of activities during a specific period. This record of events helps the user to ensure the security of documents and monitor login activities so as to avoid suspicious and malicious activities. The login history allows viruses to be traced and quickly blocked to avoid them being spread to other computers. Onunga and Shah (2005, 315–327) observe that the risks associated with network and security range from information hacking and sharing with unauthorized persons, to deletion of information and exposure to viruses. Skills in network management provide the hearing impaired with opportunities to be employed as network managers or administrators. They can get employment in banks or institutions and organizations that deal with people's personal information details.

Microsoft Word

Learning Microsoft (MS) Word is a basic step for any ICT learner. Children with HI are taken through the process of typing and saving documents in different formats on a computer or laptop. MS Word allows easy creation or publication of content. Learners with HI are able to create letters, business cards, brochures, wedding cards, etc. MS Word is easily integrated with other programs like Excel and PowerPoint and so it is easy to copy and paste from other programs. With the spell checker tool, learners can improve their spelling and grammar (BECTa, 2000b, 2). Learners with HI are empowered through ICT to make use of language and gain skills that enable them to seek employment. In the library, all learners including those with HI must gain skills in MS Word in order to continue on to other packages. Learners with HI can use their Word skills to get employment as:

- data entry officers
- minutes compilers
- online assistants
- book editors
- book formatters
- customer service assistants.

HTML

HTML has standardized markup coded language that is widely used and found on the internet. It is used to create web pages that are descriptive in structure and also consists of a series of elements that dictates to the browser on how to display the content with labels, i.e. headings, paragraphs, links and quotes among others (Astari, 2022). With the power of HTML which is beginner-friendly and has a shallow learning curve, learners with HI in Lusumu community library have been enabled to do the following with ease:

- Web development – learners make use of HTML code to design the way a browser will display web page elements. These elements include files, text, media and hyperlinks. The accessibility of rich internet applications is an element that supports a responsive design for the HI in the improvement of content on a web page (Ubah, 2021).
- Web documentation – learners are able to organize and format documents easily with HTML in the same way as Microsoft Word (Educba, 2020).
- Internet navigation – it is easy for HI learners to navigate and insert links, paragraphs and sections between related pages and websites using

tags and attributes. This aspect gives added support to the HI to access multimedia options, style sheets, facilities and documents that are helpful to their learning process (Sinha and Sinha, 2011).

Microsoft Excel

These is a spreadsheets program for performing calculations and data analysis (Onunga and Shah, 2005). A person skilled in this program has a greater advantage over those trained in other digital programs, as these skills are in high demand by employers. KNLS Lusumu library trained two of their learners with HI on this application.

Microsoft Access

Access is a relational database that can work with large amounts of information. A person with skills in Microsoft Access, is equipped for job opportunities such as quantitative analyst, IT assistant, IT solutions developer, maintenance administrator, sorting and delivery officer, among others (Baker, 2006). Hearing-impaired people with Microsoft Access skills can become self-employed.

Microsoft PowerPoint

This program is suitable for presentations in the classroom, office meetings, conferences or other gatherings. This program is suitable for use by persons with HI who are able to read, as information is generally presented in a way that is easy to understand with minimal explanations. Career opportunities for people with PowerPoint skills include office manager, executive manager, customer service officer, sales associate, etc.

Multimedia

Multimedia comprises media presentations such as images, clips, videos, text, graphics, animations and audios used to relay information to the intended audience. Multimedia presentations are mostly in visual formats and hence persons with HI can benefit from them. The hearing impaired in Lusumu library are mostly being trained on video clips, images, animation and text. Learners can earn some income through video clips uploaded to the ViuSasa application, a Kenyan digital platform that supports and displays products and services for entertainment purposes. The more views and subscriptions, the more a person gains financially. Multimedia helps in data storage, giving easy access to information and a link to the data through indexing. The persons with HI get an opportunity to explore their techno-skills, and gain the added advantage of presenting their information through technology. The chance for competition in a unique way with other hearing persons is created for them and this also creates the opportunity of coming up with interesting and appealing presentations.

Multimedia is handy for business promotions, for entertainment purposes and for emphasizing important information for public consumption. Advances in technology mean that formerly dull ways of presenting information have been taken over by lively presentations in multimedia.

Whiteboards

Whiteboards are especially handy for instructors during sessions with learners with HI. In Africa this is a new technology concept, but in advanced countries they were in use as long ago as the 1990s (Firmin and Genesi, 2012, 9). The combination of smartboard and computer creates an interactive platform for hearing impaired persons. The technology uses touch screens and special pens, and writing can be erased with ordinary erasers as well as by simply clicking on 'clear'. The boards come in various sizes and colours and are also resistant to moisture, which makes them durable.

The smartboard is connected to a desktop computer and is mainly used to display images and videos. Websites can be accessed through the internet, and this enhances the learning process. With this technology, hearing impaired learners can easily save their notes electronically for later use. This has reduced cases where learners lose their notebooks and the information they contain (Times Higher Education, 2004).

Hearing impaired learners find this technology very convenient in training programmes. Fingertips can be used to write on the smartboard and the instructor's hands can be free to use sign language. Instruction for persons with HI can be delivered easily through this visual medium. It is suitable for training on basic computer applications. In brief, the use of whiteboards is much to be recommended for learners with HI, due to the following:

- good for presentations;
- retains the attention of learners;
- very interesting;
- enables sharing of information with others;
- access to information with a touch of a finger;
- available in various sizes and colours;
- resistant to moisture;

- easy to adjust font size for learners;
- hearing impaired learn skills with which they can easily compete with others in the workplace;
- instructors are able to face the learners and remain in visual range while using sign language;
- facility to write in electronic ink on any computer application;
- enhances the learning experience for learners with HI.

Control software

This is software installed on a computer, laptop or mobile phone that is used to convert the spoken word to text, allowing persons with HI to read and follow a communication that is being relayed orally. The user controls the computer functions to enable the system to detect the human voice and automatically make the conversion to text. Learners with HI undergoing digital training are trained to follow the instruction by reading the text rather than depending on lip reading (BECTa, 2000a). This technology is enhancing the training programme running in the Lusumu community library, where the beneficiaries of training in this control software are the nine library staff, three teachers and 20 children with HI. The aim of training both staff and teachers is to ensure continuity of the training programme. Onunga and Shah (2005) state that control software training provides an essential lifetime skill to learners with HI, who can take advantage of its fast-growing and vast development platform, which fosters employment opportunities. This skill is beneficial for both employees and employers for easy and understandable communication. The platform provides a critical means of communication that should be embraced by all for the inclusion of learners with HI.

CD-ROM

Hearing impaired learners who turn up for the digital training programme in KNLS Lusumu are taken through the process of how to use and manage CD-ROMs. CD-ROMs have a large data storage capacity that enables the distribution of most types of software. They also help the hearing impaired to access information easily in a visual format. Using CD-ROMs is an essential skill for learners to be equipped with in digital training. Hearing impaired learners are trained on how to install software from CDs, and how to store and retrieve information.

Data logging

Data logging is most suitable for large amounts of data that are to be collected for analytical purposes for over a specified period of time. Uses of data logging include weather analysis and monitoring the temperatures of machines. The process of tracking and storing information is done by special sensors that produce an analogue or digital signal (BECTa, 2000a, 2). This saves on time manual monitoring and also enables a large amount and high quality of data to be gathered over a period of time. Data logging requires little verbal communication, as the machines generate the required data periodically as per the settings. This is a skill on which the library has plans to train the hearing impaired.

Microsoft Academy

In many collaborations by KNLS to streamline digital in-service provision, Microsoft Inc. came up with a free online tutor on some office applications for library users in all KNLS libraries. Clients were required to open user accounts, since this is an individual learning medium. Certification was done by Microsoft Academy on completion of the programme, which was done in segments. The course offered training in Word, Excel, PowerPoint, Access, Outlook, OneNote, Share print and Office 365, among other applications. Hearing impaired learners, with help from library staff, were encouraged to access this training when the normal digital programme was not on. This threw up many challenges for the hearing impaired, as most of the tutorials were in audio video and not in sign language. This programme with Microsoft Inc. unfortunately came to an end just as the learners were getting acquainted with it.

Digital inclusion

Inclusion is a way of ensuring that there is no discrimination or marginalization of individuals in a society. Digital inclusion gives equal rights to access and use of ICTs to all people, regardless of their status. Barriers that may hinder access to and the use of modern technology are swept away to ensure equitability in resources. The inclusive engagement of the hearing impaired in different ICT activities and programmes connects them to a brighter future that provides an opening to equal competition in all sectors.

The direction in which the world is heading now requires all individuals to acquire skills in digital technology. It is becoming a major requirement for the hearing impaired to acquire, upgrade and improve on ICT skills in order to be relevant in any field. The marginalization of the hearing impaired in communities and societies in matters of educational, social, mental and economic status has to come to an end. The main agenda for discussion in the Disability Summit held on 3 December 2018 in London, hosted by the United Nations, was inclusion in education, economic empowerment and technological innovations (UNDP, 2018).

KNLS is mainstreaming inclusive technology in its provision for the hearing impaired. The major aspect of digital inclusion is to engage youth in activities that will help in the Sustainable Development Goals (SDGs). Persons with impairment feel socially discriminated if they are separated from others, and the end result is illiteracy accompanied with low skills, which is a factor in low self-esteem. Facilitating modern technology to the hearing impaired in learning institutions and libraries is one way of addressing equity for all people (UNESCO, 2002).

KNLS as a government public institution is doing all it can to bridge the gap of the digital divide as well as to limit the discrimination that people with disabilities might face. To ensure that service provision is inclusive of all, there is clear signage in all library areas, staff are being trained in Kenyan sign language, braille and IT and awareness of people with disabilities. According to Playforth (2004), public libraries should address barriers that may interfere with service provision to people with HI. There should be good lighting and visual signage and instructions to assist self-service by the HI. At service points there should be sign language interpreters.

Projection into the future: recommendations

The following recommendations are made for the use of ICT to improve education and learning for the hearing impaired.

1   In all institutions that have learners with HI, it is essential for teachers to have ICT skills. Digital skills have become a necessity for teachers and trainers in order to give the required support in the development of digital skills of learners (Laurillard, Derrick and Doel, 2016, 9).

2   All schools with hearing impaired learners should acquire modern communication technology to enable smooth learning. Digital technology has opened up many ways of communicating with the HI, and these should be taken advantage of in the education sector so as to improve the lives of deaf people. There is a great need and demand for schools to invest more in modern technology, including by creating, maintaining and developing skills. Supporting and developing digital literacy is a worthy aim for both teachers and learners.

3   Partners need to come up with strategies for equipping libraries and

institutions with hearing impaired learners with modern technology so as to enhance digital training. ICT makes a positive contribution to raising educational, social and economic standards for persons with HI by building their self-esteem and raising their motivation to read, write and communicate (BECTa, 2001). There is a great need for funding for equipment such as whiteboards, computers and internet access so as to enable the smooth running of training programmes in schools and libraries.

4   Training on ICT and its use is needed for public library staff, through seminars, workshops and conferences. These platforms should provide opportunities to share ideas and experiences and to discuss ways forward for ICT inclusivity training programmes in all public libraries. More advocacy for digital inclusion should be addressed to all stakeholders.

5   Learners with HI should be engaged in ICT programmes for inclusivity in the era of digital literacy.

Conclusion

This chapter has provided an overview of digital training programmes for learners with HI in a public library in Kenya. Much investment in ICT has created opportunities for the inclusion of all learners, in spite any physical challenges they may face (Playforth, 2004). ICT has been adopted and is being implemented in public libraries in Kenya in order to bridge the gap of discrimination that was previously experienced by learners with HI in education and employment and in social gatherings, among others. The initiative of public libraries to train persons with HI in ICT skills has a great impact on the community and the nation at large, as has been realized during the COVID-19 pandemic.

ICT enhances the learning of all students, especially of those with HI. The Government should give special attention to these special learners through the Ministry of Education and related institutions that provide supplementary education, that is, libraries. When ICT is used adequately and appropriately, learning outcomes are bound to be enhanced; the classroom participation of learners with HI is boosted and hence they have more interest in learning (Lerslip, 2019). Language development in learners with HI has been experienced in the KNLS initiative. The incorporation of visual media with pictures, signs or text on screen allows learners to acquire general knowledge of the use of language, not necessarily depending on the spoken word, which is already a great challenge for them.

References

Astari, S. (2022) What is HTML? Hypertext Markup Language Basics Explained, www.hostinger.com/tutorials/what-is-html.

Baker, C. M. (2006) *Hearing Disabilities in Children*, John Wiley and Son.

Bhattacharjee, B. and Deb, K. (2016) Role of ICT in 21st Century's Teacher Education, *International Journal of Education and Information Studies*, **6** (1), 1–6.

BECTa (2000a) Hearing Impairment and ICT, http://tim-brosnan.net/ITPGCE/coursematerials/SEN/docs/hearing.

BECTa (2000b) Learning Difficulties and ICT, http://tim-brosnan.net/ITPGCE/coursematerials/SEN/docs/learningdiffs.pdf.

BECTa (2001) Hearing Impairment and ICT, http://becta.org.uk/technology/infosheets.

Educba (2020) Introduction to Uses of HTML, www.educba.com/uses-of-html.

Egaga, P. I. and Aderibigbe, S. A. (2015) *Efficacy of Information and Communication Technology in Enhancing Learning Outcomes of Students with Hearing Impairment in Ibadan*, https://files.eric.ed.gov/fulltext/EJ1081324pdf.

Etta, F. E. and Aligula, E. (2006) Conclusion: Mainstreaming ICT in Kenya: The Strategic Options. In Outa, G., Etta, F. E. and Aligula, E. (eds), *Mainstreaming ICT: Research Perspectives from Kenya*, Mvule.

Firmin, M. W. and Genesi, D. J. (2012) History and Implementation of Classroom Technology, *3rd World Conference on Learning, Teaching and Education Leadership (WCLTA – 2012) Cedarville*.

Gichuhi, L. and Kalista, J. (2022) The Kenya Ministry of Education's Response to the COVID-19 Pandemic, https://unesdoc.unesco.org/ark:/48223/pf0000381092/PDF/381092eng.pdf.multi.

KNBS (2019) Kenya Population and Housing Census Reports, 21 February, www.knbs.or.ke/?p=5732.

Laurillard, D., Derrick, J. and Doel, M. (2016) Building Digital Skills in the Further Education Sector, Government Office for Science, https://assets.publishing.service.gov.uk/government/uploads/system/uploads/attachment_data/file/634181/Skills_and_lifelong_learning_-_digital_skills_in_further_education_-_Laurillard_-_final.pdf.

Laws of Kenya (1965) Parliament Act cap. 225, Kenya National Library Service, https://sportsheritage.go.ke/culture-heritage/Kenya-national-library.

Lerslip, T. (2019) Use of Information Technology for Communication and Learning in Secondary School Students with a Hearing Disability, *MDPI Journal of Education Science*, **9** (1), doi: 10.3390/educsci9010057.

Masson, T. O. (2000) *Technological Intervention in Education*, Houghton Mifflin Co.

Ministry of Education, Kenya (2016) *Digital Learning Programme*, www.education.go.ke/index.php/programmes/digital-learning-programme.

Ministry of Education, Kenya (2020) *Basic Education Statistical Booklet*, 15.

Ministry of Information, Communication and Technology, Kenya (2016) *National Information, Communication and Technology, Kenya*, 8–9.

Onunga, D. J. and Shah, R. (2005) *Computer Studies*, Mariwa.

Playforth, S. (2004) *Inclusive Library Services for Deaf People: An Overview*, https://onlinelibrary.wiley.com/doi/full/10.1111/j.1740–3324.2004.00518.x

Richards, C. (2004) Using ICT Effectively with Deaf Children, *The Guardian*, 22 March, www.theguardian.com/education/2004/Mar/22/elearning.technology.

Sinha, P. K. and Sinha, P. (2011) *Computer Fundamentals: Concepts Systems and Applications*, https://learnengineering.in/computer-fundamentals-by-p-k-sinha-free-download.

Times Higher Education (2004) Transforming Education through Technology, 1 May.

Ubah, K. (2021) Learn Web Development Basics – HTML, CSS and JavaScript Explained for Beginners, www.freecodecamp.org/news/html-css-and-javascript-explained-for-beginners.

UNDP (2018) Disability Inclusive Development: Disability Summit, 3 December.

UNESCO (2002) *Information and Communication in Education. A Curriculum for Schools and Programs for Teachers' Development*.

UNESCO (2009) *Towards Inclusive Education for Children with Disabilities: A Guideline*.

Wakhaya, M. N. (2010) *Influence of the Use of Information and Communication Technology on Teaching and Learning Mathematics in Secondary Schools: A Case of Nairobi Province, Kenya*, www.semanticscholar.org/paper/Influence-of-the-use-of-Information-and-Technology-Wakhaya/782fc41a860aee36646bffdd96702cac064cd697.

10

The Role of Communities in Driving the Acquisition of Digital Literacy Skills in the 21st Century

Joshua Onaade Ojo

Abstract

Global changes and the growth of information and communication technologies have influenced largely every community in the world. The role of communities in driving the attainment of digital literacy skills in the 21st century is highly essential if no nation or group is to be left behind. This chapter focuses on the various issues surrounding the attainment of digital literacy skills, the roles of the community in providing digital materials, information literacy and education, as well as the roles of libraries in developing digital literacy skills through library instruction and user education.

Keywords: Community, digital literacy skills, 21st century, indigenous knowledge, public libraries.

Introduction

The community is one of the building blocks of a nation. Sociologically, a community is defined as a group of people who follow a social structure within a society (culture, norms, values, status). They may work together to organize social life within a particular place, or they may be bound by a sense of belonging sustained across time and space. Beyond this, the community has also been defined as a social unit with communality of norms, religion, values, customs or identity. A community may share a sense of place situated in a given geographical area or in virtual space through communication platforms (Barton and Trusting, 2005). In the context of this work, the community is regarded as a group of people with diverse characteristics who are linked by social ties, share common perspectives and engage in joint actions in a geographical location or setting.

Beyond these definitions, there are communities within cities as well as within workplaces. Community does not just denote those who live in rural areas; rather, it has a wider meaning and connotation. Community is also a set of meaningful social connections in a group of any size where members have things in common. Dwelling extensively on this notion of community, Douglas (2010) suggests positive aspects of the concept which perceive the belongingness and collective will within communities as a 'good thing' that has capacity to improve the individual wellbeing of members. Community has emotional overtones, implying familiarity, social and emotional cohesion and commitment. It implies a degree of attachment and belonging which offers a common sense of identity.

The focus of this chapter is on the role communities play in driving the attainment of digital literacy skills in the 21st century. With the outlined diverse definitions of what a community is, it is clear that the community as a whole has what it takes to drive the inculcation of digital literacy skills either in the rural or urban areas so far as the identified community has similar social, religious and/or cultural characteristics and they can take collective actions on issues that affect them. This is because commitment to shared common goals, values, beliefs, behaviour and identification of challenges has a great probability of encouraging a community to embrace collective responsibility in understanding the importance of digital skills and working towards creating an enabling environment for acquiring those skills.

Collective responsibility as a philosophical concept can be viewed positively to imply that what galvanizes a community to identify a challenge and to explore avenues for filling that gap is the belief that it will benefit everyone when solutions are provided, because in one way or another they were responsible for the existence of the challenge. It spurs a community to take account of their common problems and investigate how they can be solved in order to become a better community.

However, Giubilini and Levy (2018) argue that collective responsibility eventually boils down to individuals or a section of the community taking moral responsibility as agents that influence or drive change through taking actions that could be attributed to acts of the whole community.

Rural communities are regarded as backward, unexposed areas characterized by a lack of basic social amenities, infrastructure and services, which drives the younger members to move to urban areas to enjoy the good things of life. Thus, the benefits of information communication technology (ICT), which has transformed the way individuals, groups and societies communicate, learn, work and govern, have been mostly lacking in most underserved communities in the rural areas. That notwithstanding, the youth in many African communities yearn for skills that will assist them to engage with information in online spaces, which will in turn empower them to learn about opportunities for a better life and how to advantageously compete globally. For many, public libraries are agencies through which they can explore the possibilities of gaining digital skills that will not only enhance their knowledge but also contribute to their abilities to make use of other technological tools in the future.

Conceptualizing digital literacy skills

Gilster (1997) defined digital literacy skills in educational terms – in essence recognizing the fundamental but revolutionary uniqueness of the internet and identifying the digitally literate student as having a specific set of information skills (e.g. evaluation, searching) applied to text and multimedia information found on the internet and situated in a formal, school-based learning context. In other words, to be 'digitally literate' in this way encompasses issues of cognitive authority, safety and privacy, creative, ethical and responsible use and reuse of digital media, among other abilities. However, in recent times the definition of digital literacy has been broadened to include the awareness and understanding of how to engage responsibly in online spaces (World Literacy Foundation, 2020).

Statement of the problem

An average community in a developing country lacks the basic infrastructure that may support access to ICT, which is the basis for the acquisition of digital literacy skills. This is different from what obtains in urban areas, where ICT has been the life wire of various categories of people. This creates a huge digital gap. This disparity is a challenge that needs to be addressed in order for communities in rural areas to access opportunities online. Due to the low level of literacy and low earning power of the generality of rural dwellers, many of them do not have personal computers or mobile phones for accessing the internet. Nigeria, which is made up of 36 states and 774 local government areas, has many people in urban areas who own or have access to ICT facilities, who have the digital skills that enable them to navigate online spaces and who can cope with the high cost of data, as middle- and upper-class members of society. This helps them to fully participate in the digital information economy, unlike those in the rural communities (Ekenimoh, 2021). Definitely, this needs to be addressed so that those in the rural communities can have access to life-changing skills and opportunities. The challenge is exacerbated when there is lack of collective responsibility in communities.

Literature review

Digital literacy is conceptualized as 'the ability to understand and use information in multiple formats from a wide range of sources when it is presented via computers' (Gilster, 1997, 1). The term has evolved as technologies have provided ever-increasing capabilities for organizations, individuals and society in general. It now incorporates elements derived from other terms such as ICT literacy (the ability to use digital technologies), information literacy (recognizing when information is needed, and the ability to locate, evaluate and effectively use it) (Lankshear and Knobel, 2008), the ability to engage in constant interactions with digital technologies (e.g. using Facebook to communicate with friends), understanding how technology works (such as being able to purchase a computer to specification) and the role of technology in daily operations (including online shopping or accessing learning resources).

For a community to perform its role in the attainment of digital literacy skills, it must be empowered enough to understand the importance of those skills and the need to assume collective responsibility in seeking how to ensure that community members acquire them. This will lead the community to seek and identify agencies that would assist in this regard.

In any community, therefore, there is a need for institutions that can provide the space and ICT facilities – as well as the training on how to use them – so that community members can engage with information and opportunities online. Public libraries have the capacity to play an important role in creating inclusive, digitally literate communities via the provision of online information on health, employment, education and so on, as well as digital literacy training programmes.

The role of communities in the attainment of digital literacy skills

A community can be defined as a set of meaningful social connections in a group of any size where members have something in common. A community is social. It is also a web of relationships that provides a sense of belonging, connection, communication and interaction in all facets of life. With regard to communication, the community can improve the wellbeing of its members through the provision of digital literacy skills relevant to the 21st century. When a community is able to acquire digital literacy skills, individual wellbeing is strengthened through knowledge, intentionality and enlightenment (Kegley, 1997). The process of engaging and building connections within a community is described as 'building community' (Kelly and Sewell, 1998). A sense of community connection through networking can be built among members either accidentally or via a deliberate and informed process. This could be a systematic and deliberate community building through the teaching and acquisition of skills that involves thinking, feeling and doing things that can improve the community through innovations from information communication technologies, including digital literacy skills.

For any community to develop in the 21st century, the members of that community have a collective responsibility to understand that they have many roles to play. The United Nations' Sustainable Development Goals (SDGs) include, among others, ending poverty and hunger, fighting inequality, having access to clean water and sanitation, good jobs and economic growth, and peace and justice. Most importantly, the idea of leaving no one behind is the underlying principle, which implies mass/community movement or attainment of the goals, not just individualistic wellbeing and development (Global Goals, 2018). These goals serve as pillars for community development upon which the attainment of digital literacy can be achieved. However, good as these goals might be, they may become a figment of the imagination and unattainable if the citizens of any nation lack digital information literacy skills (Eyong, 2016).

This implies that diverse strategies need to be employed to facilitate the acquisition of digital literacy skills by different sections/members of communities, so that the SDGs will become realities at the individual level as well as at the community level. Literacy is a tool for individual and social transformation. It is an important tool for development; hence, Ayodele and Adedokun (2012) described literacy as the function of all education and lifelong learning. It is a veritable tool for the development of individuals and of society at large. However, literacy, which used to be traditionally defined as the ability to read, write and engage in numeracy, has gone beyond those levels in this age of technological innovation. Because literacy is profound to human and historical development, it should be taken beyond the traditional level to include the ability to read, write and perform other tasks in digital spaces (Adedokun, 2019).

Making communities realize how improved literacy and attainment of digital literacy can contribute to economic growth, poverty reduction and the promotion of democracy, which is very germane at the grassroots level, is most critical. Generally, the community is known for its traditional way of doing things. However, traditional literacy, for instance, which embodies the art of reading, writing and numeracy, would not be adequate to meet the present development needs and those of the future. This necessitates the role of communities in the attainment of digital literacy skills.

One of the ingredients necessary for the attainment of digital literacy skills by communities is human development in the areas of literacy and education. Education in the view of Igwe (1990) serves the purpose of inculcating in the individual the knowledge and skills required to develop individually in order to be useful not only to themselves but also to the society in which they find themselves. Using Nigeria as an example, according to Ifijeh, Iwu-James and Adebayo (2016), about 56.9% of Nigerians are illiterate. This in itself excludes them from the ability to gain access to ICTs and the ability to find and utilize information from ICT platforms which constitute digital inclusion. From Ifijeh et al.'s report, it is obvious that an even greater percentage of Nigerians may not have the requisite digital skills.

Although the Nigerian Government has made efforts to bridge the literacy gap by embarking at various times on programmes such as Education for All and Mass Literacy Campaign (MLC), one-third of the adult population still lack basic literacy. However, it should be noted that Nigeria is a multi-lingual state; some of its citizens can write and speak only in their local languages. Furthermore, it has been observed that most of the ICT facilities imported into Nigeria are configured in the English language, with no allowances for the alphabets of local languages. This excludes many in local communities; consequently, these people are digitally excluded (Intel Corporation, 2007).

Digital literacy skills and community development

ICT has affected every area of human endeavour. By implication, the level of disposition of ICT in a particular environment can be determined by its level of development. This has led to various forms of disparity between nations, leading to a digital divide. The concept of sustainability was popularized by experts who normally deploy it as a means of responding to global economic concerns, such as equity and the distribution of the common wealth of a nation. Sustainable development has been defined as development that meets the social, economic and technological needs of the present time without compromising the ability of future generations to meet their own needs. To attain development, the roles of information and digital literacy cannot be ignored (Ifijeh, Iwu-James and Adebayo, 2016).

Digital inclusion in the communities as a policy needs urgent attention, as understanding the concept and its implication could be a prelude to the attainment of digital literacy skills by all. Digital inclusion is an all-encompassing way of acquiring digital literacy skills. It involves having public policies that relate to the installation, administration, expansion, creation and development of content on wired or wireless public networks in countries, regions and communities. This includes privacy and security, training and incentives to develop new tools. The attainment of digital literacy skills can be achieved by translating the members of a community from a former state of digital exclusion to one of digital inclusion. The UK Department of Health (2014) opined that digital inclusion is a facet of social inclusion which provides the right access to the digital world for intellectual development and promotes spaces for significant cultural practices that allow individuals to be digitally literate.

ICTs have changed knowledge and technical know-how in modern society: that is, ICTs play important roles in preserving indigenous knowledge (IK) by combining scientific and technical knowledge. Digital literacy skills have also played important roles in the preservation of knowledge. According to Plockey (2015), media is a vital tool that allows individuals to have a greater understanding and appreciation of their environment, keep abreast of what is going on and act accordingly. Mass media technology, which is an off-shoot of ICTs, plays a significant role in improving the preservation of IK. Mass media technology allows indigenous communities to protect their unique cultures and knowledge through preservation.

The major uses of mass media technology for promoting IK are highlighted as follows:

- It creates easily accessible IK information systems.
- The technology captures, stores and disseminates IK so that traditional knowledge will be preserved for future generations.
- It promotes cost-effective dissemination of IK.
- It promotes integration of IK into formal and non-formal training and education.
- It provides a platform for advocating, improving and getting benefits from IK systems to the poor.

The preservation of IK in Africa has been facilitated by traditional organizations and a number of cultural industries such as museums and the mass media. One of the methods of preserving IK was through oral tradition, which has been used for centuries. Apart from oral tradition, other methods such as drama and records have been used to preserve IK in Africa. Presently, IK is also being preserved through the use of hard drives, tapes and digital video cameras, which may not be possible without digital literacy skills. Lodhi and Mikulecky (2010) observed that IK changes according to the needs of the people, due to its dynamic character. According to Nakata et al. (2014), the use of digital technologies provides means for preserving IK, thereby

making it accessible to future generations of indigenous people. Consequently, Sithole (2007) stated that IK is susceptible to slow destruction if it is
not documented and preserved for storage and wider transmission.

UNESCO (2013) states that educated people are more likely to understand,
support and create solutions that ensure the development of cities and
communities. To also do that effectively, libraries, as agents of social
communication, can help to bridge the awareness and information gap among
members of the community. For the attainment of digital literacy skills,
libraries and librarians, as information specialists and brokers, have roles to
play in identifying stakeholders who will serve as advocates in encouraging
members of the community to embrace the use of libraries, most especially
public libraries, in order to discover themselves educationally, socially,
politically etc. Libraries and their sphere of influence are defined by the type
of community/clienteles they serve. Thus, school and academic libraries cater
for students, teachers/lecturers and researchers/scholars. As the name implies,
public libraries cater for members of the public. These libraries assist members
of the community in the attainment of digital literacy skills through exposure
to a variety of information resources that help them to learn more about
digitization and the acquisition of literacy skills.

Role of libraries and digital literacy skills development

Public libraries as the local gateway to knowledge provide resources for
lifelong learning, independent decision making and the cultural development
of the individual and social groups. In rural areas, public libraries are
designed to provide information on agriculture, building, trade, health care
and other aspects of human activities which are required mostly by rural
community dwellers, because they lack access to other resources of assistance.
Rural communities in Nigeria are faced with low literacy rates and a lack of
ICTs (Ifijeh, Iwu-James and Adebayo, 2016). Perhaps one of the most
important roles public libraries can play in the acquisition of digital literacy
skills is the provision of internet services to their users. Internet provision by
libraries might serve as a source of information about health, government,
language, culture and so on.

Public libraries can also play the following roles in the attainment of digital
literacy skills in some of the information centres located in communities: teach
basic computer skills; provide information resources in various formats and
teach the proper use of the information resources; participate in programmes
to combat illiteracy; offer free or subsidized internet access alongside support
and training for users; champion programmes aimed at equipping people

with digital skills which would meet their information needs and increase their chances of enjoying community life.

Attaining adequate digital literacy among communities in any nation requires effective connections between libraries, information centres and government and non-governmental organizations, such that they will be able to serve different types of communities. To do this effectively, basic infrastructural development is needed – in this case the availability of ICTs in libraries that would not only increase and broaden the impact of information resources but also place more emphasis on the effective and efficient services needed in such communities. Ayodele (2002) defined ICT as electronic-based technology generally used to retrieve, store, process and package information, as well as provide access to knowledge. Generally, information technology is rapidly changing the whole world and creating new opportunities. Communities should therefore not be left out, and that is why it is necessary for stakeholders in the field of librarianship at all levels to play their roles.

Academic community and digital literacy skills attainment

The academic community is one of the highest-ranking communities among the different types of communities. The academic library is seen as the heart of higher education institutions today, with the community consisting of students, lecturers and other members of the university. According to Osawele and Uzairue (2013), the National Policy on Education identifies the library as one of the most important aspects of educational support service, in the sense that libraries are the medium for disseminating information and enhancing literature search, as well as a tool for the development of intellectual capabilities and promotion of cultural and social integration. Library support services include facilitating access to the library collections and instructional and reference support, including information literacy training.

Online Distance Learners (ODLs) are an integral part of the university system, and they constitute their own community, thus digital literacy is germane to that type of academic environment. Meeting ODLs' and their tutors' expectations requires facilitating the finding of, and timely access to, a broad range of relevant information, together with information enquiry and support (Secker, 2008, cited in Adigun and Tella, 2021). It is important that ODLs have access to adequate knowledge of information seeking and retrieval strategies to enable both them and their tutors to successfully search complex and multiple information systems. Digital literacy is characterized by many features that can solve some of the challenges of retrieving information resources.

Librarians should be proactive in providing library instruction through user education. This can be achieved through regular contact in virtual classrooms, but studies have shown that many librarians need more capacity-building training, since they appear to be less information literate than was assumed because of information anxiety and the complexity of the online environment. User education is an effective tool for helping distant learners and tutors to overcome library-related anxiety (Cooke, 2010). According to Primus (2009), libraries and librarians should provide a ubiquitous presence, using technologies such as blogs and social networking sites (such as Facebook, LinkedIn, Flickr etc.).

Role of non-governmental organizations and civil society

Non-governmental organizations or civil society organizations in different parts of Africa, including Nigeria, contribute to the development of communities in various ways. The major task of non-governmental organizations is to serve as an alternative means of providing help to alleviate citizens' hardships in various areas of life. They advocate for human rights, gender mainstreaming, access to education, information for development, basic infrastructure etc. Non-governmental organizations can be local or international. Some are non-political, but their impact in developing countries has been felt in such a way that society looks up to them as an alternative source to the government in making decisions concerning their lives. Notable non-governmental organizations in the academic sector include the Nigeria Library Association (NLA), American Library Association, International Federation of Library Associations and Institutions (IFLA), Association of College and Research Libraries (ACRL), Africa Library and Information Associations and Institutions (AfLIA) etc. These organizations have contributed to the development of libraries in society. The ALA took up the challenge of ensuring that library and information services are adequately provided for distance learners (Brooke, 2011; Gandhi, 2003). The requirements of extended distance learning off campus gained attention in 1931 when the ALA observed that students studying away from the main campus of their institutions were disadvantaged because of the non-availability of library resources (Gandhi, 2003). Similarly, in 1963 the ACRL developed guidelines on library services provision for this category of students. The guidelines were approved in 2008 as the ACRL Standards for Distance Learning Library Services, and revised in 2016. The NLA has initiated a number of programmes aimed at alleviating some of the challenges facing the profession.

According to Odu and Omosigho (2017), digital libraries are an emerging concept in Nigeria, and digital literacy is a necessary tool or skill needed for making use of resources in the digital library. Most Nigerian libraries are faced with challenges in library usage and services, due to an inadequate level of the literacy and digital skills required to make maximum use of digital libraries. This in turn has led to a digital divide among both users and staff. Libraries owe it to their users to make information accessible to all, irrespective of their location, language or literacy level, as libraries support all forms of literacy, from basic to digital. The NLA, through the National Library of Nigeria, has encouraged libraries to engage in literacy programmes and training in collaboration with the communities to which the libraries provide information services. Library users need to be both information and digitally literate in order to have the ability to locate, evaluate and adequately make use of needed information.

Conclusion

Competence in digital literacy skills is required for any community to develop in all spheres of life and to effectively tackle emerging developmental challenges. In the world of ICT, a fourth industrial revolution is taking place through artificial intelligence, which will significantly influence our ways of doing things in the years to come. The 21st century has seen the emergence of knowledge societies and digital economies around the world. Underpinning these changes have been the proliferation of mobile devices, increased sophistication of computers and cheaper and more widely available internet access.

References

Adedokun, M. O. (2019) The Impact of Women in Building a Formidable Community. In Sotunsi, M. and Yacob Haliso, O. (eds), *Women in Africa: Contexts, Rights*, Henemonious.

Adigun, G. O. and Tella, A. (2021) User Education and Information Literacy Instruction as Determinant of Use and Satisfaction with Library and Information Support Services at National Open University Nigeria (NOUN), *Journal of Library & Information Services in Distance Learning*, doi: 10.1080/1533290X.2021.1896621.

Ayodele, J. B. and Adedokun, M. O. (2012) Towards achieving functional adult literacy in Nigeria, *European Scientific Journal*, 8 (5), doi: 10.19044.2012.v8.5p%25p.

Ayodele, J. F. (2002) Assessment Policy in the First Twelve Years of Formal Education in Botswana and Nigeria: Practical Assessment and Research. *International Journal of Basic, Applied and Innovative Research*, 2 (1), 10–14.

Barton, D. and Trusting, K. (eds) (2005) *Beyond Communities of Practice: Language Power and Social Context. Learning in Doing: Social, Cognitive and Computational Perspectives*, Cambridge University Press.

Brooke, C. (2011) An Investigation into the Provision of Library Support Services for Distance Learners at UK Universities: Analyzing Current Practice to Inform Future Best Practice at Sheffield Hallam University, unpublished Master's thesis, University of Sheffield.

Cooke, N. (2010) Becoming an Androgogical Librarian: Using Library Instructions as a Tool to Combat Library Anxiety and Empower Adult Learners, *New Review of Academic Librarianship*, **16** (2), 208–27, doi: 10.1080/13614533.2010.507388.

Douglas, S. P. (2010) *Information Communication Technology Perspective for Developing Countries*, International Encyclopedia Britannica.

Ekenimoh, I. (2021) Overpriced: Why Nigerians Pay So Much for Data, www.stearsng.com/article/overpriced-why-nigerians-pay-so-much-for-data.

Eyong, I. U. (2016) Information Literacy and National Development in Nigeria, www.academix.ng/search/paper.html?idd-3300016544.

Gandhi, S. (2003) Academic Librarians and Distance Education: Challenges and Opportunities, *Reference & User Services Quarterly*, **43** (2), 138–54.

Gilster, P. (1997) *Digital Literacy*, John Wiley.

Giubilini, A. and Levy, N. (2018) What in the World Is Collective Responsibility? *Dialecta*, (Bern) **72** (2), 191–217, doi: 10.1111/1746–8361.12228.

Global Goals (2018) www.global.goals.org.

Ifijeh, G., Iwu-James, J. and Adebayo, O. (2016) Digital Inclusion and Sustainable Development in Nigeria: The Role of Libraries. In *3rd International Conference on African Development Issues*.

Igwe, S. O. (1990) *Professional Handbook for Teachers*, New African Publishing Company Ltd.

Intel Corporation (2007) *Leap Ahead*, www.intel.com/content/dam.doc/white-paper/learning-series-bridging-digital-divide-nigeria-paper.pdf.

Kegley, J. A. K. (1997) *Genuine Individuals and Genuine Communities*, Vanderbilt University Press.

Kelly, A. and Sewell, S. (1998) *With Head, Heart and Hand: Dimensions of Community Building*, Boolerong Publications.

Lankshear, C. and Knobel, M. (2008) *Digital Literacies: Concepts, Policies and Practices*, Peter Lang Publishing.

Lodhi, S. and Mikulecky, P. (2010) Management of Indigenous Knowledge for Developing Countries. In: *Proceedings of the 2010 International Conference on Communication and Management in Technological Innovation and Academic Globalization*, www.researchgate.net/publication/262257697_Management_of_indigenous_knowledge_for_developing_countries.

Nakata, M., Hamacher, D., Warren, J., Bryne, A., Pagnucco, M., Harley, R., Venugopal, R., Thorpe, K., Neville, R. and Bolt, R. (2014) Using Modern Technologies to Capture and Share Indigenous Astronomical Knowledge, *Australian Academic Research Libraries*, **45**, 101–10.

Odu, A. O. and Omosigho, N. A. (2017) Digital Literacy and the Implication on Nigerian Digital Library, *International Journal of Library and Information Science Studies*, **3** (2), 13–19.

Osawele, R. E. and Uzairue, L. I. (2013) The Relevance of Information and Communication Technologies in Libraries Services and Librarianship Profession in the 21st Century, *International Journal of Basic, Applied and Innovative Research*, **2** (1), 77–91.

Plockey, F. D. D. (2015) Indigenous Knowledge Production, Digital Media and Academic Libraries in Ghana, *Journal of Pan African Studies*, **8** (4), 32–44.

Primus, S. (2009) Distance Learning Library Services: Keeping Up with Campus: The Academic Library in Second Life, *Journal of Library Administration*, **50** (7–8), 909–22, doi: 10.1080/01930826.201.4888993.

Sithole, J. (2007) The Challenges Faced by African Libraries and Information Centres in Documenting and Preserving Indigenous Knowledge, *IFLA Journal*, **33** (2), 117–23.

UK Department of Health (2014) The Mandate: A Mandate from the Government to NHS England: April 2014 to March 2015, https://assets.publishing.service.gov.uk/government/uploads/system/uploads/att achment_data/file/383495/2902896_DoH_Mandate_Accessible_v0.2.pdf.

UNESCO (2013) *UNESCO Education Strategy 2014–2021.*

World Literacy Foundation (2020) *What Is Digital Literacy and Why Does It Matter?*

11

Digital Literacy, Creativity, Knowledge Sharing and Dissemination in the 21st Century
Ngozi Ogechukwu Nwogwugwu

Abstract

Digital literacy plays a critical role in information dissemination in the knowledge economy, where the possession of skills and dexterity to effectively create, share and navigate in online spaces is paramount. Digital literacy is examined as the repertoire of skills needed to maximize the usage of digital devices and gain the competitive edge needed to exploit employment opportunities in the knowledge economy. The concept of creativity is also examined and the things that can be created using digital skills are explored. These are tied in with the concept of knowledge sharing and the role libraries can play in enhancing the dissemination of knowledge and information through the exploration of digital assets. Knowledge is power, and this power becomes even more accentuated when it is effectively and efficiently shared among the people who are in need of it. Hence, libraries and library professionals have a role to play in ensuring the maximization of the potentials inherent in the digital space through empowering creativity and enabling the sharing of knowledge and information.

Keywords: Digital literacy, creativity, knowledge, social media and digital skills.

Introduction

Knowledge is said to be a powerful tool in the hands of those who can use it effectively and efficiently. Knowledge can be described as the bedrock of modern society, as it has become a highly prized commodity for diverse engagements (Khajbakteev, 2020). The era of just having knowledge without using it for anything and/or merely declaring that it is power is gradually fading away. In present times, for knowledge to be regarded as a source of power, it needs to be put to good use and, most importantly, it should be easily accessible by many. The 21st-century information, political and socio-economic landscapes are ruled by those who understand the importance of knowledge and who can key into it to create, govern and grow wealth.

The new understanding about the power of knowledge has led to a change in the way it is acquired and disseminated, as sharing knowledge through physical contact, whereby physical classes, seminars, workshops and trainings are organized, is gradually being done away with. Recent events, including the COVID-19 crisis, and evolving technologies have made virtual knowledge sharing more possible and prevalent. Teaching and learning can now be organized for different people around the world, from thousands of miles away. There is also huge buying and selling going on daily over the internet; even day-to-day communication is largely being carried out through the use of digitally enabled devices, especially for people living far apart or those who have to work from home because of the COVID-19 pandemic. This is occasioned by improvement in internet penetration around the world, mobile technologies that enable virtual meetings with a high level of interactions and a plethora of different electronic devices like smartphones, laptops, iPads and smart televisions for accessing those meetings.

The ability to read and write has led to categorizations whereby there are those seen as literate, while others could be seen as illiterates. However, the concept of literacy can be expanded to include in-depth understanding of new fields of knowledge. Therefore, the literacy of any person is relative, as someone can be literate in one field, but completely oblivious or a novice in another field. However, on a common note, a literate person is seen as someone who can at least read, write and communicate clearly with others as literacy, is the foundation of learning and being knowledgeable in different fields.

People's knowledge can be in different areas. It could be knowledge in medicine, international relations, teaching or electronics. It could also be knowledge in things that have to do with religion, government, business and other areas. Knowledge about ICTs and how to understand and use them for various purposes can come only in the form of digital literacy (DL). DL can be viewed as the ability of a person to use different ICT gadgets, devices and platforms to perform various functions; knowing how, when and where to search for, disseminate and use various data/information to execute a variety of functions to improve human lives. A person's ability to search for, find, use, create and disseminate information digitally defines their level of digital literacy. Martin (2006) opines that DL is the individual realization, attitude and capacity of digital tools usage in order to access, manage, integrate, analyse and synthesize digital information sources. Therefore, DL can be said to be playing a significant role in a world that is continuously going digital in almost all facets of life.

Digital literacy

Literacy is the ability to identify, understand, interpret, create, communicate and compute, using printed and written (and visual) materials associated with varying contexts. It involves a spectrum of continuously growing abilities that equip people with skills, knowledge and understanding to actively participate consciously and intelligibly in society (UNESCO, 2018). It can also be regarded as the ability to understand knowledge in the form and manner in which it is communicated. A person's capacity to appropriately understand or use knowledge in a particular area defines that person's literacy in that aspect. Therefore, being digitally literate is when someone has the skills and knowledge to adroitly communicate, work, create, interact and share on digital platforms. There are different levels of digital literacy; for example, a person who can use a smartphone, a laptop or a scanner can be said to be digitally literate in certain aspects. On the other hand, someone who knows only how to power up a laptop, and probably shut it down, is not on the same level with someone who can write programming code and build software.

The debate about what digital literacy is and what should be included in its definition to be seen as all-encompassing and complete has been continuing for quite some time. Kaeophanuek, Na-Songkhla and Nilsook (2018) opine that the debate surrounding the definition of digital literacy started as early as the 1990s. Being digitally literate should include the ability to navigate through certain real-world challenges using ICT and its infrastructure. This enables one to ably seek for information and data on the internet as well as to create information and disseminate information created by others online using appropriate technologies and digital platforms. Jun and Pow (2011) aver that individuals with digital literacy skills must be able to use technology as the digital age's information management tools in terms of management, evaluation and communication, and they must possess a fundamental knowledge of the laws and ethical issues concerning information access. In other words, digital literacy should encompass the application of technology for a presentation or for problem solving, co-operating and knowledge sharing, as well as an awareness of individual responsibilities and rights (Sharpe, 2010, 17). Digital literacy equips one in seeking, acquiring, creating, sharing and reformatting information in the most effective and efficient manner, using digital devices in digital spaces. The repertoire of skills makes it easier, faster and in most cases cheaper to acquire, disseminate, adapt and store information. Consequently, acquiring digital literacy skills means gaining a wide range of abilities to access various information sources, the practical capacity to use digital tools for information resources management and the ability to generate and share on different media, as well as the ability to efficiently present and communicate ideas and concepts using the proper technological processes and tools (Hague, 2010; Gee, 2012). It also involves the ability to locate and consume, create and communicate digital content (Hiller, Casey and Shea, 2017). Hence, there are various processes associated with digital literacy, as corroborated by Spires and Bartlett (2012), who divided the various intellectual processes into three categories:

1 Locating and consuming digital content: this has to do with the unique ability to find needed data or information using digital means, and comprehending such information to make for use. That is, being able to sift through enormous amounts of data and information to know what is accurate so as not to disseminate falsehoods or deceive others. It entails strategically searching for information and evaluating its accuracy and relevance for use (Leu et al., 2008, 324).
2 Creating digital content: this entails the ability to create or develop materials, ideas and information that will be required and/or accessed digitally by others. This is of course through the help of various ICT tools and digital media. Bakkenes, Vermunt and Wubbles (2010) state that digital content is easily created by teachers and students alike using multiple media and a variety of Web 2.0 tools. The implementation of digital content can be an important and effective method of enhancing teaching and learning and enabling the dissemination of knowledge.
3 Communicating digital content: it is not enough to locate and assimilate digital content, it is also crucial for that content to be interpreted appropriately and communicated in an understandable way so as to elicit the desired results.

Digital skills for employment

The era of having knowledge in the various fields of human endeavour without supporting it with digital skills and knowledge is fast disappearing. This is because, with digital skills, one can reach a greater audience, collaborate more and have wider access to resources, organizations and people with less stress, time and cost, as well as greater productivity in the workplace, both quantitatively and qualitatively. According to the ITU (2021), possession of digital skills has become critical for professional growth and success. Having digital skills is an added advantage to many in the overcrowded employment market in developing nations such as Nigeria and other African countries. This is highlighted by Laar et al. (2019), who point out that knowledge of ICT and digital literacy support economic growth by generating business and employment opportunities. Similarly, Gómez, Tobarra and López (2014) opine that digital skills have become a key element in opening up employment opportunities for the mass of unemployed youth. Furthermore, there cannot be a knowledge economy without a vast number of people with digital skills. These skills are not only vital for participating in the knowledge society, but also crucial in contributing significantly to the economy's social discourse (van Deursen and van Dijk, 2011).

Skills that are required for the effective functioning of today's economy are referred to as 21st-century skills, as described by Greiff, Niepel and Wüstenberg (2015) and by Griffin, Care and McGaw (2012), who jointly explicate that the skills needed for navigating the contemporary world and the workplace have been labelled 21st-century skills. Prominent frameworks that promote and discuss 21st-century skills cover those related to the use of ICTs, collaboration and communication, creativity, critical thinking, problem solving, being productive and acting in a socially and culturally responsible manner both physically and virtually (Dede, 2010; Ferrari, Punie and Redecker, 2012; Voogt and Roblin, 2012).

Some of the skills necessary for today's knowledge economy include, but are not limited to:

- internet usage skills
- content creation
- software building
- artificial intelligence skills
- computer programming
- digital business analysis and simulations
- digital data science and analysis
- digital design and data visualization
- digital project management
- editing skills (video, picture and audio)
- digital marketing
- digital currency navigation
- web design skills
- graphics designing
- application building

- social media handling and management skills
- ICT gadget-handling skills
- maintenance and repair of ICT devices skills.

Creativity

Creativity is the ability to imagine, generate and/or understand different or alternative avenues, ideas and concepts for solving problems or doing things. Creativity has two integral aspects – thinking and producing (Naiman, 2014). Digital skills have great potential for breeding ingenuity and creativity as more and more digital tools are produced that enable people to turn their ideas or imaginative concepts into reality. Such skills also provide or make for a larger audience to showcase creativity, and probably at less cost. Digital skills can increase creative abilities. For example, those who have the skill of graphic design when combined with digital skills can produce new, improved and innovative designs because technology can imbue digital devices with features that enhance designs. The same goes to those with video, picture and audio editing skills; the acquisition of digital skills can boost their creativity and help them to remain relevant in their field of work.

ICT makes it possible for millions of people to see an idea or a creative work from anywhere in the world. It makes people part of a global village, where time and space has been shrunk and made irrelevant. That is, people can now showcase their work virtually to a global audience through different digital platforms like Zoom and Facebook. Such is the power of ICT in today's world. As a result of the endless possibilities offered by ICT, people have become more creative, because the competition and market space has been widened. Competition and products and/or services marketing is no longer limited to the local or immediate environment or market, but with global and more sophisticated competitors, clients and platforms.

Having digital skills enables inclusion, as individuals from diverse communities learn how to use digital devices to tell their own stories on global platforms; these are stories, opinions and perspectives that ordinarily would not have not been shared outside of certain locales. With the application of digital skills, these stories are being heard because under-represented communities and individuals whose viewpoints had hitherto been ignored can now have visibility. This creates inclusiveness as people participate in social discourses that affect them and understanding is built (AfLIA, 2020).

Things that can be created digitally

A plethora of things can be created digitally using the power of ICT and the internet. These include the following.

Text: Ideas can be converted to text so as to store them and make them reach a wider audience. An idea cannot materialize if it is not shared with others, both those within a specified area and those outside. With text, collaboration is aided and advanced for better creativity and sustainability.

Posters: Creative ideas can be conveyed in the form of posters, flyers and billboards. All these are only possible with the aid of digital devices, supported by digital skills to bring such ideas to life. Interestingly, using other digital tools, these posters can be animated and made into stories or short films.

Maps: Maps can also be created digitally to help people navigate through areas that were hitherto unknown to them or which they do not know very well or may have forgotten. All the person needs is an internet connection and for the location to be mapped on a map such as Google Maps.

Stories: Stories can also be created using digital skills, to entertain and inform others. They can be animated or even translated from one language to another on digital platforms.

Software programs: Software programs that can be used for a variety of purposes can be created using digital technologies and skills. These could be for educational uses, entertainment, medical and governmental purposes.

Animations and games: Games and animations can also be created using digital technologies to stimulate people's minds to think critically, or just for entertainment and to lower stress levels.

Online interactive activities: Interactive sessions, conversations, training and hook-ups can be driven digitally. People no longer have to be in the same location in order to converse, and applications and software are now being developed to deal with the issue of time and space.

Libraries encouraging creativity

Libraries are not only a place of learning, but also institutions that allow users to be curious, to experiment and to get creative (Korbey, 2014). Libraries are tapping into the idea that digital skills can help to grow creativity, as they create spaces for collaborative gaming and problem-solving activities with digital devices. This spurs users to think and be creative with the use of digital skills to find solutions. The University of North Texas Digital Library has such a space which is designed to provide 'an immersive, real-life gaming experience' (Falcon, 2017). The internet creativity ecosystem could be anchored in libraries, especially in communities where the library is the only place where one has access to facilities and to free or low-cost internet. This has potential for growing the numbers of people with digital skills and of those who can use their acquired skills to be creative.

Makerspaces in libraries also promote creativity, as users are allowed to tinker with ideas and make things. Some makerspaces promote digital creativity. According to Burke (2014, 4), makerspaces may have tools for robotic programming and working with 3D, among other things.

Knowledge sharing

Today's world is referred to as a knowledge economy because knowledge is the key factor that drives all processes of production, where intellectual capital and the skill to manipulate various things, including digital devices, is critical. For knowledge to be useful, it needs to be shared and communicated to others, so as to help other people to solve real-world problems. Turban, McLean and Wetherbe (2004) opine that knowledge sharing is the wilful application and transfer of one or more person's ideas, insights, solutions and knowledge to another person(s), either directly or via an intermediary, such as a computer-based system. The number of persons that get to know about your knowledge depends largely on the medium used for sharing the knowledge. Therefore, one has to be discerning in choosing the channel for sharing knowledge, depending on the target audience

In the past, knowledge has been shared through face-to-face contact, through physical platforms, meetings, seminars and conferences, books, journals and other physical containers of information, but with the advent of ICT knowledge sharing has been made very easy, with wider coverage and at lightning speed. By improving access to services, enhancing connectivity and changing the ways in which people communicate, interact and engage with one another, ICTs have become a central contributor to social transformation and knowledge sharing (Laar et al., 2019). Today, virtual meetings can be organized for thousands of people in different parts of the world, thereby saving the costs of travel and accommodation, and the time and risk involved. Different online media such as Facebook, Twitter, LinkedIn can be used to share enormous amounts of knowledge with millions of people. Therefore, social media play a pivotal role in the dynamics of information dissemination. A simple creative image shared on Instagram, for example, can potentially reach millions of people within a short period of time. People are only a click away from getting crucial messages and information online. Facebook, Twitter, YouTube, Telegram and other social media platforms also play significant roles in the quest to share knowledge and information. The interesting thing about sharing knowledge through these media is that a wider audience is reached at a reduced cost, and this continues to breed more creativity.

The place of libraries in ensuring digital literacy and knowledge sharing

Libraries are known as places where different materials about different subjects and concerns can be obtained; they are known as a repository of knowledge. This presupposes that those institutions have a role to play in knowledge sharing and the acquisition of digital skills, whether directly or through some form of intermediary, where they provide the electronic platforms to disseminate information or for storing information for easy access. They are also fundamental in the digital literacy mix. This is because materials and facilities that can play a part in equipping people with the digital knowledge they seek can be found in libraries.

Some libraries played an active role and are still playing a role in lessening the impact of the lockdown during the peak period of the COVID-19 pandemic by providing people with electronic materials that kept and are still keeping them actively engaged mentally. For example, in Germany, the Netherlands, Norway, Nigeria, South Africa and Spain, social media was used to offer story-time through Facebook groups and YouTube profiles, or for library exchange and (re)use of digital products (Bulgaria). Sometimes stories were distributed through library websites, for instance in Switzerland, Germany and many other countries; digital storytelling as a new library service is becoming popular. These are some of the roles libraries have played in disseminating knowledge during the pandemic.

Conclusion

Information and knowledge are said to be power, and this power becomes accentuated when it is effectively shared among people in a swift manner. With innovation and ingenuity, information sharing has been made easier in the digital eco-system, where information travels at lightning speed. However, in order to maximize the potential inherent in the digital space, digital literacy is paramount. Digitization has facilitated the delivery of people's creativity and ingenuity to a global audience, by the means of various digital media with global coverage and accessibility to all who are technologically and digitally inclined. In order that no one is left behind, libraries and their professionals have a role to play in making sure that people can access materials required to help them to become digitally literate enough to participate actively in the digital space.

References

AfLIA (2020) *Wikipedia for African Libraries: Liberating Knowledge*, https://web.aflia.net/wikipedia-project-for-african-librarians-liberating-knowledge.

Bakkenes, I., Vermunt, J. D. and Wubbles, T. (2010) Teacher Learning in the Context of Educational Innovation: Learning Activities and Learning Outcomes of Experienced Teachers, *Learning and Instruction*, **20** (6), 533–48.

Burke, J. J. (2014) *Makerspaces: A Practical Guide for Librarians*, Rowman & Littlefield Publishers, https://rowman.com/ISBN/9781442229686/MakerSpaces-A-Practical-Guide-for-Librarians.

Dede, C. (2010) Comparing Frameworks for 21st Century Skills. In Bellanca, J. and Brandt, R. (eds), *21st Century Skills: Rethinking How Students Learn*, Solution Tree Press.

Falcon, J. (2017) Libraries Unlocking Creativity, www.ilovelibraries.org/article/libraries-unlocking-creativity.

Ferrari, A., Punie, Y. and Redecker, C. (2012) Understanding Digital Competence in the 21st Century: An Analysis of Current Frameworks. In Ravenscroft, A., Lindstaedt, S., Kloos, C. D. and Hernández-Leo, D. (eds), *21st Century Learning for 21st Century Skills*, Springer, doi: 10.1007/978–3-642–33263–0_7.

Gee, J. P. (2012) The Old and the New in the New Digital Literacies, *The Educational Forum*, **76**, 418–20.

Gómez, N., Tobarra, M. Á. and López, L. A. (2014) Employment Opportunities in Spain: Gender Differences by Education and ICT Usage, *Regional and Sectoral Economic Studies*, **14**, 105–30.

Greiff, S., Niepel, C. and Wüstenberg, S. (2015) 21st Century Skills: International Advancements and Recent Developments, *Thinking Skills and Creativity*, **18**, 1–3, doi: 10.1016/j.tsc.2015.04.007.

Griffin, P., Care, E. and McGaw, B. (2012) The Changing Role of Education and Schools. In Griffin, P., McGaw, B., and Care, E. (eds), *Assessment and Teaching of 21st Century Skills: Methods and Approach*, Springer, doi: 10.1007/978–94–007–2324–5_1.

Hague, C. (2010) *It's Not Chalk and Talk Anymore: School Approaches to Developing Students' Digital Literacy*, www.nfer.ac.uk/publications/FUTL09/FUTL09.pdf.

Hiller, A. S., Casey, M. P. and Shea, N. K. (2017) Digital Literacy for the 21st Century, *Encyclopedia of Information Science and Technology*, 4th edn, doi: 10.4018/978–1-5225-2255-3.ch194.

ITU (2021) Digital Inclusion of Youth, www.itu.int/en/mediacentre/backgrounders/Pages/digital-inclusion-of-youth.aspx.

Jun, F. and Pow, J. (2011) Fostering Digital Literacy through Web-based Collaborative Inquiry Learning: A Case Study, *Journal of Information Technology Education*, **10** (57–71).

Kaeophanuek, S., Na-Songkhla, J. and Nilsook, P. (2018) How to Enhance Digital Literacy Skills among Information Sciences Students, *International Journal of Information and Education Technology*, **4** (8), 292–7.

Khajbakteev, B. (2020) *How the Commodification of Knowledge is Creating a New Age of Colonialism*, www.opendemocracy.net/en/oureconomy/how-commodification-knowledge-creating-new-age-colonialism.

Korbey, H. (2014) *How Libraries are Advancing and Inspiring Schools and Communities*, www.kqed.org/mindshift/38418/how-libraries-are-advancing-and-inspiring-communities.

Laar, E. V., Deursen, A. J. A. M., Van Dijk, A. G. M. and Haan, J. (2019) Twenty-first Century Digital Skills for the Creative Industries Workforce: Perspectives from Industry Experts, *First Monday*, **24** (1–7).

Leu, D. J., Coiro, J., Castek, J., Hartman, D., Henry, L. A. and Reinking, D. (2008) Research on Instruction and Assessment in the New Literacies of Online Reading Comprehension. In Collins-Block, C., Parris, S. and Afferbach, P. (eds), *Comprehension Instruction: Research Based Best Practices*, Guilford Press.

Martin, A. (2006) *A European Framework for Digital Literacy*, www.semanticscholar.org/paper/A-european-framework-for-digital-literacy-Martin/f83e53af6e453519aa9adc9960cc826fa7dc93c3.

Naiman, L. (2014) *What Is Creativity? (And Why is it a Crucial Factor for Business Success?)*, www.creativityatwork.com/what-is-creativity.

Sharpe, R. (2010) *Conceptualizing Differences in Learners' Experiences of e-Learning: A Review of Contextual Models*, www.heacademy.ac.uk.

Spires, H. and Bartlett, M. (2012) *Digital Literacies and Learning: Designing a Path Forward*, Friday Institute White Paper Series, North Carolina State University.

Turban, E., McLean, E. and Wetherbe, J. (2004) *Information Technology for Management: Transforming Organizations in the Digital Economy*, 6th edn, John Wiley and Sons.

UNESCO (2018) *Digital Skills Critical for Jobs and Social Inclusion*, https://en.unesco.org/news/digital-skills-critical-jobs-and-social-inclusion.

van Deursen, A. J. A. M. and van Dijk, J. A. G. M. (2011) Internet Skills and the Digital Divide, *New Media & Society*, **13** (6), 893–911, doi: 10.1177/1461444810386774.

Voogt, J. and Roblin, N. P. (2012) A Comparative Analysis of International Frameworks for 21st Century Competences: Implications for National Curriculum Policies, *Journal of Curriculum Studies*, **44** (3), 299–321, doi: 10.1080/00220272.2012.668938.

12

Underscoring the Value of Digital Literacy as a Tool for Reducing Unemployment and Enhancing Workplace Productivity

Lanre Abubakar Folorunso and
Emmanuel Omeiza Momoh

Abstract

In recent times, unemployment has become a persistent challenge. Many African countries have tried to unravel its causes and arrive at sustainable solutions. Several propositions, research studies and in-depth analyses have been conducted to find ways to end the scourge which has affected mostly the younger generation. This has not achieved anything worthwhile, as the rate of unemployment is increasing all over the continent. The inability to reduce unemployment has fuelled crime rates and other forms of social unrest/distress. This chapter examines the connection between digital literacy and its value in ending the scourge of unemployment. It also brings to the fore ways in which digital literacy can be used to increase employees' productivity especially in the 21st century when advancement in the workplace may be measured through skills that promote productivity and not mere academic qualifications, and the function of digital literacy both as an instrument and a concept in bringing about the desired reduction of unemployment in Africa.

Keywords: Digital literacy, unemployment, underemployment, workplace productivity.

Introduction

Unemployment or underemployment is the bane of many countries in Africa and the world in general as it continues to be a major cause of poverty, economic impoverishment and an abrupt increase in the rate of crime and other forms of social unrest. Sub-Saharan Africa may be the worst hit by unemployment and underemployment with the International Labour Organization (ILO, 2019) observing that the youth unemployment rate in sub-Sahara Africa (SSA) was 13.27% in 2018, exceeding the rate recorded on other continents.

Poor economic policies, political unrest, large-scale conflicts and poor management of resources may be the cause of this high rate of unemployment and under-employment in Africa. However, there is also a high probability that the lack of technological skills, experience and knowledge of digital skills in many job seekers is another cause of the spike in the rate of unemployment, as many job seekers rely on their certificates without acquiring or honing relevant technological skills that are not taught in schools. This, according to Metu et al. (2019), results in a disparity between employers' demands and the available skills.

The issue of unemployment is of particular importance to policy makers and economic experts in Africa because of the growing quest to acquire an education or be regarded as literate, which liberates many from ignorance and opens up a wealth of opportunities that can boost economic survival and reliance, on both personal and national levels. Many organizations require their employees to have educational qualifications, the least being a bachelor's degree in the desired field.

Many countries have developed different strategies for reducing both unemployment and underemployment. Ogungbile (2021) includes among these strategies public private partnerships (PPPs), which facilitate the establishment of industries by private individuals while the government gives necessary support, and the inclusion of entrepreneurship in the educational curriculum so as to inculcate the principle of economic self-reliance from a young age (Onwuka, 2020). However, laudable as these initiatives may be, they appear not to have yielded the desired results.

Unemployment, underemployment and digital literacy

Ever-evolving technologies have led to the invention of many concepts. One of such is digital literacy, which has been affirmed as a subset of literacy and offers a ready-made tool for addressing the common challenges of unemployment and underemployment and to enhance workplace productivity. Many organizations have included digital literacy as a prerequisite for employment and for the promotion of employees.

Unemployment, as defined by Westfall (2020), is a situation where an individual actively searching for employment is unable to find a suitable job to meet their daily needs and demands. The ILO's metadata glossary (ILO, 2020), also defines the term as the share of the labour force that is without work but available for and seeking employment. Underemployment, which is a milder form of unemployment, is a situation where an individual engages in a job that offers either few work hours or meagre wages or salary. According to Amadeo (2020), underemployment happens when a person desires a full-time job but is working for half of the time he is available, or is employed in a job that does not make full use of his skills and knowledge.

Hcareers (2019) also defines underemployment as a situation in which a job prevents an employee from utilizing their potential, skills, qualifications and experiences to the maximum. They categorize underemployment into visible underemployment, which includes employees who are working fewer hours than are normal in their field, and invisible underemployment, which is when a full-time employee is not using their skills. The latter may be because the employee was not able to find work in their chosen field, and in many such cases people receive pay below the industry standards.

There seems to be an unending controversy over the definition of the term 'digital literacy'. This could be due to the use of the term literacy, the definition of which has not been totally and aptly captured. Literacy has been referred to as a person's ability to read and write. However, this definition fails to capture essential concepts, especially within the African context, where the chances of daily survival depend not solely on educational attainment, but on skills and knowledge of manual work, which are all classified under the informal sector. Furthermore, it is necessary to consider the four communication skills, which are speaking, reading, writing and listening, and which are deemed to define literacy. While being mindful of the fact that these skills are closely related to one another, it will be wrong to conclude that an individual who possesses two of these four skills is literate. However, for the sake of this discussion, literacy will be defined as the complex constellation of cognitive, social, and affective competencies that involve the use of symbol systems for expressing and sharing knowledge and ideas, information and experiences (Hobbs, 2016).

Digital literacy can therefore be regarded as the ability to use information and communication technologies to find, evaluate, create and communicate information, requiring both cognitive and technical skills (American Library Association, 2017). Khan and Waheed (2015) also define digital literacy as the ability to effectively perform tasks in the present digital information environment. In 2018, the United Nations Educational Scientific and Cultural Organization (UNESCO, 2018) gave an all-encompassing definition of digital literacy as the ability to define, access, manage, integrate, communicate, evaluate and create information safely and appropriately through digital technologies and networked devices for participation in economic and social life. UNESCO stated further that digital literacy is synonymous with other forms of literacy, which include information literacy, computer literacy, data and media literacy. It can then be assumed that an individual may be literate in other terms, but not digitally literate.

General observations over time indicate that there may be a correlation between the rate of unemployment and high numbers of graduates from tertiary institutions. This makes many doubt the necessity of education or being literate when their main objective, to enhance economic survival, has been partially defeated. From the foregoing, it may not be an exaggeration to conclude that either possessing or lacking educational qualifications is not related to being gainfully employed; that is, that there is no significant relationship between unemployment, underemployment and literacy.

Through the years, the term 'literacy' has been used synonymously with other close concepts. Some of the literature has justified the assertion that literacy is a broad concept which encapsulates other related terms such as digital literacy, media and information literacy, financial literacy. The different terms associated with digital literacy have been used interchangeably. However, close observation reveals that there are areas where the differences between these terms come into play. Media literacy is the ability to produce both academic and professional communication materials by utilizing a wide range of media such as newspapers, e-mail, broadcasting, social media, internet etc. It also deals with the knowledge of both printed and non-print (digitized) media of communication. On the other hand, information literacy is the ability to find, locate, share and manage information, especially on the world wide web, which has an avalanche of information resources. That is, an information literate individual is said to possess the skill of being able to select and synthesize relevant and factual information. This skill is paramount in formal organizations where valuable information has to be extracted from large data sets in order to make decisions. Digital literacy has great potential for boosting employability and productivity on an individual level, as elucidated by Vrana (2016), as well as on an organizational level. Attahiru (2018), in his study listed, some of the benefits of digital literacy to include the following:

- improved quality and quantity of research;
- efficient and effective time management strategies as a result of having the requisite skills for information retrieval;
- improved quality of teaching and discharge of duties;
- increased usage of e-resources;
- better decision making: when you have limited ways of getting information, your choices are also limited.

Models of digital literacy

Garcia-Giron and Navarro (2014) submitted that just as several models have been postulated to understand information seeking, so also there are models for understanding digital literacy. Such models include the project DQ (digital quotient) and the JISC (Joint Information Systems Committee) models, respectively. They further noted that digital literacy models provide an anchor to previous genre knowledge of the concept and allow for an understanding of learning-style shifts and blends.

JISC model

The JISC model of digital literacy seeks to explain the interrelationship between the different concepts of digital literacy, as well as why some individuals are able to adapt quickly to the digital environment, while some others are not. The model outlines six key elements that can be used to define a digitally literate person. These are as follows:

Information and Communications Technology proficiency

A digitally literate person defined by this parameter is one who is able to utilize computer software and applications, digital devices and other associated services. On a primary level, they have knowledge of the various devices and are also able to utilize the internet effectively. On an advanced level, information and communications technology (ICT) proficiency has to do with systems analysis, troubleshooting, fault detection and correction and, most importantly, systems and applications upgrading. It is generally evident that not many are acquainted with some of the advanced digital skills. This may well be the reason many are unemployed, especially within the information delivery sector including libraries, and explains why library operations such as systems and server configuration and networking are carried out by experts in the field of ICT rather than by librarians.

Information, media and data literacy usage

In this regard, a digitally literate person is able to find, access, utilize and share data, knowledge and information, especially in digital formats. This aids co-operation and collaboration, especially in conducting research. Other things that align with this factor are copyright, patents and open access. Librarians in special and academic libraries who are engaged in research studies are hampered by lack of the ability to fully make use of media and data. The consequences include poor research output, lack of diversified knowledge about individual disciplines, etc.

Digital creation and innovation

At a basic level, digital creation and innovation entails the capacity to design digital artefacts and materials; digital writing; digital imaging; video and audio, which are some formats for presenting data. At higher levels, it encompasses the ability to code and to design apps/applications, games, virtual environments and interfaces. As the world progresses and advances and inventions occur, the ability to generate scripts and codes and develop programs seems to be the new oil. Nonetheless, research studies and observations have revealed that many people may be unable or unwilling to key into these advancements. Lack of skills in this area may hinder employment opportunities for many people, even as there are concerns about how to increase the number of people with creative digital skills in Africa (Adegoke, 2021).

Digital communication, collaboration and participation

A digitally literate person in this context is able to utilize social media and other relevant platforms to build valuable networks and communities of practice which speed up research tasks, information sharing and delivery, etc. Other issues within this context are privacy, password management and web analytics. This is most applicable to librarians in academic and public libraries who have a diverse audience. Thus, lacking skills in this area could result in poor client and customer relationship management. This could affect productivity in the workplace.

Digital learning and professional development

This has to do with the ability to explore and utilize different opportunities for learning in the digital environment. Beyond utilizing such opportunities is the ability to put into practice what has been learned in order to improve workplace productivity and meet organizational goals and objectives. The 21st century has seen a rise in the development of digital learning platforms, which make learning easily affordable for people at free or reduced rates. However, many researchers are of the opinion that not many people are aware of these platforms and that the few who are aware have not made best use of them for self-development. This in the long run will lead to an increase in unemployment and underemployment rates and a reduction in workplace productivity.

Digital identity and wellbeing

Digital identity and wellbeing relates to the ability to exercise restraint and caution and to remain safe in the digital world. The digital environment is seen as a replica of the physical environment; that is, what applies to the physical must be in the digital. A lack of skill in this area results in hacking and piracy attacks, distractions and digital stress, which all distort the processes of work. It is therefore understandable that 21st-century employers will want to know if prospective employees have this digital skill.

Project DQ model

The project DQ (digital quotient) model is an extension of the JISC model. According to the Institute (2021), the model is a comprehensive set of technical, cognitive, meta-cognitive and socio-emotional competencies that are grounded in universal moral values and that enable individuals to face the challenges as well as harness the opportunities of digital life. Furthermore, the United Nations Department for Economic and Social Affairs (UNDESA, 2019) asserts that the model is divided into three core areas of proficiency, which are digital entrepreneurship, digital creativity and digital citizenship. The model contains three levels, eight areas and 24 competencies, which are made up of skills, knowledge and values.

Essential digital literacy skills for reducing unemployment

Digital literacy according to Attahiru (2018) is paramount, and it is a survival skill for professionals, including librarians. This is largely because digital literacy is a subset of skills for using ICT, which is now essential in many professions. To this end, relevant digital skills need to be inculcated at different levels of education and in-job training, not only to reduce rates of unemployment but also to enhance workplace productivity among professionals in different fields. Use of the internet, which is a subset of digital literacy, cuts across all fields of human endeavour and is not the exclusive reserve of professionals in the information sector. A cogent point to note, however, is that the importance of the library in assisting professionals in different fields to acquire relevant digital literacy skills to enhance workplace productivity cannot be overemphasized.

Momoh and Folorunso (2019) in their study observed that 21st-century professional, commercial and individual demands and realities have made it critical for libraries to begin to map out ways to help their users acquire and hone digital literacy skills. This is necessary in order to reduce the alarming rate of unemployment, as an individual's employability in current times may depend on his or her possession of digital literacy skills. Labbo et al. (2003) and Schumar-Dobler (2003) held the opinion that any professional, regardless of their discipline, should have a range of digital literacy skills beyond the mere ability to operate a computer or access the internet. As such, they recommend skills such as information evaluation, electronic communication, etc., due to the fact that unemployment is not limited to the information sector but is an ever-present factor in all disciplines.

The rate of unemployment varies from one country to another, for a variety of reasons including favourable government policies that boost local production and encourage entrepreneurship, socio-political stability and others. The World Bank (2015) reported that small and medium-size enterprises account for up to 60% per cent of total employment and up to 40% per cent of gross domestic product in emerging economies. Closely related to this is the diversification of the economy so that it is not dependent on a single major product or industry. According to the *World Youth Report* published by the United Nations Organization (UNDESA, 2019), the year 2017 recorded the highest rate of youth unemployment in Northern Africa, at 29.5%. This has remained high and increasing over the years and can be attributed to political instability as a consequence of insurrections and mass civil actions.

The present global pandemic, according to official statistics released by Bloomberg (2021), has also caused the unemployment rate to rise. This is because of pay cuts, downsizing and mergers, which were some of the strategies utilized by many industries to stay afloat.

Arab countries faced an unemployment rate of 24.9%. Unemployment rates for Lesotho, Mozambique and Namibia are estimated at 38.5%, 42.7% and 45.5%, respectively. In addition, young people in developing economies, when compared to their counterparts in developed economies encounter different employment and work-related scenarios. This is largely due to the fact that employment opportunities in many developing economies are in the informal sector, which faces challenges such as wage fluctuations, and lack of standards and work regulations, as well as lack of pensions and insurance packages in times of disasters (UNDESA, 2019).

Youth in developed economies have an edge over their colleagues in the developing world, due to advancements in technology, globalization and industrial development that have provided viable means of being gainfully employed, which contributes to the nation's internal revenue. This is most applicable to the countries of Europe, Southern and Northern America and Asia (World Economic Forum, 2020).

Reducing unemployment rates in Africa: The Nigerian experience

In recent times, the rate of unemployment in Nigeria has been alarming. James (2021) observed that it is almost impossible to give clear statistics for unemployment and underemployment. The Nigerian Bureau of Statistics in a 2020 report pegged the rate of unemployment at 33.3%. This was an increase over the 27.1% recorded in the first quarter of 2020. One of the many reasons attributed to this, according to the Borgen Project (2020), is over-dependence on oil as the main source of revenue and the global coronavirus pandemic, which culminated in mergers, downsizing and pay cuts.

Apparently aware of the hazards of unemployment, the Nigerian Government initiated several schemes such as the Youth Enterprise with Innovation in Nigeria (YOUWIN), the Subsidy Reinvestment and Empowerment Programmes (SURE-P) and, most recently, the N-Power Programmes (Ibrahim, 2021; Nwosu and Ugwuerua, 2014). Laudable as these schemes may be on account of their aim to drastically reduce unemployment, they have been criticized by economic and developmental experts for failing to integrate digital literacy skills. This is evident from the fact that many participants in the different schemes, even after the expiration of the contract, still lack relevant digital skills that could have made them economically self-reliant in the long term. Many of the schemes are tailored towards awarding grants to innovative ideas, especially with regard to agricultural development. The N-Power scheme, which could have helped the majority of the populace to acquire digital skills, was faced with the challenges of lack of equipment and human power. In the end, many of the beneficiaries of the scheme were sent to remote villages to teach inside the four walls of a classroom without even having the requisite teaching qualifications or experiences.

Technology companies in Nigeria, such as Microsoft and Google, inter alia, are gradually realizing their role in providing opportunities for Nigeria's teeming population by opening up internship opportunities of 3–4 months for interested youths as a way for them to gain knowledge, skills and work experience. Some areas of interest are data science, web analytics, product design and management, social media marketing, artificial intelligence and machine learning. After concluding their internship, some are absorbed into the host organization as permanent staff members, while others are given the necessary support to become self-reliant and provide opportunities for others. That is, a single individual is trained and the trained individual trains others, and so the cycle continues on a geometric progression.

Digital literacy and workplace productivity: the nexus

It is paramount to note that digital literacy is a means to an end, and not an end in itself. According to the World Economic Forum (2016), five million jobs in the world's leading economies could disappear over the next five years due to redundancy and automation. Apparently aware of this, Bynghall (2016) was quick to note that surviving in the current work environment, which he defined as highly dynamic and competitive, requires the highest measure of innovation and flexibility, which could be made possible only by utilizing technological facilities and digital skills.

Furthermore, organizations with larger workforces more often than not experience information and knowledge gaps with respect to the digital skills management of older staff members who are not digitally inclined and the new generation who do have experience and are well equipped with digital literacy skills. Leaving this challenge unaddressed could lead to internal issues such as conflict, and affect workplace productivity and employee performance. The best strategy for addressing this challenge is to move away from the manual environment and migrate to the digital one. The cost may be in terms of the various processes and equipment involved, but it has been proven to save huge costs in the long run.

In the context of organizational management, it has been proven that adopting digital literacy reduces drudgery at work, which in turn promotes efficiency, and this is aside from increasing the speed and rate of work. This could be the reason why many organizations encourage their workers to take additional courses on navigating the digital environment. Some other organizations provide digital refresher courses at intervals for their staff. A high premium has been placed on this in the library environment, as it is most important if not compulsory for library workers to be able to carry out basic operations in the digital environment. This is just one of many requirements that must be met in order to be promoted.

Balch (2013), in a *Guardian* feature article, opined that digital literacy is the main skill of the present century and is paramount to success in the modern world. As such, it is a priority for anyone who desires to be a high achiever to acquire these skills. Research studies have proven the fact that workers who have digital literacy skills are much better than those who do not. This, in the end, sharpens their innovative and creative abilities as well as aiding better and quicker decision-making processes and workplace productivity (AATPowerup, 2019).

Different workplaces and the corresponding digital literacy skills needed

In different sectors of a nation's economy, there are different sectors with different individuals and different levels of digital literacy skills (Jose, 2016). Jose further asserts that 21st-century realities reveal that the lack of these digital literacy skills has had a profound effect on a worker's productivity. JISC (2014) corroborated this fact by submitting that digital literacy is an essential qualification that makes an individual capable of living, learning, working and participating in a digital society.

Highlighted in Table 12.1 are some of these sectors or workplaces and the different skills needed.

Table 12.1 *Digital skills for different workplaces*

Workplace	Digital literacy skill
Construction and manufacturing	Robotics, artificial intelligence, data analysis, machine learning and configuration, cyber security and risk management, ethical hacking, web hosting, app development.
Educational institutions and libraries	Information and web retrieval, data processing and management, use of virtual learning platforms, intellectual property management and copyright, Office 365
Research organizations	Data analysis, information retrieval, use of statistical packages, social media management for collaboration with other researchers and organizations, Web 3.0, micro blogging
Policy/decision makers, government agencies	Microsoft Office packages, digital communication, Web 3.0, internet and web design
Agriculture and transportation	Stock and inventory management using automated systems, social media marketing, e-mails
Banking, finance and insurance	Information brokerage and dissemination, digital customer relationship management systems, electronic order processing, app development and management
Health sector	Database management, electronic customer relationship management systems
Informal sector (artisans, market women etc.)	Microsoft Office tools, mobile phone usage and data subscription, brand management, copy-editing

Source: futurelearn.com/info/courses/career-credentials-digitalliteracy

Continental bodies and their role in reducing unemployment: the present and the future

Several continental bodies, such as the Economic Community of West African States and the African Union among others, are gradually taking measures to contain the widespread effects of unemployment in the continent. These measures come in the form of providing internship opportunities and organizing programmes and initiatives especially for the teeming youths. The African Union, for instance, organizes a yearly Youth Volunteer Corps programme, which aims to bring youths from the countries under the Union to serve as volunteers in a variety of organizations for a year (African Union, 2021). The African Development Bank also provides job opportunities such as the young professionals programme, and internship offers for interested people to join its workforce. This can be on either a contract or full-time basis (African Development Bank, 2021).

Edudzie (2019) notes that continental bodies must embrace digital reality. He further asserts that education and training programmes should be upgraded to keep up with the technical and higher-level skills demanded by jobs in the digital economy. Similarly, Metu et al. (2019) revealed that information technology devices and data usage have had a profound effect on reducing unemployment in sub-Saharan Africa. They therefore suggested an increase in budget allocations for information technology by governments in sub-Saharan Africa, because the region was lagging behind in digital literacy when compared with regions such as Asia, Europe, America and the Middle East. They claimed that doing this would help to reduce the scourge of unemployment and boost workplace productivity towards optimal performance.

Carboni and Schiff (2020) in their review highlighted strategies for the mass inculcation of digital literacy, including the following.

Starting early: Starting early entails beginning the teaching of digital skills in primary school. This is deemed especially necessary for girls so they can build confidence in using digital devices, and to prevent digital divide with respect to gender.

Adaptive curriculum: This has to do with building skills for employability, through practical projects, collaborative problem-solving sessions and presentations at all levels of education. Teachers also have a role to play with regard to incorporating new ways of learning educational content through 'real life' projects that can build skills in teamwork, communication and critical thinking.

Exposure to digital businesses: Through this medium, young people will be exposed to adventures, ideas and concepts in the digital world. Today's world, especially due to the COVID-19 crisis, has seen the necessity of going digital. This undoubtedly is the reason why many organizations are shifting their operations from the physical environment to virtual platforms.

Providing an enabling environment: The provision of an enabling environment where individuals and communities can access internet-enabled devices freely or at minimal cost, such as in libraries, can help with teaching digital literacy skills. Issues relating to the availability of devices and the cost of data are the bulk of challenges faced by young people in acquiring digital skills, and these need to be nipped in the bud.

In the same vein, workers in the library environment can also take advantage of learning different skills related to the digital world, so as to make them more digitally inclined. Folorunso and Momoh (2020) observed that the coronavirus pandemic has forced many libraries to shift their operations online. Hence, it is essential that workers acquire and hone relevant skills to make them more productive. They further argued that skills such as information marketing, which is intertwined with digital literacy, are of paramount importance to librarians in all libraries. This in the long run will reduce unemployment and enhance workplace productivity, thus reducing redundancy. The onus is binding on library management to provide the facilities and environment necessary for librarians to embrace digital literacy.

Corroborating the above point, Cordell (2013) noted that librarians need skills related to navigating the library website, how to access a search page or find the advanced search page, how to find the help files, how to save or export citations and full text, how to set up an account on a social media site, how to upload files to that site, how to comment on others' postings. Being equipped with all these skills will help them help their users to access the desired information at the right time (Abertawe, 2013). These upskilled librarians will also be able to help their user communities to gain digital skills.

Different countries both within and outside the African continent have taken giant steps towards ensuring that individuals have relevant digital literacy skills. In Nigeria there is what is known as Information Technology Infrastructure. This is an initiative geared at improving people's digital literacy skills by providing facilities at discounted rates (Digital Future Initiative, 2021). The Federal Government has launched the Digital Future Initiative Skills to allow young professionals to develop and enhance their digital skills as a means to solving practical challenges in society. Both programmes have been able to meet the needs of several communities in reducing unemployment and enhancing workplace productivity (NITDA, 2021).

Several academic libraries in collaboration with their parent institution now offer a general mandatory course on digital literacy for their students. This is to provide the students with the basic skills needed to explore and navigate the digital environment. This in the long run presents them with diverse opportunities for employment. The University of Ilorin, Nigeria, for instance, has a course with code GNS 312 to be taken by students in their third year. This provides them with digital literacy skills such as using Microsoft software packages (UNILORIN, 2021).

Some public libraries are partnering with organizations whose activities revolve around the digital world to train their users in digital literacy. This is mostly at a discounted rate to allow everyone to make use of the opportunity. Sharma (2019) observed that public libraries can help their users to learn about digital literacy and to use modern technologies to their best advantage. This will allow them both to use digital information and also to build an information society. Morgan (2018), for instance, reported that the Willoughby Eastlake Public Library partnered with the Mozilla Inc. to train its staff and users on the use of digital technologies.

Conclusion

Digital literacy is important for reducing unemployment and enhancing workplace productivity. Much still needs to be done with respect to developing and implementing long-term programmes in order to achieve the goal of digital literacy both within and outside the library environment. This is because a gap exists between those who possess the requisite digital literacy skills and those who do not. Strategic plans involving libraries that are tailored towards inculcating digital skills at all levels of education, as well as for those already in the workforce, need to be developed as a means to reducing unemployment and underemployment and boosting economic self-reliance and reducing drudgery in the workplace.

References

AATPowerup (2019) Why Digital Skills Are Important for You and Your Workforce, www.aatcomment.org.uk/aatpowerup/why-digital-skills-are-important-for-you-and-your-workforce.

Abertawe, P. (2013) *Information and Digital Literacy Strategy*, Swansea University.

Adegoke, Y. (2021) The Truth about Africa's Tech Shortage, https://restofworld.org/2021/the-truth-about-africas-tech-talent-shortage.

African Development Bank (2021) Career Information, www.afdb.org/en/about-us/careers.

African Union (2021) African Union Youth Volunteer Corps, https://au.int/en/volunteer/african-union-youth-volunteer-corps.

Amadeo, K. (2020) Underemployment, its Causes, and How it Affects You, www.thebalance.com/underemployment-definition-causes-effects-rate-3305519.

American Library Association (2017) Definition of Digital Literacy, https://literacy.ala.org/digital-literacy.

Attahiru, I. S. (2018) Digital Literacy: Survival Skills for Librarians in the Digital Era, *Journal of Information and Knowledge Management*, **9** (4), 107–16.

Balch, O. (2013) Youth Unemployment: Could Technology Hold the Answers? *The Guardian*, 20 June, www.theguardian.com/sustainable-business/youth-unemployment-digital-literacy-technology.

Bloomberg (2021) Nigeria Unemployment Rate Rises to 33%, Second Highest on Global List, *Bloomberg*, 15 March, www.bloomberg.com/news/articles/2021-03-15/nigeria-unemployment-rate-rises-to-second-highest-on-global-list.

Borgen Project (2020) 5 Facts about Unemployment in Nigeria, https://borgenproject.org/5-facts-about-unemployment-in-nigeria.

Bynghall, S. (2016) Digital Workplace Fundamentals, https://digitalworkplacegroup.com.

Carboni, I. and Schiff, A. (2020) How Do We Develop Work-ready Youth in a Digital Age?, https://cenfri.org/articles/how-do-we-develop-work-ready-youth-in-a-digital-age.

Cordell, R. M. (2013) Information Literacy and Digital Literacy: Competing or Complementary? *Communications in Information Literacy*, **7** (2), doi: 10.15760/comminfolit.2013.7.2.150.

Digital Future Initiative (2021) https://digitalfutureinitiative.com.

Dqinstitute (2021) What is the DQ Framework?, www.dqinstitute.org/dq-framework.

Edudzie, E. (2019) *Transforming Education for Youth Employment in Africa: Challenges for and Pathways to Success*, www.africaportal.org/features/transforming-education-youth-employment-africa-challenges-pathways-success.

Folorunso, A. L. and Momoh, E. O. (2020) Underscoring the Importance of Information Marketing as a Vital Skill by Librarians in Post COVID-19 Era, https://web.aflia.net/underscoring-the-importance-of-information-marketing-as-a-vital-skill-by-librarians-in-post-covid-19-era.

Garcia-Giron, C. and Navarro, I. (2014) *Digital Literacy and Metaphorical Models*, www.researchgate.net/publication/287444000_Digital_Literacy_and_Metaphoric al_Models.

Hcareers (2019) Underemployment: What Causes it and Who Does it Affect? www.hcareers.com/article/employer-articles/underemployment-what-causes-it-and-who-does-it-affect.

Hobbs, R. (2016) Defining Literacy, *The International Encyclopedia of Communication Theory and Philosophy*, 1–11, doi: 10.1002/9781118766804.wbiect162.

Ibrahim, Y. (2021) Understanding the Impact of N-Power on Youths, https://thenationonlineng.net/understanding-the-impact-of-n-power-on-youths.

ILO (2019) *Global Employment Trends for Youth,* www.ilo.org.

ILO (2020) *Glossary of Metadata,*
https://databank.worldbank.org/metadataglossary/world-development-indicators/series/SL.UEM.TOTL.NE.ZS.

JISC (2014) *Developing Digital Literacies,* www.jisc.ac.uk/guides/developing-digital-literacies.

James, P. (2021) The Federal Republic of Unemployed Nigerians,
https://qwenu.com/2021/03/31/the-federal-republic-of-unemployed-nigerians-by-patrick-james.

Jose, K. (2016) Digital Literacy Matters: Increasing Workforce Productivity through Blended English Language Programs, *Higher Learning Research Communication,* **6** (4), https://files.eric.ed.gov/fulltext/EJ1132743.pdf.

Khan, S. A. and Waheed, A. (2015) *Digital Literacy Practices for Library Users at Government College University Libraries,* University Libraries, Lahore.

Labbo, L., Leu, D., Teale, W. H. and Kinzer, C. (2003) Teacher Wisdom Stories: Cautions and Recommendations for using Computer-related Technology for Literacy Instruction, *Reading Teacher,* **57** (3), 300–4,
www.researchgate.net/publication/292370120_Teacher_wisdom_stories_Cautions_and_recommendations_for_using_computer-related_technologies_for_literacy_instruction.

Metu, A. G., Adujua, G. A., Eboh, I. E. and Ukeje, C. (2019) *Ending Youth Unemployment in Sub-Sahara Africa: Does ICT Development have any Role?* Presentation at the African Economic Conference, Egypt,
https://aec.afdb.org/en/papers/ending-youth-unemployment-sub-sahara-africa-does-ict-development-have-any-role-98.

Momoh, E. O. and Folorunso, A. L. (2019) The Evolving Roles of Libraries and Librarians in the 21st Century, *Journal of Library Philosophy and Practice,*
https://digitalcommons.unl.edu/libphilprac/2867.

Morgan, K. (2018) Bridging the Digital Divide by Building Digital Literacy Skills,
www.webjunction.org/news/webjunction/building-digital-literacy-skills.html.

NITDA (2021) Digital States Initiative,
https://academy.nitda.gov.ng/public/digital-skills.

Nwosu, O. C. and Ugwuerua, E. (2014) Challenges of Subsidy and Reinvestment Programme (SURE-P) towards Youth Employment in Nigeria 2012–2014, *Researchjournali's Journal of Public Policy,* **1** (2), 1–10,
www.researchjournali.com/pdf/1167.pdf.

Ogungbile, E. O. (2021) Public Private Partnership and a Developing Nigeria,
https://qwenu.com/2021/04/14/public-private-partnership-and-a-developing-nigeria-by-ogungbile-emmanuel-oludotun.

Onwuka, E. (2020) The NYSC Entrepreneurship Programme is Good but …, https://qwenu.com/2020/12/03/the-nysc-entrepreneurship-programme-is-good-but-by-ezinwanne-onwuka.

Schumar-Dobler, E. (2003) Reading on the Internet: The Link between Literacy and Technology, *Journal of Adolescent and Adult Literacy*, **47** (1), 80–5.

Sharma, J. (2019) Role of Public Library to Growing Digital Literacy in Our Society, *International Research Journal of Multidisciplinary Science & Technology*, **1** (6), 295–7.

UNDESA (2019) *World Youth Report: Youth and the 2030 Agenda for Sustainable Development*, Chapter 3, https://bit.ly/3kGILCX.

UNESCO (2018) *A Global Framework of Reference on Digital Literacy Skills for Indicator 4.4.2*, Information paper no. 51, http://uis.unesco.org/sites/default/files/documents/ip51-global-framework-reference-digital-literacy-skills-2018-en.pdf.

UNILORIN (2021) GNS 312 Course Description, www.unilorin.edu.ng/index.php/gns312-digital-skill-acquisition/6013-gns312-course-description.

Vrana, R. (2016) Digital Literacy as a Boost Factor in Employability of Students, www.researchgate.net/publication/313031140.

Westfall, P. (2020) Guide to Unemployment, www.investopedia.com/terms/u/unemployment.asp.

World Bank (2015) Doing Business: Going Beyond Efficiency, www.openknowledge.worldbank.org.

World Economic Forum (2016) The Future of Jobs, Employment, Skills and Workforce Strategy for the Fourth Industrial Revolution, www3.weforum.org/docs/WEF_Future_of_Jobs.pdf.

World Economic Forum (2020) Future of Work: 5 Things to Know about the Future of Jobs, www.weforum.org/agenda/2020/10/5-thing-to-know-about-the-future-of-jobs.

13

Backward Design Modelling of Digital Literacy in Africa

Oluwaseun David Adepoju

Abstract

Since the early 2000s, digital literacy has been widely discussed in academic and policy circles in Africa, and many conferences and workshops have been held to explore and teach digital literacy skills to professionals and the general public. Financial investments have also been made into various training initiatives at societal and organizational levels. While we pursue digital literacy projects in Africa, we often leave out the more critical conversation on technology readiness and all it entails to be technologically ready. Research has shown that a technologically developed country will bridge the digital literacy gap faster and more efficiently. Despite all the investments, curriculums and digital policies in African countries, most are still far behind in bridging their digital literacy gaps. This chapter seeks to apply the backward design model to digital literacy curriculums in Africa. This model helps to guide the learning process in such a way that it considers the bigger goals and the important components of the learning experience. Backward design can help to push the reset button of the digital literacy curriculum in Africa and refocus digital literacy intentions across the continent. This chapter is a contribution to thought leadership on digital literacy in Africa and the conversation in relevant policy circles. The chapter develops an adaptation of Wiggins and McTighe's (1998) original backward design model.

Keywords: Digital literacy, backward design, digital design, digital curriculum.

Introduction

It has been observed that there is a greater tendency to lose track of the learning outcomes and objectives in a learning process if the proper guideposts are not in place. The backward design model helps educators to stay on track and ensure that the most important aspects of their curriculum are delivered without faltering. The original proponents of the Backward Design Model, Wiggins and McTighe (1998), stated that backward design is a method of designing an educational curriculum by setting goals before choosing the instructional methods and forms of assessment. In addition, McTighe and Thomas (2003) stated that in backward design, the educator starts with goals, creates or plans out assessments and finally makes lesson plans.

The above literature points to some important information that must be critically looked at. Unlike the traditional curriculum-building system, where a list of typical items is made before identifying the instructional methods to deliver those topics and the assessment strategies for the same, backward design starts by setting the goals of the learning module. Setting goals helps to start the learning process from the end in mind, and with a breakdown of what the journey will look like on a day-to-day or lesson-by-lesson basis. Backward design thus involves three main processes: identifying the desired results, determining acceptable evidence and planning the learning experience and instructions (Wiggins and McTighe, 1998).

The backward design model has been adopted and applied by several educational institutions since its first proposition and continues to be relevant. In addition, several researchers have explored the use of the model in troubleshooting new knowledge areas. Examples of such research are Armes (2020) in his study of Repertoire Selection; Davis and Austin (2020) in their study on formative assessment and differentiated instructions; Bitetti (2019) in his study of the flipped classroom; and Hills et al. (2020) in their study on anticipated learning outcomes. While these and many other studies have applied the backward design model to studying a variety of subjects, it is difficult to find a study that explores the application of backward design to digital literacy instruction.

Digital literacy is probably one of the most used phrases since the early 2000s. Despite the investments of international organizations, African governments, non-governmental organizations (NGOs) and several others to try to bridge the digital literacy gaps in Africa, the outcome has been slower than expected. This begs the question, 'What are we doing wrong?'

According to do4africa.org (2020), the digital literacy rate goes hand in hand with access to digital means. To understand where Africa currently stands in bridging the digital literacy gap, the internet world statistics by

Statista (2020) stated that internet penetration in Africa in 2020 was estimated to be 47.1%, and that at the end of 2019, 45% of the population in sub-Saharan Africa subscribed to mobile services. The report further noted that as digital penetration remains low, as compared to other continents, digital literacy is also behind. However, a variety of initiatives have been put in place to leverage digital accessibility and affordability. Different schools, institutions, NGOs and many others are pushing hard to bridge the digital divide in Africa and increase digital literacy among the population for capacity building.

Despite the continuous struggle by various institutions to bridge the digital literacy gaps, the question should be asked again: 'What are we doing wrong, and what can we do to accelerate success?'

Theoretical framework: Parasuraman's Technology Readiness Index Model (TRIM)

According to Parasuraman's (2000) TRIM, a multiple-item scale to assess people's readiness to interact with technology, there are predictors for the adoption of innovative technologies. He states further:

> The proliferation of technology-based products and services, and evidence of the challenges and frustrations associated with using them effectively, suggest an urgent need for scholarly inquiries on several important issues: How ready are people to embrace and effectively use new technologies? What are the primary determinants of technology readiness? Is it possible to group people into distinct segments on the basis of their technology readiness, and, if so, do those segments differ meaningfully on demographic, lifestyle, and other criteria? What are the managerial implications for marketing to and serving customer segments that differ on technology readiness?

Based on the above, Table 13.1 on the next page shows the TRIM analysis of digital literacy in Africa.

Putting the cart before the horse: technology readiness as a precursor to digital literacy implementation

Several studies and reports on digital literacy in Africa have noted that the inability to afford digital infrastructure has been a major impediment (World Bank, 2018). The World Bank report further states that schools are trying to provide sustainable access to information and communications technology infrastructure by assessing the additional costs to students. However, this practice is widely criticized as discriminatory to those who cannot afford it

Table 13.1 *Technology Readiness Index analysis of digital literacy in Africa*

Merits	Demerits	Opportunities
Highlights clear indicators of technology readiness as the contributors and the inhibitors.	It does not consider 'human' or 'corporate' intentions as among the indicators for technology readiness.	Considering technological intentions as a precursor for technology readiness.
The Model gives general and logical indicators for technology readiness.	The Model does not make provision for contextual indicators for technology readiness.	Introduce context indicators such as demographic and socio-economic conditions in technology readiness.
The indicators presented are self-explanatory.	The Model does not clarify whether some inhibitors can actually serve as a motivation for technology readiness.	Subject the conclusion tracks of technology readiness indicators to the probability of possibility rather than an outright decision.

in lower-income countries. An additional issue is that electricity coverage is still fragmented in various areas of the continent. According to the World Bank report, only 31.5% of the rural parts of Africa were covered in 2018.

The work of Maden and Kanos (2020) focusing on digital literacy and the future of works noted that sub-Saharan Africa ranks the lowest both in the percentage of the labour force that uses LinkedIn – only 4% of the total population – and in terms of the level of digital skills, with about half the average global level of digital skills adoption. The report further highlights that there is a higher level of digital skills in Nigeria, Kenya and South Africa than in the rest of sub-Saharan Africa, on average. In their examples, they state that although only 17% of South Africa's labour force is on LinkedIn, the country's relative penetration of digital skills is slightly above the global average. Residents of Nigeria and Kenya also possess relatively high levels of digital skills but there is a smaller percentage of LinkedIn users within the total labour force.

The above two pieces of research show that something needs to be done before digital literacy initiatives are increased. It seems that the issue of technology readiness and digital infrastructure development is frequently overlooked in the initial project and curriculum design of digital literacy programmes in Africa. Backward design helps by starting from the bigger picture of goals rather than the frenzy of implementing digital skills initiatives. The World Bank's *Future of Work* report for 2020 (World Bank, 2020a) reported digital literacy skills across African countries in the chart reproduced in Figure 13.1 opposite. Insights from the data show clearly that the countries that seem to be leading the pack are also performing poorly when it comes to global digital literacy standards. Figure 13.1 confirms the struggles that have already been pointed out in this chapter. What is more

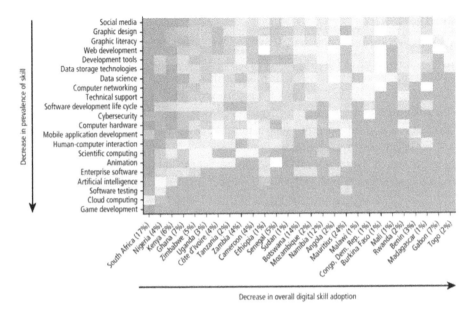

Figure 13.1 *Future of work in Africa, 2020*
Source: Future of Work in Africa (World Bank, 2020a)

worrisome is that these kinds of data have been consistent for a decade, with almost no noticeable progress. Could there be something that has been wrong over the years that has not been noticed?

The value of bridging the digital literacy gap in Africa is not just for the sake of it but also for the economic prosperity of Africa. Research has shown that there is a strong correlation between digital literacy skills and a transformative work environment. To corroborate this, the World Bank's *Future of Work* report for 2019 stated that technology is reshaping the skills needed for work. While the demand for less advanced skills is declining, the demand for advanced cognitive, socio-behavioural and adaptable skills is rising. It is not just that new jobs are replacing old jobs, but also that existing jobs increasingly require a different set of skills.

Reimagining digital literacy curriculums, initiatives and projects in Africa

In this chapter I would like to adopt and adapt by adding a new component to the original model by Wiggins and McTighe (1998) for the purpose of reimagining digital literacy plans and curriculums across all sectors of interest. The strength of the backward design model is that it starts by identifying desired results, a process that is very germane to the success of learning, training or teaching. It has been noticed that many digital literacy projects and training efforts in Africa fail because the plans start with activities such as setting up a physical space for training, conferences, etc. Starting a learning journey from learning experiences without first of all setting the goals for the programme or initiative may lead to a waste of time and resources or worse still, building a redundant system.

Building on the issues addressed above, the 'technology readiness' component will be added to the original backward design in order to create a somewhat 'worthy of exploration' playbook for digital literacy in Africa, going forward. The model will also suggest some key performance indicators for a digital literacy curriculum and project implementations.

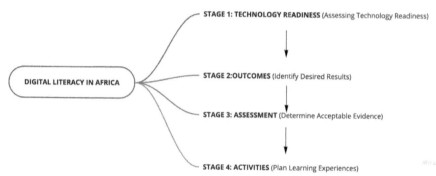

Figure 13.2 *Adapted backward design model for digital literacy in Africa*

Technology readiness

The definition of technology readiness is not limited to the propensity of people to adapt and use new technologies but also includes digital infrastructure readiness. Terminologies such as 'technology readiness index' and 'technology readiness levels' have been used as part of the technology readiness understanding across several spectrums of technology. Parasuraman (2000) proposed the Technology Readiness Index and defined technology readiness as the people's propensity to embrace and use new technologies to accomplish goals in their home life and at work. The construct can be viewed as an overall state of mind resulting from a gestalt of mental enablers and inhibitors that collectively determine a person's predisposition to use new technologies. Bakirtaş and Akkaş (2020) state that research on the Technology Readiness Index and the Technology Acceptance Model have overlooked the potential role of technology readiness and acceptance. In the same vein, Damerji and Salimi (2021) note that technology readiness has a significant influence on technology adoption.

If the standpoint of the above literature is true, it is important for the design of any digital literacy project, initiative or curriculum to start with the issues of technology readiness in their entirety. The reimagined backward design model suggests that before any steps are taken towards the formulation and implementation of digital literacy activities, there should first of all be a set of research and psychosocial analysis to ascertain the levels of technology readiness of the people the intervention is designed for. This will not only help in optimizing the curriculum for the project but also give insights into the right sets of learning goals and expectations to be laid down.

On the digital infrastructure side, many studies have reported that some of the major challenges hindering the massive bridging of the digital literacy gap in Africa are low internet penetration and an epileptic electricity supply. Implementing a digital literacy skills acquisition programme without first of all ensuring that the people have continuous access to the necessary digital tools and infrastructure is a case of putting the cart before the horse. According to the World Bank's (2018) report, electricity and the internet remains a major issue in most parts of Africa, especially in the rural areas. It should be noted that once the technology readiness has been assessed, all the digital literacy projects, interventions and initiatives will be able to get their priorities right.

Outcomes

The outcomes in the backward design are identification of the desired results for the learning process. While several amazing digital literacy skills training and curricula have been developed in Africa over the last decade, it has been observed that the curriculum has no content on digital philosophies and indigenous innovation. The importance of these is that they will help digital skills students to understand the foundational and theoretical knowledge of digital technologies and this in turn will fire their interest in the development of new digital tools, rather than just using what already exists. Before the first digital decade for most African countries, Adubifa (1986) stated that Africa is a laggard in innovative technologies because it imports a lot of technologies that are not fit for the African context and culture. Rather than consume existing digital solutions, it would be more beneficial to adapt and innovate by hybridizing the technologies that already exist and developing applications for our context and culture.

In addition, including digital philosophies and indigenous innovation among the main outcomes on any digital literacy curriculum in Africa would not only reduce digital scepticism and technophobic attitudes but also lay the foundation for a smart understanding of the other practical digital skills in the curriculum. These two are like the operating systems on which the skills will run.

Assessment and activities

While assessment is the evaluation of what the learners have learned by means of an evidence-based assignment, if care is not taken, it can be skewed towards creating the good feeling of having delivered a curriculum without actually having achieved the necessary learning outcomes. According to The Edvocate (2017), the foundation of digital literacy has four factors. Technological skills and access, authorship rules, representation rules and online social responsibility. For students and employees to interact responsibly in a digital society, it is imperative to understand all four elements. These four fundamental areas of digital literacy are very important if digital literacy curriculums, projects and initiatives are to have a greater impact in Africa. Rather than crunching data on the numbers of people that have been trained and the number who have been reached by a digital literacy intervention, the assessment should focus on these four core areas.

It should also be noted that oftentimes, the digital literacy evaluation process may be satisfied with the fact that people have started using the technology and some digital tools. However, The Edvocate (2017) states that the ability to use technology is not enough to advance individuals. Technology use comes with many possible hurdles which can halt progress when they present themselves. Things like improper research practices can harm student performance. Additionally, unsafe internet practices and inappropriate online activity can harm employees. To avoid these common missteps, people need proper education on digital citizenship and literacy. In addition, in order to design the best assessment approach to measuring digital literacy training, initiatives and interventions, there should be a clear distinction between digital literacy for everyday life and digital literacy for core technology careers.

The World Bank (2020b) stated that the 2020 digital literacy workshop co-organized by Mozambique and Rwanda redefined what digital skills are. According to their report, the workshops allowed them to distinguish between two categories of digital skills: (1) digital skills for all occupations, or digital literacy, and (2) digital skills for information and communications technology career paths. This kind of redefinition will go a long way towards redesigning the digital literacy assessment approach and success metrics in Africa.

Digital literacy frameworks and their implications for Africa

Several digital literacy frameworks (DLFs) have been designed, globally, for the purpose of accelerating, understanding and mainstreaming digital literacy. This section reviews three DLFs and their implications for bridging the current digital literacy gaps in Africa. The DLFs reviewed here are:

- the '8 Cs' model by Doug Belshaw;
- the Joint Information Systems Committee '7 elements' model;
- the New Media Consortium '3 stages' model.

Table 13.2 *Implications and implementations in Africa*

	The '8 Cs' model by Doug Belshaw (Belshaw, 2014)	Joint Information Systems Committee '7 elements' model (JISC, 2018)	The New Media Consortium '3 stages' model (Educause, 2017)
Strengths	There are many different, competing definitions of 'digital literacies'. Co-created definitions have more power than those that are simply adopted or imposed. A definition of digital literacies can be found by applying the eight essential elements of digital literacies to a particular context.	Digital literacies are those capabilities that fit an individual for living, learning and working in a digital society. Digital literacy looks beyond functional IT skills to describe a richer set of digital behaviours, practices and identities. What it means to be digitally literate changes over time and across contexts, so digital literacies are essentially a set of academic and professional situated practices supported by diverse and changing technologies.	Curricular infusion across the disciplines. Rather than assigning the topic to a single institutional unit, digital literacy as a curriculum is diffused throughout different classes in appropriate ways that are unique to each learning context. Universal literacy applies to learners and creators of all ages and is based on inculcating a critical stance towards the increasingly immersive world of digital media.
Summary	Design any digital literacy intervention in the 'context' and the 'culture' of the society in which it is to take place.	Technology is changing at a fast pace so there is a need for evolution in digital literacy plans and interventions.	Digital literacy should not be a stand-alone curriculum, training or intervention but, rather, an infusion into already existing systems and structures.
Implication for Africa	It will be beneficial to design the African digital literacy playbook in the context of African skills level, needs, education, innovation ecosystem and job environments. Borrowing foreign models, curriculums and playbooks may not produce any change in the current situation of heavy investment but little result.	The rate at which technology is changing is so fast-paced that digital literacy curriculums must change at the same pace. In order for Africa to stop playing slow followers or laggards in the rapidly changing digital society, it must change its digital literacy playbooks to an evolving one. In a nutshell, this will help to avoid giving old training to do new jobs.	Digital literacy should not be a once-a-year intervention or a tenured-based intervention funding but rather a systematic integration into already existing curriculums and structures.

Conclusion

According to Future Agenda (2021), 'With a steadily growing population heading towards 2bn, Africa's 1.1bn workforce will be the world's largest by 2040. Equally, with a collective GDP of $2.6 trillion by 2020 and $1.4 trillion of consumer spending, many see the impact of around 500m new middle-class consumers'. The predicted statistics above show that Africa has a great potential to ride on the Digital Dividends to prepare for its time to shine as the place with the largest workforce in the world. The future skills that will be needed by 2040 in Africa are embedded in the continent's ability to restructure, re-imagine and redefine its Digital Literacy environment and investment to be more strategic, inclusive and impact-driven. This chapter has been able to adapt the Backward Design Model to include Technology Readiness in re-imagining what Digital literacy programs and curriculums in Africa should be modelled after.

References

Adubifa, A. (1986) Research Proposal for the Study of Science and Technology Assets in Sub-Saharan Africa, Nigerian Institute of Social and Economic Research.

Armes, J. W. (2020) Backwards Design and Repertoire Selection: Finding Full Expression, *Music Educators Journal*, **106** (3), 54–9, doi: 10.1177/0027432119893735.

Bakirtaş, H. and Akkaş, C. (2020) Technology Readiness and Technology Acceptance of Academic Staffs, *International Journal of Management Economics & Business*, **16** (4), 1043–58, doi: 10.17130/ijmeb.853629.

Belshaw, D. (2014) *The Essential Elements of Digital Literacies*, https://dougbelshaw.com/essential-elements-book.pdf.

Bitetti, L. (2019) Activate Business Model Learning through Flipped Classroom and Backward Design, *Journal of Business Models*, **7** (3), 100–10.

Damerji, H. and Salimi, A. (2021) Mediating Effect of User Perceptions on Technology Readiness and Adoption of Artificial Intelligence in Accounting, *Accounting Education*, **30** (2), doi: 10.1080/09639284.2021.1872035.

Davis, T. C. and Austin, N. P. (2020) The Cognitive Trio: Backward Design, Formative Assessment, and Differentiated Instruction, *Research Issues in Contemporary Education*, **5** (2), 55–70.

do4africa.org (2020) Digital Literacy and Digital Channels, www.do4africa.org/en.

Educause (2017) *Digital Literacy in Higher Education, Part II: An NMC Horizon Project Strategic Brief*, https://library.educause.edu/resources/2017/8/digital-literacy-in-higher-education-part-ii-an-nmc-horizon-project-strategic-brief.

Future Agenda (2021) Foresights and Africa's Growth,
www.futureagenda.org/foresights/africa-
growth/#:~:text=With%20a%20steadily%20gro
ing%20population,500m%20new%20middle%20class%20consumers.

Hills, M., Harcombe, K. and Bernstein, N. (2020) Using Anticipated Learning
Outcomes for the Backward Design of a Molecular Cell Biology Course-based
Undergraduate Research Experience, *Biochemistry & Molecular Biology Education*,
48 (4), 311–19, doi: 10.1002/bmb.21350.

JISC (2018) *Developing Digital Literacies*, www.jisc.ac.uk/full-guide/developing-
digital-literacies.

Maden, L. and Kanos, G. (2020) Figures of the Week: Digital Skills and the Future of
Work in Africa, *Brookings*, 22 July, www.brookings.edu/blog/africa-in-
focus/2020/07/22/figures-of-the-week-digital-skills-and-the-future-of-work-in-afri
ca.

McTighe, J. and Thomas, R. (2003) Backward Design for Forward Action, *Educational
Leadership*, **60** (5), 52–5.

Parasuraman, A. (2000) Technology Readiness Index (Tri), *Journal of Service Research*,
2 (4), 307–20, doi: 10.1177/109467050024001.

Statista (2020) Number of Internet Users Worldwide from 2005 to 2021,
www.statista.com/statistics/273018/number-of-internet-users-worldwide.

The Edvocate (2017) Digital Literacy is the Most Important Lifelong Learning Tool,
The Edvocate, 30 December, www.theedadvocate.org/digital-literacy-important-
lifelong-learning-tool.

Wiggins, G., and McTighe, J. (1998) *Understanding by Design*, Association for
Supervision and Curriculum Development.

World Bank (2018) Learning to Realize Education's Promise,
www.worldbank.org/en/publication/wdr2018.

World Bank (2019) The Changing Nature of Work,
www.worldbank.org/en/publication/wdr2019.

World Bank (2020a) *The Future of Work in Africa: Harnessing the Potential of Digital
Technologies for All*, https://openknowledge.worldbank.org/handle/10986/32124.

World Bank (2020b) Digital Skills for all African Students: What Will it Take? 28
February, www.worldbank.org/en/news/feature/2020/04/14/digital-skills-for-all-
african-students-what-will-it-take.

Index